The Fall of the Pagans
and the Origins
of Medieval Christianity

Kenneth W. Harl, Ph.D.

THE
GREAT
COURSES

PUBLISHED BY:

THE GREAT COURSES
Corporate Headquarters
4840 Westfields Boulevard, Suite 500
Chantilly, Virginia 20151-2299
Phone: 1-800-832-2412
Fax: 703-378-3819
www.thegreatcourses.com

Kenneth W. Harl, Ph.D.

Professor of Classical and Byzantine History
Tulane University

Professor Kenneth W. Harl is Professor of Classical and Byzantine History at Tulane University, where he has taught since 1978. He earned his B.A. from Trinity College and his M.A. and Ph.D. from Yale University.

Professor Harl teaches courses in Greek, Roman, Byzantine, and Crusader history from the freshman to graduate levels. A recognized scholar of coins and classical Anatolia, he takes Tulane students to Turkey on excursions and as assistants on excavations of Hellenistic and Roman sites.

Professor Harl has published numerous articles and is the author of *Civic Coins and Civic Politics in the Roman East, A.D. 180–275* and *Coinage in the Roman Economy, 300 B.C. to A.D. 700*. His current work includes publishing the coins from the excavation of Gordion and a new book on Rome and its Iranian foes. Professor Harl also serves on the editorial board of the *American Journal of Archaeology*.

Professor Harl has received numerous teaching awards at Tulane, including twice receiving the coveted Sheldon Hackney Award for Excellence in Teaching (voted on by both faculty and students) and receiving the Student Body Award for Excellence in Teaching on multiple occasions. He was also the recipient of Baylor University's nationwide Robert Foster Cherry Award for Great Teaching. In 2007, he was the Lewis P. Jones Visiting Professor in History at Wofford College.

Professor Harl is also a fellow and trustee of the American Numismatic Society. ■

i

Table of Contents

INTRODUCTION

Professor Biography..i
Course Scope...1

LECTURE GUIDES

LECTURE 1
Religious Conflict in the Roman World...4

LECTURE 2
Gods and Their Cities in the Roman Empire.....................................12

LECTURE 3
The Roman Imperial Cult...21

LECTURE 4
The Mystery Cults...28

LECTURE 5
Platonism and Stoicism...37

LECTURE 6
Jews in the Roman Empire...47

LECTURE 7
Christian Challenge—First Conversions...55

LECTURE 8
Pagan Response—First Persecutions..63

LECTURE 9
Christian Bishops and Apostolic Churches.......................................70

LECTURE 10
Pagan Critics and Christian Apologists..79

Table of Contents

LECTURE 11
First Christian Theologians...86

LECTURE 12
Imperial Crisis and Spiritual Crisis..94

LECTURE 13
The Great Persecutions...103

LECTURE 14
The Spirit of Late Paganism 111

LECTURE 15
Imperial Recovery under the Tetrarchs..120

LECTURE 16
The Conversion of Constantine..129

LECTURE 17
Constantine and the Bishops...136

LECTURE 18
Christianizing the Roman World...144

LECTURE 19
The Birth of Christian Aesthetics and Letters 150

LECTURE 20
The Emperor Julian and the Pagan Reaction...................................157

LECTURE 21
Struggle over Faith and Culture...165

LECTURE 22
New Christian Warriors—Ascetics and Monks 174

LECTURE 23
Turning Point—Theodosius I 181

Table of Contents

LECTURE 24
Justinian and the Demise of Paganism 190

SUPPLEMENTAL MATERIAL

Timeline 198
Glossary 234
Biographical Notes 252
Bibliography...288

The Fall of the Pagans
and the Origins of Medieval Christianity

Scope:

The conversion of the classical world to Christianity is one of the fundamental changes in Western civilization that has been matched only by the discovery of the New World and the industrial revolution. This course will explain the reasons for the clash between the pagans and the early Christians that ended in the Christianizing of the Roman world between the 4th and 6th centuries A.D.

The opening lectures define paganism and explain the piety and the appeal of the pagan cults of the Roman world. It is often assumed that these cults were inferior to Christianity in their cosmology, spiritual values, and moral precepts and therefore doomed to fail before the superior faith of Christianity. Scholars writing under the influence of Franz Cumont (1868–1947) have long argued that many pagans discarded the empty communal cults of their ancestral gods either for the charismatic mystery cults, with their promises of moral rejuvenation and ecstatic rites or, for the intellectuals, the doctrines of Stoicism and Platonism. This vision of paganism has, in the past generation, been called into question in the light of ever-growing evidence from archaeology, inscriptions, documentary papyri, Roman legal texts, and coins, as well as a reexamination of classical texts.

A more modern view sees mystery cults as simply cults with initiation rites that were neither exclusive in membership nor distinct in their rituals and sanctuaries from the civic and family cults. Instead, the major change in pagan worship was the Hellenization or Romanization of cults. Provincials in the eastern provinces assimilated their native cults to those of Hellenic ones, whereas the provincials in the western provinces interpreted their gods in Roman guises. All communities across the Roman world also linked their ancestral gods to the veneration of the spirit (*genius*) of the emperor who, on his death, would be enrolled among the gods.

To the Romans, the Christians presented a unique threat by their proselytizing among pagans to deny worship of the ancestral gods. In contrast, Jews were perceived by Romans as practicing a legitimate religion that posed no such threat. In turn, Christians had to come to terms with both the Roman state and the pagan cults. Therefore, the next six lectures deal with how Romans and Christians clashed, why Roman authorities singled out Christians for persecution, and what institutions Christians evolved to ensure their survival in a hostile pagan world.

Christians claimed to be the third race, distinct from Jews and pagans. In the two centuries before the conversion of Constantine, Christians were restricted in their efforts of proselytizing. Christianity had been outlawed as a superstition in A.D. 64; then the Roman governor of Bithynia-Pontus in 112–113, Pliny the Younger, created the sacrifice test and judicial proceedings to punish Christians. Persecutions were sporadic, local outbreaks; martyrs numbered at most in the dozens rather than the hundreds. Far more significant was the emergence of monarchical bishops in the apostolic churches, who also determined which texts were canonical and consistent with what would become mainline Christian doctrines.

Bishops held together their churches in times of persecution. The theologian Origen, in his *On First Principles*, expounded the Christian faith in Platonic terms so that henceforth Christianity was ever more accorded by intellectual pagans the status of a philosophy rather than superstition. These developments were far more significant than winning numbers of converts because bishops and theologians could explain to Constantine why he had converted and why he should promote the new faith.

Four lectures are devoted to the crucial turning point in the 3rd century, between 250 and 313, when emperors conducted empire-wide persecutions to compel Christians to sacrifice to the gods. While apologists claimed the blood of the martyrs was the seed of the church, pagan authors, such as Galen of Pergamum and Celsus, were unimpressed. Romans, long accustomed to the cult of blood in the arena, viewed Christian martyrs as criminals and outcasts who worshiped a weak god unable to protect them. For Christians, the persecutions defined their faith, and martyrs became examples to follow. At the same time, faith in the ancestral gods did not wane. The soldier-emperor and reformer Diocletian, who ended a military crisis, sponsored a revival of the cults. Neoplatonic thinkers, commencing with Plotinus, devised henotheistic schemes of cosmology consistent with the ancestral cults and interpreted myths and rituals in moral terms in the system known as theurgy.

Paganism was spiritually and intellectually vibrant when on October 28, 312, Constantine converted to Christianity. The emperor's conversion offers the best insight into how many pagans could be brought to consider the Christian god legitimate and powerful. His conversion proved a decisive turning point. The final lectures, comprising the last third of the course, therefore concern the Christianizing of the Roman world between the reigns of Constantine (306–337) and Justinian (527–565). Constantine effected a religious revolution. He created the imperial Christian church, giving bishops the means to claim control of the empire's cities and its high culture for the new faith. He also relocated the Roman autocracy, with its powerful bureaucracy and army, at a new Christian capital, Constantinople. At the same time, in the deserts of Egypt arose the ascetics and monks who defined holiness in a Christian society and became the missionaries who converted villages and towns across the Roman world.

Although pagans were long in the majority, they failed to reverse Constantine's revolution during the reign of the pagan emperor Julian the Apostate (360–363). With Julian's death and failure, Christian emperors ever more suppressed the pagan cults, promoted missionaries, and supported bishops in turning pagan cities into Christian ones. Later emperors, prelates, and monks not only completed the conversion of the Roman world, but created the new world of medieval Christendom. ■

Religious Conflict in the Roman World
Lecture 1

The traditional narrative of the conversion of the Roman world to Christianity is of the inevitable success of a superior religion over a corrupt and declining faith—a narrative inherited from the first scholar of Christianity, Eusebius. Our task in this course will be to take a closer look at the vision of Rome's history we have inherited from Eusebius and reexamine a host of different sources—Christian, Jewish, and pagan—to understand this great historical change.

The Conversion of Constantine

- On October 28, 312, the Roman emperor **Constantine** defeated a rival named Maxentius, who controlled the city of Rome, in an ambush at the **Milvian Bridge**, just north of the city. This battle was not particularly remarkable in its fighting, but it was significant because on the previous day there had been a miracle.

- **Eusebius**, the first historian of the Christian movement, wrote an account of this battle that he claims was given to him by Constantine himself, although he wrote it some 30 years after the event. According to to Eusebius, the day before the battle, Constantine and his entire army saw the skies part and saw an image of the **Christogram**,

Constantine's conversion revolutionized Roman culture.

©Photos.com/© Getty Images/Thinkstock.

the Greek letters chi (χ) and rho (ρ), the first two letters of "Christ" in the Greek alphabet.

- Along with this came a message in Latin: *In hoc signo victor eris*, "In this sign, you will conquer." Constantine thus put the Christogram on his labarum, or banner, and won the battle under a Christian symbol.

- Eusebius hailed Constantine's conversion as the triumph of Christianity. This report of Constantine's conversion, however, has produced a lot of controversy among scholars and popular writers. Many have questioned Constantine's motives. But there was little doubt until quite recently that his conversion was the final act of a rising powerful Christian movement.

- In some ways, accepting the interpretation that Constantine gave his approval to a successful, important Christian movement produces more problems than it solves given the existing evidence: He did not make Christianity Rome's official religion; that was Emperor Theodosius I, three generations later (391–392). He did not ban pagan worship or close pagan temples. Above all, he was a pragmatist.

- It is now clear, to scholars at least, that there were far fewer Christians in the Roman world in 312 than has previously been assumed. Christians did not occupy any significant positions in the imperial government or the army.

- Even more perplexing, Constantine's nephew, Emperor Julian, was baptized and reared as a Christian but embraced the worship of the old gods at the age of 20 and sought to restore their worship when he took the throne. Had he not died in battle after a brief reign, he might have reversed the conversion of the empire.

- Therefore, our task is to explain how the Roman world became Christian. This is a fundamental question because the Roman world at the start of the empire—more or less the time of the birth of Christ—was a traditional, hierarchical, conservative society in which the vast majority of peoples worshiped ancestral gods, bound up with rites, traditions, and social values that went back centuries.

In the Footsteps of Eusebius

- The conversion of the Roman world to Christianity between the 1st and 6th centuries A.D. was a major turning point in the Western tradition. This change would dictate the course of Western civilization thereafter.

- Eusebius is the prime source for the conversion of the empire; in fact, he is the only narrative account of the first three centuries covered in this course. He compiled many of the original documents that explained the rise of the Christian movement.

- There was never a doubt in Eusebius's mind that Christianity was the superior faith, that pagan cult statues were idols, and that Christians were the heirs

Eusebius was a Christian and a contemporary of Constantine.

to the Hebrew prophets. He also has a vision of a single Christian church. Yet Christians were by no means unified even well after Constantine's conversion.

- Eusebius drew upon the writings of earlier Christian authors, notably the **apologists**—authors who wrote early defenses of the faith. Two of the earliest apologists we know of are Justin Martyr and Tertullian.

- Justin and Tertullian agreed that the blood of the martyrs is the seed of the church. Thus the Roman imperial government, which persecuted Christians starting in A.D. 64, was actually assisting the spread of the faith. For every Christian martyr who went into the arena and died for his faith, many pagans were moved to inquire about Christianity, perhaps even to convert.

- This vision of the power of martyrdom is presented by Eusebius and has influenced modern and popular scholars down to this day. This course will question this vision.

- Eusebius continued to influence scholars into the 19th and 20th centuries. These include Adolf von Harnack, author of *The Mission and Expansion of Christianity in the First Three Centuries*. Von Harnack did a major service to all scholars by compiling an enormous array of Christian and pagan sources for others' use.

- The most brilliant exposition of Eusebius's position drawing on von Harnack's work was by British scholar W. H. C. Frend, *Martyrdom and Persecution in the Early Church*.

The Differing Perspective of Classical Scholars

- Scholars with a classical background come at the question from a different angle and look at the issue of paganism and religious change in general. One such crucial work by Arthur Darby Nock is called *Conversion*; it looks at the various forces bringing about religious change in the Roman world between the reigns of Alexander the Great and Constantine.

- Nock argues that the paganism of Rome is not the paganism of Greek mythology. Numerous pre-Roman cults—neither Greek nor Roman in origin but part of a wider Roman world, from the British Isles to North Africa—acquired a classical tinge. Thus the diversity of paganism at the time of the Roman Empire was considerable.

- Nock was also one of a number of important scholars who argues that there may already have been a spiritual crisis in the Roman world at the time of Jesus—a decline or flight from the beliefs in the traditional gods. This approach was pioneered by another leading scholar, Franz Cumont.

- Cumont studied the god Mithra, or Mithras, who was worshiped in the Roman army and by various peoples of the empire but was Persian in origin. Cumont suggested that this Mithras was the same Mithras referred to in the Avesta, the Zoroastrian text.

- Cumont also studied other cults, which he called **mystery cults**. These cults had initiation rites; members chose to join them, whereas traditional cults were a matter of birth or residence.

- Cumont built up an image that dovetails well with notions of spiritual crisis among the pagans: There was a new wave of enthusiastic, irrational cults attracting pagans away from their traditional gods and preparing them (albeit unwittingly) to accept Christianity.

- Some scholars have gone so far as to claim that Christianity was just the most successful mystery cult; this is one of the major positions this course must look at and reinterpret in light of new evidence and new scholarship.

Conversion Was about More Than Religion

- Another important trend noticed by scholars was the development of philosophies, particularly Roman Stoicism and Neoplatonism. This is not a philosophy course any more than it is a theology course, but it is important to understand these doctrines because they were embraced by the literate classes of the Roman Empire and acted as a bridge between the elite and Christianity.

- Christian faith is based on dogma, text, and universal morality and institutions, as opposed to pagan cults that varied from one city to another and from one god to another. How pagan Romans overcame this barrier to conversion will be a major question this course addresses.

- Furthermore, Christians see God as a transcendent being, beyond this world, whereas the pagans see the divine and the human as intermingled in the material world. It was very hard to convince many pagans to worship a transcendent, singular god so distant from Roman cultural and social values. One of this course's tasks is to look at how closely and deeply embedded pagan worship was in the entire fabric of Roman life.

- The modern West has inherited many assumptions from Eusebius, down to the novels of the 19th century and the books and films of the 20th and 21st centuries: *Quo Vadis?*, *Ben-Hur*, *The Passion*, and *The Last Temptation of Christ*, to name a few. This course's primary task is to examine this vision in the light of evidence from Christian, pagan, and Jewish sources and to thoroughly evaluate what we really know about this great historical change.

Important Terms

apologist: Defender; a Christian writer who penned defenses against pagan criticism. The most important of the early apologists were Justin Martyr (103–165), who wrote in Greek, and Tertullian (160–220), who wrote in Latin.

Christogram: The combined Greek letters chi and rho, the first two letters of *Christos*. Before the Battle of Milvian Bridge, Constantine applied this symbol to his military standard (vexillum) and so created a Christian labarum, or banner.

Milvian Bridge, Battle of: The victory of Constantine the Great over his rival Maxentius north of Rome on October 28, 312. Constantine credited his victory to the Christian God.

mystery cults: In older scholarship, this name was given to certain pagan sects seen as ecstatic, irrational cults that displaced traditional worship in anticipation of Christianity. Mystery cults had initiation rites and conformed to general pagan expectations of piety.

Names to Know

Constantine I (a.k.a. **Constantine the Great**; after 280–337; r. 306–337): Emperor who first legalized Christianity in the Roman Empire. Declared emperor by the Western army, Constantine reunited the empire in 324. In 312, after the Battle of Milvian Bridge, he was convinced his victory was the gift of the Christian God and converted to Christianity. The first Christian emperor, he created the imperial church. In 325, he summoned and presided over the First Ecumenical Council at Nicaea, which declared heretical the views of Arius. In his later years, Constantine was won over by the Arians, so that on his deathbed he was baptized by an Arian bishop. He built a new Christian capital at Constantinople on the site of Byzantium in 330.

Eusebius (260–340): Bishop of Caesarea (314–340) and friend of Emperor Constantine. He composed important pastoral theological works, the most important of which was his *Ecclesiastical History*, the prime source for early Christianity. Eusebius set the standard for later Christian historians. He also composed a life of Constantine, the main source for the emperor's conversion in 312, and the *Tricennial Oration* (336), praising Constantine as the ideal Christian ruler.

Suggested Reading

Augustine of Hippo.

Brown, *Body and Society in Late Antiquity*.

———, *The Making of Late Antiquity*.

Cumont, *The Mysteries of Mithra*.

Dodds, *Pagan and Christian in the Age of Anxiety*.

Frend, *Martyrdom and Persecution in the Early Church*.

MacMullen, *Paganism in the Roman Empire*.

Nock, *Conversion*.

Potter, *The Roman Empire at Bay*.

von Harnack, *The Mission and Expansion of Christianity*.

Questions to Consider

1. How has Eusebius influenced historians to this day on the nature of religious change and conflict in the Roman world? What are the virtues of Eusebius's historical vision? What are the shortcomings of his interpretation?

2. What other sources bear on the religious change and conflict of the Roman world? What are their value and their limitations?

3. Was the demise of paganism inevitable? What were the turning points in the conflict? How has each generation of scholars since the 19th century reinterpreted the conflict?

Gods and Their Cities in the Roman Empire
Lecture 2

P agan worship in the Roman world served not only a religious function but social, economic, and political functions as well. The extraordinary expense of processions and festivals was shouldered by the Roman elite, who were rewarded for their outlay with power and prestige. The syncretic nature of Roman paganism, with its roots in Hellenistic Greece, meant that all local religious customs eventually were subsumed into the support of the state and the worship of the emperor.

The Basic Roman Temple

- We have two major types of evidence for how pagans worshiped in the Roman world from the 1st into the 4th century A.D.: literary evidence and archaeological evidence. These offer a composite idea of how pagans viewed the divine world and how they communicated with their gods.

- There were enormous differences among the cities and peoples of the Roman Empire, which comprised perhaps a fifth of the world's population and stretched from Britain to Egypt. But there were several commonalities. Foremost were their temples and sanctuaries.

- Temples in the pagan world were homes of the gods, not places for congregational worship. All a sanctuary needed was a temenos wall to block out the mundane world and an altar on which to sacrifice. The temple is an addition to a sanctuary where the god's possessions were stored, such as the *kosmos*—the robe put on the cult statue for processions—and votive offerings.

- Temples in the Roman Empire tended to look like a Greek temple in the eastern provinces or an early Roman-style temple in the western provinces. By A.D. 200, most sanctuaries presented a generally uniform look.

Greek temples were intended as places to house the cult statues, not as places for worshipers to congregate.

- The temple to Zeus and Rhea at Aezanis in Asia Minor provides a good example of a Greek-style temple. It is situated on a hill. Around it is the temenos wall and before it is the altar. The temple is the focus of the city; it is a major monument, but it does not match our modern idea of a place to pray or worship.

- The town of Thamagaudi (now Timgad), in modern Algeria, provides an example of a Roman-style temple. The city is a miniature Rome with a temple to Jupiter Capitolinus, a geometric street plan, public baths, an amphitheater complex, and all the standard features of a Roman city. All Roman cities and colonies were built on essentially the same plan.

- The cities of the empire present their temples and sanctuaries in a Roman or **Hellenistic** (Greek) style because that was high architecture—the architecture of the emperors and success. Therefore, long before the arrival of Christianity, change was already taking place in Roman paganism in the form of Hellenization and Romanization.

The Gods of the Cities

- Temples were only one part of pagan worship. Other city monuments were just as important, particularly theaters. These were assembly points for religious worship and political meetings, not just entertainment.

- Equal in importance to temples and theaters were the colonnaded streets because the real worship of the gods involved rituals and processions. These were presided over by the elite members of the society: **decurions**, **equestrians**, **senators**, and ultimately the imperial family.

- We have a description of one such procession in the city of Ephesus, in modern Turkey, from the novelist **Xenophon of Ephesus** in his romance *Ephesian Tale*, or *Anthia and Habrocomes*, written around the 2nd century A.D.

- The main sanctuary—the **Artemision**, dedicated to Artemis Ephesia—is outside the city. On the high holidays, the cult statue was dressed in its *kosmos* and paraded through the city in a sacred cart drawn by stags. It entered through the *magnesia*, or east gate, near the upper agora, or marketplace, and wound around the various districts, ending up at the theater.

- In the theater, sacrifices would be offered to the goddess, and the goddess would make an epiphany, an appearance; the statue would become the receptacle for receiving the divinity. With minor variations, this scenario characterizes all Roman pagan worship: public procession, public ritual, prayer, sacrifice, and the appearance of the deity.

The Festival Distributions

- Above all, these rituals were accompanied by distributions—gifts from the festivals' sponsors to the city's thousands or tens of thousands of residents, including meat, grain, money, and perfume.

- Inscriptions and coins (described from Stratonicea in Asia Minor) report a distribution by a husband-wife team, Tiberius Claudius Aristeas Menander and Aelia Glycinna, who held a festival in honor of the witch goddess Hecate for the entire city. The details of the inscription match the ritual at Ephesus and also describe the distribution.

- The people were summoned to the theater by means of placards placed in the deme—the residential districts. Every citizen was given two denarii, the standard silver coins of the empire. The couple also gave the city 1,000 denarii for the construction and upkeep of the public bath, and Claudius Aristeas's grandfather erected an honorary monument to the city at his own expense.

- Obviously, pagan worship was very expensive, and much of the cost fell on the landed elite, who also controlled the city government. There was no distinct clergy. One more thing Claudius Aristeas and Aelia Glycinna did: They handed out large bronze coins commemorating the festival as well as their own generosity in hosting it.

- Festivals were not always one-time affairs. The importance of these festivals and distributions is borne out by an inscription that was uncovered at the city of Oenoanda, in Asia Minor, around A.D. 125. Gaius Flavius Demosthenes set up an endowment for a four-week festival, including a tax-free market, to be held in perpetuity. Perhaps ironically, the city is abandoned today.

The Family Gods and the Pagan Afterlife

- Family and ancestor worship was widespread in the Roman world. The ancestors were known in Latin as the *maiores*, "the greater ones." There were also ancestral gods, such as the **Lares** and **penates** guarding every Roman household. The herms were the Greek protector spirits.

- Funerary monuments abounded, and a lesser Roman city had a **necropolis**—a city of the dead. Sarcophagi and funerary monuments could be quite opulent but made little comment about the afterlife; rather they were memorials to the family's wealth and position and were virtually public monuments in themselves. Many were guarded with curses against defacement.

- The purpose of these monuments was to do what in Greek is *eudoxos*, or appropriate—to perpetuate the family well-being. This included burying the ancestors appropriately and appearing each year to carry out celebrations with them. One widespread Roman practice was the Rosalia—that is, the placing of roses on a grave.

- This piety is seen in a number of ways in inscriptions. For example, many inscriptions were set up to make sure that everyone arrived on time and the appropriate dinner was arranged at the temple-tomb. Yet these family-oriented practices never developed into private devotional worship; they were always side by side with the public cults.

Faith without Dogma

- The Roman pagans revered the texts of Homer and Hesiod, who revealed the gods, as well as the early Latin texts, but they had no religious canon. They had no authoritative sacred texts. They learned the morality of the gods, as well as rituals, socially.

- Polybius, a Greek historian of the 1st century B.C., was stunned at how pious the Romans were, even compared to his fellow

Greeks. Morality and piety were taught in the home, on the street, everywhere. It was part of the fabric of society.

- Some historians have argued that the Greeks and Romans did not have a sense of right and wrong rather had a shame culture; that is probably going overboard.

Syncretism and the Cult of the Emperor

- **Syncretism** is the process of assimilating local gods into the gods of another (often dominant) culture. The Greeks made equivalents between their gods and the Egyptians', for example. Syncretism is premised on diversity; it is not an incipient monotheism.

- Syncretism in the Mediterranean world started with Alexander the Great, and the Hellenization and Romanization of temple architecture is an example of syncretism as well: Roman and Greek gods are the most powerful; therefore, we will make our local gods' versions of the Roman gods.

- In some instances, the Romans were willing to accept a god that had no equivalent. Pagans in general accepted a new god if its power and validity could be proven. This would be important during the conversion to Christianity.

- In many instances, we find the Roman emperors themselves giving approval to various local gods. The Romans had a very pragmatic view of the gods. By the 1st century A.D., all the gods in the Roman world had essentially been enrolled as Roman protectors and had assumed Roman qualities.

- The Romans had a ceremony known as the *evocatio*, the summoning out, to summon the gods of foes or rebels onto the Roman side. This is an extremely important concept in the Roman world, that all cults are legitimate if they have age and tradition behind them (that is why Judaism was legitimate to the Romans) and that all gods were able to defend the emperor. By extension, city worship and imperial worship were linked.

- Christians not only denied the pagan gods but, as we shall see, they also did not want to venerate the emperor. That meant that the Christian movement from the start was on a collision course with not only the pagan gods but the Roman emperor as well.

Important Terms

Artemision: A temple of Artemis, more specifically the one near Ephesus considered one of the Seven Wonders of the Ancient World.

decurions: The landed civic elites defined as capable of holding municipal office with wealth assessed in excess of 25,000 denarii or one-tenth the property qualification of a Roman senator.

equestrian: The landed property class of Roman citizens (assessed at 100,000 denarii) who stood below the senatorial order in the Principate. They provided the jurists, officials, and army officers of the imperial government.

evocatio: Latin for "calling out"; the Roman ceremony of winning over the gods of a foe with promises of temples and votive offerings. The ceremony was performed by a magistrate with imperium—the right to command an army.

Hellenistic: Greek-like; the period between the death of Alexander the Great and the Battle of Actium (i.e., 323–31 B.C.). It also denotes the civilization of this period, which was fusion of Hellenic and Near Eastern traditions.

Lares: The guardian spirits of Roman homes, settlements, and roads.

necropolis: Greek for "city of the dead"; cemeteries outside the walls of a Greek or Roman city. This was intended to prevent ritual pollution of the living.

penates: Roman guardian spirits of the hearth.

senator: A member of the aristocratic families of Rome of the highest property qualification (250,000 denarii) who sat in the Senate and served in the high offices of state.

syncretism: From Greek for "mixing with"; the identification of one's national gods with their counterparts of other peoples, so that Roman Jupiter was equated with Greek Zeus, Syrian Baal, and Egyptian Amon, for example. Such an outlook encouraged diversity in pagan worship rather than an incipient monotheism.

Name to Know

Xenophon of Ephesus (fl. early 2nd century A.D.): Novelist of the Second Sophistic movement who wrote the *Ephesian Tale*, a fanciful romance between Anthia and Habrocomes. The story provides details of cult practices and social mores in the Roman East.

Suggested Reading

Dodds, *The Greeks and the Irrational*.

Harl, *Civic Coins and Civic Politics in the Roman East*.

Fox, *Pagans and Christians*.

Liebschuetez, *Continuity and Change in Roman Religion*.

MacMullen, *Paganism in the Roman Empire*.

Naiden, *Ancient Supplication*.

Swain, *Hellenism and Empire*.

Vermeule, *Aspects of Death in Early Greek Art and Poetry*.

Questions to Consider

1. How did pagans define piety? Why were rituals and sacrifices so important in communication with the gods? How spiritually fulfilling were public rituals?

2. What was the nature of prayer, and what did pagans expect from their gods? How do votive offerings reveal pagan religious sensibilities?

3. What do funerary monuments and inscriptions reveal about pagan conceptions of the divine and the afterlife? How were such monuments expressions of social rank and membership in the ruling circles rather than expressions of piety?

4. How did Romans view the gods of other peoples? Did syncretism allow for enrolling all gods of the Roman world as imperial protectors? Why did Roman emperors seek to link themselves with the many gods of the empire?

The Roman Imperial Cult

Lecture 3

From a modern, cynical standpoint, the Roman cult of the emperor might be viewed as a top-down propaganda effort by which a tyrant imposed his rule on the populace. Nothing could be further from the truth. While the elites of the city of Rome were suspicious of the idea of a god-emperor, deified rulers were part of a long tradition in the Mediterranean world, and the imperial cult served an important purpose in fostering Roman identity and enforcing the political pecking order in the far-flung provinces of the empire.

The Pre-Roman Origins of Ruler Cults

- The Roman imperial cult was established by Augustus, the first Roman emperor. He set up an institution for the veneration of the emperor's spirit, or **genius**. On the emperor's death, if he had been a pious and good emperor, he would join the gods.

- After a formal ritual of *consecratio* and a vote of the Roman Senate, the emperor's genius would become a *divus*—a god. This was a new institution in Rome, but it drew on many older practices in the Mediterranean world and the Near East.

Emperor Augustus was not worshiped as a god during his life.

- Alexander the Great established the Hellenized version of the ruler cult in the 4th century B.C. In 324 B.C., he was proclaimed not a god but someone who would join the gods after death by virtue of his great deeds. He was considered a descendant of Achilles and Heracles, the latter of whom had his own apotheosis—Greek for "joining the gods."

- Apotheosis was a widespread tradition in what became the eastern half of the Roman Empire by the 2nd and 1st centuries B.C. These regions were ruled by the Macedonian kings—families descended from Alexander the Great's generals: the Ptolemies in Egypt, the Seleucids in Asia, and the Attalids in northwestern Asia Minor.

- Asia Minor in particular had a long-established tradition of ruler cults before Alexander. These can be seen through a succession of archaeological monuments, starting in the 13th century B.C. with Hittite kings at Yazılıkaya. In Egypt, from the Third Dynasty on, the pharaoh was believed to be a living god who became the god Osiris in death.

- All of these traditions were accommodated by the Greeks in the Hellenistic Age, from the death of Alexander the Great to the final Roman conquest in 31 B.C. It was a way of adapting their republican or democratic traditions to their Macedonian or Iranian overlords. So there were both political and religious dimensions to these ruler cults.

Augustus Initiates the Imperial Cult

- The Roman ruler cult established by Augustus was based on the veneration of Julius Caesar, his adoptive father. Caesar was believed to be taken up to join the gods shortly after his death when a comet was seen at the Latin Games in the summer of 44 B.C. Augustus took as one of his titles Filius Divi, "son of a deified one."

- Before Augustus, Rome was a republic. The Romans detested monarchy, and the Roman upper classes detested anything that smacked of ruler worship. Roman emperors had to project themselves as magistrates of the republic to the aristocracy in the city of Rome, but to the rest of the Roman world, ruler worship made sense.

- Invariably, the emperor's spirit was worshiped in tandem with other gods, usually the goddess Roma, who represents the city of Rome. The oldest example of this comes from Pergamon in 25 B.C. Augustus ensured that the provincials understood this was not a temple to a living god but to venerate a spirit.

The Imperial Cult Rituals and Temples

- The *consecratio* was carefully elaborated and formalized over the course of the 1st century. It was purported that at an emperor's funeral pyre, you would know he was deified when an eagle appeared and took him up to the heavens. In the case of empresses, it would be a peacock.

- Many of the monuments built in Rome in the imperial age had a religious dimension to them. Trajan's ashes were deposited beneath his famous column; the memorial not only celebrates his achievements but marks the fact that those achievements entitle him to join the gods.

- Emperors took pains to deify their predecessors. In some cases, these were overt political acts. Macrinus, who had ordered the assassination of his predecessor, Caracalla, promptly had Caracalla deified to throw suspicion off his involvement in the plot. Trajan Decius came to the throne by civil war; he struck coins celebrating all his deified predecessors as a way of stressing his legitimacy.

- The cult required a minimal bureaucracy, at least in Rome itself. To make the imperial cult function, the emperor depended on the same local elites who had the property, wealth, social prestige, and influence to support the other pagan cults.

- Without local initiative there probably would be no imperial cult. That fact alone vitiates arguments that the cult was imperial propaganda. The initiative for emperor worship came from below.

- Dramatic examples of imperial cult worship in the colonies are found in Ephesus. Its agora boasts temples to Augustus, Domitian, and Hadrian as well as a fountain to Trajan. These monuments made the city a showplace.

- At Pergamon, the great Attalid citadel was converted for the imperial cult, extended with a temple to Trajan and Roma that turned the Hellenistic citadel into a Roman center. Similarly, Pisidian Antioch built a Roman civic downtown with an elevated temple to Augustus made out of the rock excavated to build the city.

- Many times, an existing temple became *synnaos*; that is, cult statues of the imperial family were put into the existing temple. In Sardis, in Asia Minor, the heads of five colossal statues were dug up in the late 1990s that were given a ritual burial in the 4th or 5th century A.D. These represented Antoninus Pious and his wife, Faustina the Elder; Marcus Aurelius and his wife, Faustina the Younger; and Commodus.

Why Worship the Emperor?

- Decurions advanced their rank by their efforts to set up imperial cult temples and host processions and festivals, which were similar to those of other cults. An important inscription from a benefactor named Opramoas in Lycia, Turkey, describes giving money to imperial cult temples in the lesser cities of Lycia.

- Many moderns would take a cynical view of this behavior; writers of the time, like the historian Tacitus or the biographer Suetonius, as well as some members of the Roman senatorial upper class, would also have seen this as overt flattery of a despot, but they represent a tiny minority.

- A more common view is given by the author Seneca, who tutored the future emperor Nero. His *Apocolocyntosis*, at first glance, is a spoof on the *consecratio*. On closer inspection, however, it is a spoof of the deification of Emperor Claudius specifically, not the concept of the imperial cult itself.

- Greek intellectuals long accepted and justified the apotheosis of an emperor; in part, this is a result of the Greek language. The Greeks had a single word, *theos*, meaning "god" or "goddess." Latin has *deus*, meaning "god," and *divus*, meaning "deified one." So the Greeks were forced by the language to be hyperbolic about their patron.

- That fed into the veneration of the emperor, as for example in this loyalty oath to the emperor Caligula: "The rule of [Caligula], hoped and prayed for by all mankind, has been proclaimed, and the cosmos has found unbounded joy, and every city and people have been eager for the sight of the *theos* … the happiest age of mankind has now begun."

- The oath drives home the stereotypes about Greek hyperbole, but also the religious associations of the emperor. These oaths were taken very seriously and sanctified by sacrifices; if they did not go correctly, the gods would punish you; they were, in effect, prayers.

- It is worth noting that emperors who overtly claimed they would be gods in their lifetime—including Caligula as well as Commodus—were assassinated by the Roman elites. Other emperors, as outrageous as they were—such as Nero, Domitian, and Caracalla—never made overt claims of divinity.

- Particularly in Asia Minor, the imperial cult was assimilated with local cults. Furthermore, the ambitions of the local elites were channeled toward carrying out the activities of the imperial cult. They could not express civic loyalty by fighting their neighbors, who were also Romans, so they had to express it in other ways.

- Having an imperial cult title or the imperial title of *neokoros*, meaning "temple warden"—that is, the whole city is a protector of the temple—was a way of expressing the greatness of your city. Therefore, local elites and their cities benefited by putting on these rituals and processions to the imperial cult, and the cult was woven into the religious, social, and political fabric of cities.

Jews, Christians, and the Imperial Cult

- For the Jews, the imperial cult did not pose a problem. They were recognized in Roman law as a legitimate religion. Yahweh, his temple at Jerusalem, and the hereditary priesthood all made sense to the Romans, and the Jews would offer up prayers on behalf of Rome and the emperor, which was sufficient.

- The Christians, however, refused to participate in the imperial cult. Their refusal to participate is closely linked with their refusal to worship the pagan gods, whose statues stood side by side with the emperors'. In the Romans' eyes, therefore, the Christians were atheists, denying the gods. They were regarded as traitors, with no loyalty to Rome or the emperor.

Important Terms

consecratio: Consecration; the rite of deifying a deceased emperor.

divus/diva (m. pl. *divi*; fem. pl. *divae*): Latin for "defied one"; the spirit (*genius*) of an emperor or member of the imperial family that was, on his funeral pyre, taken to join the gods. This deification was confirmed by a decree of the Senate.

genius: Latin for "spirit"; The spirit of each man. The genius of the emperor may be defied upon his death and consecration. Juno is the spirit of each woman. *See* **divus**.

neokoros: Greek for "temple-warden"; A Greek city possessed of a temple dedicated to the Roman emperor.

synnaos: Greek for "temple sharing"; the placement of a cult statue of the Roman emperor within a temple of a city god.

Suggested Reading

Burrell, *Neokoroi*.

Fishwick, *The Imperial Cult in the Latin West*.

Harl, *Civic Coins and Civic Politics in the Roman East*.

L'Orange, *Studies on the Iconography of Cosmic Kingship in the Ancient World*.

MacCormick, *Art and Ceremony in Late Antiquity*.

MacMullen, *Enemies of the Roman Order*.

Price, *Rituals and Power*.

Taylor, *The Divinity of the Roman Emperor*.

Weinstock, *Divus Julius*.

Questions to Consider

1. What led peoples of the Roman Empire to venerate or worship the emperor? Was this an act of political loyalty or belief?

2. How did the rites, sacrifices, and temples to the imperial family conform to traditional worship? What was the impact of associating the emperor with local gods?

3. What were the practical limits emperors faced in disseminating their worship in the provinces? How did the civic elites use the imperial cult to their own advantage and to advance their cities?

4. How did Jews and Christians perceive the imperial cult? What objections would they raise against its practices? Why could Jews accommodate themselves to the imperial cult?

The Mystery Cults
Lecture 4

In the late 19th century, the Belgian scholar Franz Cumont introduced the idea of the mystery cult: a new form of religion that emerged in the early Roman Empire out of pagan malaise. These cults focused on initiation rituals and ecstatic worship and seemed to prepare Roman culture for the coming of Christianity. But were these cults really new and nonclassical? In fact, more recent research indicates that they are a divergent set of faiths, many of which antedate Roman rule by centuries, and are no more similar to Christianity than to each other.

Mystery Cults—A Modern Concept

- The so-called **mystery cults** are cults associated with initiation rites—in fact, the word "mystery" comes from the Greek word for "initiation." Members of these cults chose to join them and to worship these particular divinities.

- Mystery cults are a very controversial subject in the history of the religion. In many ways, they are the creation of a Belgian scholar named Franz Cumont, who wrote at the end of the 19th century. The term "mystery cult" was not used by the Romans themselves.

- The mystery cult is seen as an indication of pagan spiritual malaise; it is often viewed as a bridge whereby many pagans became accustomed to an idea of the divine that drew them toward Christianity in the 3rd, 4th, and 5th centuries A.D.

- Cumont started his work on **Mithraism,** the cult of Mithras, a god of Persian origin. Mithras is seen as a creator god who fights a great cosmic bull and in dying carries out an act of creation. Cumont concluded that the cults of Mithras, Aphrodite and Adonis at Paphos, Artemis Ephesia, **Cybele** (the great mother goddess of Asia Minor), and Dionysus all had one thing in common: A creator divinity who went out of its way (usually by dying) to benefit mankind.

The Allure of the Mystery Cults

- Another feature among the mystery cults was a connection between the afterlife and redemption. The pagans had a sense of afterlife; what that notion was is still debated, and as best we can tell it was somewhat contradictory and did involve physical resurrection.

- The earliest description we have of the Greek afterlife is in the *Odyssey*, book 11, when Odysseus goes to the underworld and calls up the spirits of the deceased. He sees many ghosts, including Achilles, who says, "Would I were the slave of a landless man than lord of all the dead."

- These notions of afterlife, in Cumont's and others' opinions, meant that the mystery cults offered something new: a connection between death, redemption, and a pious life. Sin took on a much more moral connotation; it was not simply performing the proper rites to the ancestors and the gods.

- The most important rite was the **taurobolium**, associated with the myth of Cybele. A bull or pig was sacrificed while the initiate stood underneath it. One Christian writer, Prudentius, writing at the end of the 4th century A.D., said this was the pagan equivalent of baptism, which was probably a Christian misunderstanding.

- There are also references to redemption in *The Golden Ass*, the novel by Apuleius set in Tunisia in the 2nd century A.D. The protagonist, Lucius, is turned into an ass and has many misadventures. He is restored to human form and joins the cult of the Egyptian goddess Isis, the implication being Lucius has entered a new life by joining this cult.

- The mystery cults were also seen by scholars as enthusiastic, irrational, and nonclassical. E. R. Dodds argued that the communal and family cults in the Roman world were not fulfilling, whereas mystery cults had a foreign tinge to them, making them exotic and exciting.

- Members chose to join mystery cults. There were initiation rites; Cumont and others have gone so far as to say that the mystery cults proselytized, acting as models for later Christian missionaries. When you add up these features, the mystery cults were seen as prefiguring Christianity, as well as being index to something that was wrong with the traditional pagan cults.

Some Specific Mystery Cults

- The mystery cult model—foreign, nonclassical, enigmatic— has been constructed by looking at many cults. Some of them, however, were Greek and very well known in the Greek and Roman world, such as the cult of Demeter and Persephone at Eleusis (the Eleusinian Mysteries) and the rites of Dionysus preserved in the Villa of the Mysteries frescoes at Pompeii.

- Both of these Greek cults are seen as mystery cults and somehow not classical. Yet these divinities were worshiped well into the Bronze Age—between 1600 and 1225 B.C. So how long do you have to be a cult in Greece before you become Greek?

- The most famous mystery cult is that of the Persian god Mithras. Mithras is known from the Avesta, an ancient religious text of Zoroastrianism that was redacted (edited and reformed) in the 3rd and 4th centuries A.D. He was a guardian angel figure in Zoroastrianism, but he was a prime god in the Roman world.

- The cult of Mithras emerged in Rome in the Flavian Age (A.D. 69–96) and was particularly popular with Roman soldiers, customs officials, and imperial freedmen. The ruins of many Mithraea (temples) are found on Rome's borders, near old Roman army camps in Italy, the Upper Danube, and the Rhine.

- The cult involved many oaths and a hierarchy similar to the Roman military. The priestly garb of the Mithras cult was superficially Iranian; Mithras himself wore a Phrygian cap, which was the Romans' stereotype of what Persians wore. No actual Persian dressed this way. So the Mithras cult was, in structure and style, quite Roman.

The cult of the Persian god Mithras was the prototypical mystery cult.

- The cult of Cybele arrived in Rome in 204 B.C. during the Second Punic War. It came from the sanctuary of Pessinus in western Asia Minor. She is a mother goddess typical of the region. Her priests were the Galli—foreign eunuchs. The poet Catullus wrote about her lover, Attis, who castrated himself with a flint knife; that mutilation was seen by Cumont and others as another form of the dying savior god. Yet Attis was not a god, just a mortal.

- Serapis and Isis were the original divinities of Egypt. Serapis, iconographically, was an Egyptianized version of Zeus or Hades. Isis was sometimes worshiped alone, sometimes with Serapis as consort, and sometimes with her child, almost like the Madonna and child of Christianity.

Does the Mystery Cult Model Hold Up?

- Scholars have argued that this general picture demonstrates Roman pagan malaise—the flipside of Eusebius's vision. As Christianity is rising, paganism is in trouble, and the mystery cults are seen as proof of this.

- Roman authors like **Vergil** and **Horace** lamented the decline of piety during the civil war, and Augustus carried out a huge effort to rebuild temples in Rome. Many see this as part of a rearguard action—pagan cults were already on the wane at the dawn of the empire.

- In 235, there was a major political and military crisis that engulfed the empire for the next 50 years. We have very little statistical documentation for the period, but Eusebius's picture indicates that between 235 and 312, paganism, including the mystery cults, began losing out to Christianity. This included the cult of Sol Invictus, the unconquerable sun god, much of whose solar imagery came to represent the triumphant Christ.

- The cult of Sol Invictus is sometimes classified as a syncretist cult representative of all the various sun gods and therefore of an incipient monotheism. Technically, however, this is **henotheism**—a single divine power manifested in many ways. Syncretism and henotheism are premised on diversity; it is misleading to think that they lead inevitably to monotheism.

- The problems with the mystery cult idea have become ever more evident as historians have applied two points: One, they have looked at the worshipers themselves rather than the gods. Two, the way scholars have approached the cults is not how the ancients did. No ancient ever compared Christianity to a mystery cult, nor did any ancient say the mystery cults were in competition with the other cults.

The Great Diversity of Roman Religion

- The mystery cult idea operated on a modern assumption that unless religion is personal and brooded on the great questions of cosmology or questions of sin and redemption, it is not really religion. This is actually a 17th-century idea, coming mainly from Dutch theologian critics of the Thirty Years' War and an increasing sense that religion should be a matter of conscience and choice.

- Efforts to show mystery cults on the rise by the number of Mithraea or the number of inscriptions have failed; in fact, the most numerous dedications in the early empire are to the traditional gods: Jupiter, Mars, Juno, and so forth.

- Many of these mystery cults have been selectively studied to act as a parallel to Christianity rather than seen on their own terms, particularly the Mithras cult. When studied in a broader context, it becomes clear that the Mithras cult arose in Rome and relied heavily on imperial patronage, as did the cult of Cybele.

- In the case of Serapis and Isis, 85 percent of the cult's members were from Roman Alexandria; that is, expatriates worshiping their traditional divinities in their new home, not Roman converts to a foreign cult. Those non-Egyptians who did convert seemed to be suffering from general Aegyptomania—an obsession with all things Egyptian that is not unheard of in the West today.

- When you take a look at the cults themselves, they do not add up to a coherent whole. Each is quite distinct, and most importantly, wherever they go, they are assimilated to their setting. In fact, with the exception of Mithras, all of these cults long antedated Roman rule, much less the empire.

- One cult that emerges in the Roman world is described by **Lucian of Samosata**, the cult of the serpent god Glycon, set up by the charlatan prophet **Alexander of Abonoteichos**. The cult centered on a snake with a human head that delivered oracles via Alexander's ventriloquism. Alexander was clever enough to occasionally have Glycon refer a seeker's question to one of the more established oracles at Delphi or Claros and thus receive their support.

- Several Roman senators were attracted to the cult as well as Emperor Marcus Aurelius. The cult continued long after Alexander's death, reaching as far as the Bulgarian shore and northern Turkey. So even in this era of so-called pagan malaise, traditional cults were growing and thriving.

- The mystery cults, therefore, were not in competition with traditional paganism. Nor were they a measure of decline. They were simply part of the vast diversity of religious experience available to pagans of the Roman world.

Important Terms

Cybele (a.k.a. **Kubaba**): The great mother goddess of Anatolia, whose principal shrine was at Pessinus. She was known to the Romans as the Great Mother (Magna Mater).

henotheism: The religious outlook regarding traditional pagan gods as aspects of a single transcendent godhead. This was the religious vision of the Neoplatonic philosopher Plotinus and the emperor Julian II.

Mithraism: The Roman cult of the god Mithras, originally a Persian god of oaths. The cult was popular among Roman soldiers and customs officials in the 1st–4th centuries A.D.

mystery cults: In older scholarship, this name was given to certain pagan sects seen as ecstatic, irrational cults that displaced traditional worship in anticipation of Christianity. Mystery cults had initiation rites and conformed to general pagan expectations of piety.

taurobolium: A votive sacrifice of a bull or pig to the goddess Cybele; it was misrepresented by the Christian critic Prudentius, writing around A.D. 400, as distorted blood baptism.

Alexander of Abonouteichos (c. 105–c. 170): Charlatan philosopher who founded the cult of the serpent god Glycon in northern Asia Minor. He gained the patronage of Emperor Marcus Aurelius and the contempt of Lucian, who wrote a satirical critique of Alexander and the cult of Glycon.

Horace (a.k.a. **Quintus Horatius Flaccus**; 65–8 B.C.): Poet and soldier. Born at Venusia and son of a freedman, Horace fought for the Republican cause at Philippi (42 B.C.), but he was pardoned and promoted at the court of Augustus through the efforts of Maecenas. His works include *Carmen Saeculare* (chorus for the Saecular Games of 17 B.C.), *Odes*, Epodes, Epistles, Satires, and *Ars Poetica*. He is considered the master of the Roman lyric and poet laureate of the Golden Age.

Lucian of Samosata (c. 125–180): Greek satirist and brilliant prose stylist, he composed works on religious themes, including *Dialogues of the Gods*, *Banquet of Philosophers*, and a life of the false prophet Alexander of Abonouteichos.

Vergil (a.k.a. **Publius Vergilius Maro**; 70–19 B.C.): One of the most important poets of ancient Rome. Born at Mantua in Cisalpine Gaul (northern Italy), he was a friend of Horace. His patrons included Maecenas, Asinius Pollio, and Augustus. A poetic genius, Vergil composed the national Roman epic the *Aeneid* and the pastoral poems *Eclogues* (or *Bucolics*) and *Georgics*. He shares with Horace the rank of poet laureate of the Augustan court.

Suggested Reading

Apuleius, *The Golden Ass*.

Burkert, *The Ancient Mystery Cults*.

Cumont, *The Mysteries of Mithra*.

———, *Oriental Religions in the Roman Paganism*.

Dodds, *Pagan and Christian in the Age of Anxiety*.

Jones, *Culture and Society in Lucian.*

Lucian, *On the Syrian Goddess.*

————, *Works.*

MacMullen, *Paganism in the Roman Empire.*

Nock, *Conversion.*

Plutarch, *Moralia*, vol. 5.

Roller, *In Search of God the Mother.*

Wilken, *The Christians as the Romans Saw Them.*

Witt, *Isis in the Ancient World.*

Questions to Consider

1. Why was the vision about mystery cults offered by Franz Cumont so convincing? How have excavations and new sources of information transformed this vision?

2. What were the specific appeals of the cults classified as mystery cults? How did they differ from civic and family cults? Did any of these cults offer a distinctively different vision of the divine?

3. How does the cult of Glycon reflect pagan religious views? What accounted for this cult's success?

4. How did the Romans accept new gods? Did the Romans have a sense of religious conflict? Why did the Romans regulate the actions of worshipers but never rites and belief?

Platonism and Stoicism
Lecture 5

The two most important philosophical schools of the Roman Empire were Platonism and Stoicism—related philosophies inherited from the Athenian Greeks. While not religions in themselves, the Roman ruling classes applied these philosophies to the practice of traditional paganism, which affected their views of morality, duty, piety, and cosmology. Neither Platonism nor Stoicism was inherently hostile to Christianity, and in fact both schools would influence early Christian thinkers, although those thinkers first had to learn to write in the language of Plato before Roman philosophers would take them seriously.

Greek Thought Conquers Rome

- Among the various philosophies practiced by the ruling classes in the Roman world, the two most important were Platonism—particularly middle Platonism and **Neoplatonism**—and **Stoicism**. Platonism is of course traced to **Plato**; Stoic doctrines go back to **Zeno of Citium** but were modified greatly by the 2nd century B.C., so Roman Stoicism is really a separate school of thought.

- Most people who used philosophy as a moral guide in the Roman world were among the upper, educated classes. They were eclectics, rather than strict adherents of one philosophy or another.

- Plato was the most influential philosopher to the Romans for several reasons. First, he established the philosophical language, writing in perfect, pristine Attic Greek. In the dialogue *Timaeus*, he puts forth the first scientific cosmology, one that did not resort to allegory, myth, or sexual imagery. He also tried to create a coherent body of all knowledge to that point, particularly mathematics.

- Within Plato's philosophical system, which is an open philosophy, are a lot of points Plato does not bother to explain. He is essentially an optimist; not everything needs to be explained. Instead, he focuses on *mythos*—that is, a plausible explanation or speculation, not hard and fast canonical truths.

- In the *Timaeus*, Plato describes three ultimate realities: a **Demiurge**, the Greek word for craftsman. This is a passive creator god who made the universe in a single act by using all available material; the ideas, or forms, eternal patterns that exist forever for the material world we experience; and finally the receptacle, which is the space that gives shape to the ideas.

- Plato's successors often replaced the ideas and the receptacle with the **nous** (intelligence), or thought in its purest form, and psyche, meaning "spirit" or "soul," respectively.

Plato's philosophies affected early Christian thinkers.

- Plato thought that evil is the absence of good, not a force as argued by some later philosophical systems, certain Christian sects, and the Gnostics, who saw the material world as innately evil. Pagan philosophers agreed with Christian thinkers that the Gnostics and others who renounce the material world are renouncing God's (or the gods') creation.

- Plato drew a strong distinction between the three realities and the physical world. The eternal world was *to einai* (the world of being), and the physical world was *gignesthai* (the world of becoming, of flux and change). What we see in this physical world is nothing but an imperfect reflection of reality. The informed individual who has *gnōmē*, "knowledge," can perceive beyond the physical world the eternal patterns and the true reality.

- One of the most important innovations on Plato's theory was made by Aristotle. Aristotle, a materialist, defined the creator god as a rational god whose thought is fully actualized—that is, the Aristotelian god is essentially a computer with eternal input going into eternal output. By the act of pure thought, he moves the universe.

- To Aristotle, the middle Platonists, and the Neoplatonists, the individual souls of humans are fragments of the world's soul imprisoned in the body. This is the beginning of a notion that will be expressed by Plotinus in the 3rd century as the Great Chain of Being. The duty of the informed person is to ascend the chain through understanding.

Plato's Ideas and Rome's Religion

- Platonic mysticism is very intellectual. It requires a great deal of discipline, learning, and training. Furthermore, Platonic philosophy in its later guises was readily adapted to the traditional cults.

- **Plutarch of Chaeronea**, who wrote biographies of the Greeks and Romans as well as moral tracts, wrote that Platonism was a way of understanding the cults and the myths. For instance, he wrote an essay on Serapis and Isis in which he reinterpreted the combat between Serapis and his brother Seth, the evil god of the desert, as a Platonic allegory in which Serapis represents the yearning to understand and Seth represents the physical world holding us back.

- Plutarch (who was also a priest of the Eleusinian Mysteries) was offering a way of using philosophy not only as a moral guide to your personal life but as a way of interpreting the cults in a higher reality—as allegorical, symbolic, and therefore worthy of perpetuation. Philosophy was not a copout; it was a way of coming to terms with and giving new moral meaning to the traditional cults and myths.

- **Philo of Alexandria** was a Jew living in the Greek city of Alexandria, Egypt, who wrote a work on the creation. He used the doctrines of Plato to understand his own Jewish faith. Philo is a pivotal figure because he shows how Platonic philosophy can be divorced from worship of the traditional gods and applied to a monotheistic creed.

- Platonic doctrines tended to prevail in the eastern half of the Roman Empire. They began to arrive in the city of Rome in the 2nd century A.D. as seats in the senate opened to provincials from the East. So the popularity of Platonism reflects the changing makeup of the Roman aristocratic class.

The Evolution of Roman Stoicism

- Roman Stoicism can be traced not only to the Stoic teacher Zeno of Citium but also to **Chrysippus**, both of whom were writing in the 3rd century B.C. and considered themselves students of Plato. Greek Stoicism had a very complicated cosmology; when the Romans first encountered it in the 2nd century B.C., they did not know what to make of it. Cato the Elder simply ran the Greek philosophers out of Rome.

- Later Stoics realized that the Romans were far more interested in morality and practical philosophy than explanations of how the world came to be. One of the most important figures behind this was **Posidonius of Apamea**, writing in the 2nd and 1st centuries B.C.

- In Roman Stoic doctrines, the creator god is the **Logos**, the word; this rational act is often identified with Jupiter. A logical order is created by the Logos; that is, what happens in the physical world matters, and each person is born into a position and should follow the divine plan. Stoicism is also an optimistic philosophy; it does not reject the physical world.

- **Epictetus of Hierapolis**, writing in the 2nd century A.D., was a slave, turned philosopher, turned Roman citizen, who summed up the earlier Stoic doctrines for the Romans. He said the divine plan was much like the Roman army: You have your rank; you might be promoted, or you might be demoted if you do not do what you are supposed to.

- Roman Stoics cultivated *apatheia*—not "apathy" in our modern sense but keeping an even keel emotionally. They believed every person contained a divine spark from the Logos; ergo, every human had a certain capacity for divinization that would be identified with the soul in the Platonic system.

The "Golden Slavery"

- It is hard to say how many Romans were really Stoics. Most of them were probably eclectics. There were probably many more Platonists because there were many more people in the eastern half of the empire. The men who were Roman Stoics were from the ruling class and ran the Roman imperial government for almost 250 years, even under the corrupt emperors, out of an obligation to family, nation, and ancestral custom, justified by Stoic doctrines.

- Roman Stoicism is best expressed in the *Meditations* of Emperor Marcus Aurelius, who was a practicing Stoic. Aurelius wrote *Meditations* while he was battling the Germans on the northern frontier of the Danube in the 160s and 170s. For him, contemplation was a luxury; this is in contrast to the Platonic view, in which contemplation was a holy attempt to reach the creator god.

- Marcus Aurelius's philosophy stresses the importance of duty, honor, and the traditional cults. This is why he persecuted Christians. He also called the emperorship "golden slavery," a duty he must perform because he was born to it.

- The Romans never believed in equality; there was always a hierarchy. The people of the upper classes had more of the divine spark than the lower classes. But each had a duty to play a part in the divine plan. You can understand why the British of the 19th century, especially those involved in the colonial government, saw in Marcus Aurelius and the Roman Stoics the models for their own governors.

The Intersection of Philosophy and Religion

- Some scholars have wondered whether philosophy was a substitute for religion for the elite or if educated Romans really believed in their gods. It seems the vast majority of them did believe. **Dio Chrysostom**, a middle Platonic scholar of the early 2nd century A.D., argued that one could not know whether the traditional rites work or whether the gods heard them, but they were ancestral and therefore it was appropriate to continue them.

- In this same period, Cynic philosophers throughout Rome rejected or renounced the world. Cynics tended to be individuals who would show up in cities and cause riots. They were unpopular with the vast majority of Roman citizens. Sometimes a Christian missionary would be compared to a Cynic, but Diogenes of Corinth, who supposedly lived in a barrel, is the classic example.

- Neither the Platonists nor the Stoics ever formed a clergy. Most of them were engaged in the wider world as teachers or as part of the ruling class. What is more, they were not necessarily hostile to Christians.

- Philosophers did not have a canon like the Christians and Jews. They had a number of important texts that were read, shared, and discussed, but no one work was considered sacred scripture, and no one teacher had a monopoly over what was taught. Instead, the philosophers shared their positions with grammarians, rhetoricians, and teachers of oratory.

- Despite this intellectual freedom, proper philosophy had to be written in proper Attic Greek, the Greek of Plato, or no one took you seriously. This was the fallout of the Second Sophistic movement of the 1st and 2nd centuries A.D.

- Mastery of all Attic Greek was part of being trained as a gentleman; it did not have a religious connotation, and eventually the Christians learned it and became learned gentlemen, just like their pagan counterparts. Until that time, however, the Romans would be hostile to the representatives of the new Christian movement.

Important Terms

Demiurge: "Craftsman"; the term used by Plato in his dialogue *Timaeus* (c. 360 B.C.) to describe the creator God.

Logos: Greek for "word"; in Stoic philosophy, the divine active intelligence of the universe. Christians (based on John 1:1) applied the term to Christ as the second person of the Trinity.

Neoplatonism: The Platonic philosophical doctrines as interpreted by Plotinus (205–270) and later philosophers.

nous: Greek for "mind": The second level of reality—rational intelligence—in middle Platonic and Neoplatonic philosophy.

Stoicism: The philosophical doctrines of Zeno of Citium (334–262 B.C.). Zeno could not afford a school, so he taught under the public stoas—hence the name of the philosophy.

Names to Know

Chrysippus (c. 280–207 B.C.): Native of Soli in Cilicia and a leading Stoic philosopher who taught at Athens, perfecting Stoic physics and logic.

Dio Chrysostom (a.k.a. **Dio the Golden Mouthed**; c. 40–120): Greek sophist and philosopher born at Prusa, Bithynia, in northwestern Asia Minor.

Dio taught at Rome until he was banished by Emperor Domitian. A convert to Stoicisim, Dio left some 80 orations on a host of subjects.

Epictetus of Hierapolis (55–135): Stoic philosopher who arrived at Rome as the slave of Epaphrodites, freedman secretary of Emperor Nero, studied Stoic philosophy with Gaius Musonius Rufus, and acquired his freedom. In 93, Epictetus, along with several other philosophers, were banished from Rome on the orders of Domitian. His writings on moral conduct gained him admirers among the senatorial class and from Emperor Hadrian.

Philo of Alexandria (c. 15 B.C.–45 A.D.): Jewish thinker and Platonist who headed the prosperous Jewish community of Alexandria and represented Jewish interests in the embassy to Emperor Caligula in protest of the laws requiring sacrifice in A.D. 39–40. A prolific writer, Philo used Platonic analysis and schemes in *On the Creation* to elucidate the Jewish faith and so set the model for Christian Platonic thinkers.

Plato (428–348 B.C.): Athenian philosopher and disciple of Socrates (470–399 B.C.) who founded the Academy and defined Western philosophy. He was from a noble family and despised the Athenian democracy. His dialogue *Timaeus*, composed around 360 B.C., defined all subsequent Greek and Roman speculation on cosmology and morality. His philosophical dialogues also set the standard of literary Attic Greek prose.

Plutarch of Chaeronea (c. 45–120): Platonic philosopher, biographer, and scholar born at Chaeronea, Boeotia, in central Greece. He studied at both Athens and Rome and was a friend of Emperor Trajan. His works include the *Moralia*, 60 essays on a wide range of topics, and *Parallel Lives of Greeks and Romans*.

Posidonius of Apamea (135–51 B.C.): Stoic philosopher, historian, and astronomer who studied under Panaetius at Athens. Favorable to Rome, he traveled the lands of the western Mediterranean, writing on geography and ethnography. In his philosophical writings, he refined Plato's doctrine on the soul (*pysche*) and Stoic cosmology.

Zeno of Citium (335–263 B.C.): A merchant turned philosopher and founder of Stoicism. From 301 B.C., he taught in the Stoa Poikile at Athens because he could not afford a proper school. His ethnical and philosophical writings survive in fragments.

Suggested Reading

Arnold, *The Physical World of the Stoics*.

Dillon, *The Middle Platonists*.

Kaster, *Guardians of Language*.

MacMullen, *Enemies of the Roman Order*.

Marcus Aurelius, *Meditations*.

Philo of Alexandria, *On Creation*.

Philostratus, *The Life of Apollonius of Tyana*.

Plato, *Timaeus and Critias*.

Plutarch, *Moralia*.

Rist, *The Stoics*.

Swain, *Hellenism and Empire*.

Questions to Consider

1. How was the cosmology of Plato in *Timaeus* adapted by later thinkers in the Hellenistic and Roman ages? What were the concerns of these so-called middle Platonists? To whom did such doctrines appeal?

2. What did Zeno of Citium teach as the primary Stoic principles? Why did Romans initially find these doctrines unappealing? How did later Stoic thinkers adapt their philosophy to Roman political and social values?

3. In the imperial age, how did senators and equestrians adapt Stoic principles to conduct a moral life as a governing class devoted to traditional worship? How did they influence the very nature of imperial government?

4. Why is it misleading to see Platonic and Stoic philosophy as a bridge to Christianity? Why would pagan philosophers reject Christianity?

Jews in the Roman Empire

Lecture 6

The Romans thought they understood the Jews, but the relationship between the two cultures was fraught with many misunderstandings. Sometimes this led to conflicts, wars, and rebellions; other times, it allowed the Jews to quietly practice their faith under a deluded but satisfied imperial patron. The chronic mismanagement of the Jewish homeland, however, would ultimately lead to tragedy, and the Romans' failure to comprehend Jewish religion would leave them further baffled when they confronted the 1st-century pacifist sect of Judaism known as the Christians.

The Jewish People at the Dawn of the Empire

- Judaism was a very important faith in the Roman Empire; some estimate perhaps as much as 10 percent of the population of the empire was Jewish in the 1st century A.D. Understanding Judaism in the Roman Empire is obviously important to this course because Christianity emerged out of Judaism during this period.

- For the Romans, contact with Judaism was the first instance in which they dealt with members of monotheistic faith, as well as a nation that defined itself overwhelmingly by religion. Unfortunately, Romans actually misunderstood Judaism in a number of ways, and some of those misunderstandings carried over into their dealings with the Christians.

- The 4th century B.C. to the 2nd century A.D. is arguably the period in which the national worship of Yahweh as the god of the Hebrews turned into Judaism as we understand it: A monotheistic faith depending on text and moral purity and—as important as the Temple of Jerusalem was—not necessarily tied to any locale.

- Judaism is a faith that is carried everywhere; it is within the heart and mind. That resulted from the redaction of Judaism's sacred texts during the Babylonian Captivity—that is, the period from 586 to 539 B.C. when the Jews were deported to Babylonia. A religion based on canon is something quite distinct from paganism.

- When the Jews were allowed to return to their homeland by the Persian king Cyrus around 539 B.C., they rebuilt their temple in Jerusalem. The **Sadducees** were the priestly caste that administered the temple sacrifices, maintained ritual purity, and interpreted the Torah.

- The Persian kings respected Judaism, in part because the Jewish homeland was not of strategic importance to them. To the Romans, the region they called Palestine was an important route for moving their armies, and thus they had an interest in controlling the region and their people. (Please note: The term "Palestine" as used in this course refers to the Roman political division, a corruption of the word "Philistine," and should not be interpreted in a modern political context.)

The Jews of the Diaspora

- By the 2nd century B.C., many Jews had emigrated and had become members of the **Diaspora**, meaning "scattering" in Greek. Many of them left as mercenary soldiers, serving in Hellenistic armies and being rewarded with land. In the Diaspora, they quickly had to come to terms with Greek language and culture.

- In Alexandria, Egypt, the Jews were a powerful intellectual community. It is estimated that a third or more of the city's population of 750,000 to1,000,000 people were Jewish. In lesser cities scattered throughout Asia Minor and Greece, Jewish communities set up **synagogues** side by side with Greek temples and gymnasia.

- Most of these Jews spoke Greek, which is why the Septuagint was created. Many of them adhered to the Pharisee tradition, the broader and more generous interpretations of Jewish law.

The Jewish Revolt agains the Syrians led by Judas Maccabaeus in the mid-2nd century B.C. added to the tradition of Jewish apocalyptic literature.

The Hasmonaean Kingdom of Israel

- Roman Palestine was an unruly place. A century and a half earlier, the Jews had been ruled by the Seleucid kings of Syria. After 190 B.C. and a defeat at the hands of the Romans, the Seleucids were in constant fiscal and military crisis. King Antiochus IV Epiphanes tried to address this problem by imposing an active Hellenizing process on his lands, including Jerusalem and its temple, by sponsoring cults to Zeus.

- The Orthodox Jews, the Hasidim, raised the call for national resistance in 167 B.C. The Jews flocked to the banner of **Judas Maccabaeus**, who was of the House of Hashmon, or the **Hasmonaeans**. In 164 B.C., the Jews won a significant victory, destroyed the mercenary army of Antiochus IV, reoccupied Jerusalem, and rededicated the temple to Yahweh. This victory is still commemorated at Hanukkah.

- The Maccabees not only liberated Jerusalem; they expanded the kingdom, brought Samaria under Judean rule, subjected the pagan towns of the coast, and colonized the northern regions of Galilee. Rome, which had no love of the Seleucids, recognized the independent Jewish state.

- This national struggle was often seen in apocalyptic terms. There is a powerful apocalyptic tradition of Jewish texts talking about final judgments and the end of days, starting with the Maccabees and ending in the early 2nd century A.D. These texts included notions of a **Messiah**, a member of the house of David who would restore the kingdom of Israel. In more cosmic terms, he was the "son of man" who would preside over the final judgment. This tradition had a powerful influence on early Christianity.

- Eventually, the Hasmonaeans failed to keep order, and in 63 B.C. the Roman general Pompey stepped in to secure the coastal highway—the *Via Maris*—from Alexandria to Antioch and Syria. Eventually the Romans placed a half-Jewish mercenary general on the Jewish throne, a man known as **Herod the Great**.

The Romans Take Control of Israel

- The Jews had many reasons to dislike Herod, but he was the only man who could keep order among the various Jewish regions. The Romans liked Herod because he spoke Greek and understood the Roman political system. Herod kept order until his death in 4 B.C.; then the Jewish kingdom was partitioned among his three sons, who were eventually deposed for incompetence.

- The religious running of the Jewish homeland was given to the Sanhedrin, a high council composed of the Sadducees and Pharisees. This is the council that, according to the Gospels, put Jesus on trial. They administered the temple and ran Jerusalem.

- For civil administration, the Romans sent in governors called procurators. These were low-level equestrians. Procurator of

Judaea was a dead-end appointment; it meant you had washed out of the Roman imperial system. **Pontius Pilate** was a perfect (and incompetent) example.

- The Roman military presence in Palestine was minimal. The soldiers were inept locals, and some of them virulent anti-Semites. Their behavior contributed to the outbreak of the great national rebellions. Overall, the Romans mismanaged the province entirely.

Roman Culture and Jewish Faith

- For all that Rome tolerated and respected (or thought they respected) Judaism, the Romans did not understand it. To the Romans, Judaism looked legitimate: It was an ancestral national religion. Although they found the idea of a single god and the lack of images peculiar, they respected the fact that the rituals had gone on for centuries and believed that they had worked.

- They also misunderstood the Sadducees. They thought of them as some variety of Stoic and believed they were loyal to Rome because they were not in open rebellion. The Sadducees were merely ignoring Rome; Rome was just one of the many trials God had given them to overcome.

- Outside the Jewish homeland, the Pharisees were able to reconcile Judaism to the wider Roman culture, including the Greek language and philosophy. The Romans misunderstood this, too, as a gesture of loyalty. They saw the historian **Flavius Josephus**, for example, who wrote in Greek, as a Pharisee who could accommodate himself to the Roman world.

- Not all Jews complied with Roman rule. The Zealots wanted to restore the House of David and, in Josephus's opinion led the Jewish nation down to the sack of Jerusalem in A.D. 70. Ascetics such as the Essenes lived apart from the wider Jewish community. Judaism was very diverse, but the Romans felt that the ruling classes were cooperating.

- The Jews offered sacrifices on behalf of the emperor at the temple, but there were certain things they could not do. A strict Jew could not serve in the Roman army because there were too many pagan cults associated with it. They also tended to give charity in local settings, rather than participate in the grand distributions and festivals of the pagan cults.

- By the time the First Jewish War of 66–73 broke out, it was driven by national outrage over the mismanagement and stupidity of the Romans, perhaps best symbolized by Emperor Caligula's attempt to have his statue placed in the Holy of Holies of the Temple of Jerusalem some 25 years before.

- The final insult was Procurator Gessius Florus raiding the sacred treasury of Jerusalem. When the rebellion broke out, Gessius Florus did what all procurators did: He made a beeline to the coast, to Caesarea Maritima, and ignored it, resulting in a major war. Two other rebellions broke out in the following century, both fueled by the same national and religious sentiments.

- The Romans treated these wars as mere rebellions in their official iconography, depicting defeated Judaea as a seated figure in mourning. They even respected the Jews for fighting for their traditions. The fact that the Romans only took actions against those Jews who rebelled and not the Diaspora Jews is a pagan outlook; their treatment of the Jews was not anti-Semitism in the modern sense.

- The Romans learned very little from their dealings with the Jews, and they were completely baffled when they met the Christians. Unlike their Jewish cousins, the Christians would defy Rome, but they would never resort to arms, and this type of resistance was something totally new to the Romans.

Diaspora: "Scattering"; the settlements of Jews living outside the homeland in the Hellenistic and Roman ages.

Hasmonaean: The royal dynasty of Judaea, founded by Simon Maccabaeus in 165 B.C. and ruling until 37 B.C. when Herod the Great seized power in the Jewish homeland.

Messiah: Hebrew for "anointed one"; in Jewish Apocalyptic literature, the Messiah is a descendant of King David who will restore Israel. The Greek equivalent is *Christos*.

Sadducees: Members of the Jewish upper classes from the mid-2nd century B.C. through the late 1st century A.D. who practiced strict ritual purity, maintenance of the sacrifices at the temple, and adherence to the Torah.

synagogue: From Greek *synagoge*, "gathering together"; a consecrated prayer space in Judaism. The synagogue did not replace the Temple of Jerusalem.

Names to Know

Herod the Great (74–4 B.C.; r. 37–4 B.C.): Second son of Antipater of Idumaea who rose in Hasmonaean service and was appointed governor of Galilee in 49 B.C. From 43 B.C., Herod adroitly exploited his friendship with leading Romans, first Marc Antony and then Octavian, so that he ousted the Hasmonaean dynasty and ruled the Jewish lands from 37 B.C. in the interests of Rome. Herod built on a grand scale, notably Caesarea Maritima and the fortress of Masada. He was despised by his Jewish subjects as a tyrant and a slack adherent to Judaism. In the Gospel of Matthew, he is charged with the Slaughter of the Innocents.

Josephus (a.k.a. **Flavius Josephus**, b. c. 37): A prominent Pharisee and historian of the first rank who composed an eyewitness account of the Jewish War of 66–73 A.D. His *Antiquities of the Jews* is invaluable for Jewish religious attitudes and customs. He also composed an apology for Judaism in two books, *Contra Apionem*.

Judas Maccabaeus (a.k.a. **Judah Maccabee**; d. 160 B.C.): Jewish priest and son of Mattathias of the Hasmonaean house who led the revolt against Seleucid king Antiochus IV Epiphanes (175–164 B.C.), who sought to Hellenize the cult of Yahweh at Jerusalem. In 167–163 B.C., Judas won spectacular victories, acquiring the nickname Maccabaeus ("hammer" in Aramaic), and he reoccupied and rededicated the Temple at Jerusalem.

Pontius Pilate (r. 26–36): Roman procurator of Judaea and fifth equestrian governor of Roman Palestine (Judaea and Samaria, notorious for his inept and venal rule. In the Synoptic Gospels, Pilate is presented as reluctant to order the crucifixion of Jesus.

Suggested Reading

Goodman, *The Ruling Classes of Judaea*.

Josephus, *Antiquities of the Jews*.

————, *The Jewish Wars*.

Nikelsburg, *Jewish Literature between the Bible and the Mishnah*.

Segal, *Rebecca's Children*.

Sherwin-White, *Racial Prejudices in Imperial Rome*.

Smallwood, *The Jews under the Roman Rule from Pompey to Diocletian*.

Vermes, *The Complete Dead Sea Scrolls in English*.

Question to Consider

1. How did Jews view the rule of Rome? How accurate is Josephus as a source in reporting the views of the Sadducees, Pharisees, Zealots, and Essenes?

Christian Challenge—First Conversions
Lecture 7

E arly Christianity was not an organized or unified faith. The religion we know today arose out of the apostolic church, led by three men: James the Righteous, who led the Jerusalem Church, which was composed of Jews and was wiped out in one of the rebellions; and Saints Paul and Peter. Paul became the Roman world's first missionary, circling the Mediterranean three times to spread his understanding of Jesus's message to Jews and gentiles. By his execution around A.D. 67, he had established what became the mainstream Christian faith.

The Original Christians

- In the immediate aftermath of the crucifixion, usually dated to around A.D. 26–27, the followers of Jesus had a debate: What was the nature of Jesus's message? Immediate leadership of the group fell to James, often known as **James the Righteous**, sometimes called James the brother of Jesus.

- James's title caused some debate in late antiquity. Saint Jerome, writing at the end of the 4th century A.D., believed James was a cousin of Jesus because he accepted the doctrine of the perpetual virginity of Mary. Others noted that a brother succeeding to his late brother's position was part of the Pharisee tradition, giving weight to James being Jesus's biological brother.

- James assumed his leadership role in what is often called the Jerusalem Church, whose members were in close association with the temple and continued to practice the Jewish dietary traditions, follow the Torah, and so forth. They were suspicious of apocalyptic traditions but accepted Jesus as the son of man and did await the impending *eschaton*.

- This group included Saint Peter, who on two occasions in the New Testament (in the letter of Paul to the Galatians and in the Acts of the Apostles) clearly defers to James's authority.

The Political Church and the Gospel of Mark

- The group's position seems to be reflected in the **Synoptic Gospel** of Mark. Mark is regarded as the oldest gospel. It was written in a simple form of Greek influenced by Aramaic grammar—Aramaic being the language that Jesus taught in. It includes appeals to an impending *eschaton*, Greek for "great reckoning," when God will reveal himself, the hypocrites will be punished, and the humble faithful will be uplifted.

- Mark also mentions the son of man, the mortal figure who will preside over the end of days; alludes to the suffering servant of the book of Isaiah; and uses the term "Messiah," which many Jews would have understood as the leader of a rebellion from Rome.

- When Jesus was crucified, it was not a Jewish punishment. Crucifixion was the Roman penalty for *seditio*—sedition, or treason. The two men crucified beside him are typically referred to as thieves; that was the Romans' euphemism for guerillas.

- The Jerusalem Church continued until around A.D. 60 or 65; then, **Hegesippus**—an early writer whose work does not survive but was used by Eusebius—tells us that the Christians at Jerusalem moved to the city of Pella, where they were destroyed in one of the great rebellions. There were tensions within the group even before this; Saint Stephen was murdered around the year A.D. 35, apparently for arguing that Jesus's message is universal.

Paul's Christianity

- A huge change in the church came with the career of **Paul of Tarsus**. Saint Paul was one of the great religious mystics and intellects of all time. He was a Pharisee Jew who, in his early life,

Saint Paul's missionary journeys created a network of churches—called the apostolic churches—throughout the empire, particularly the eastern half.

was suspicious of the Christians and took part in persecuting them. After a mystical vision on the road to Damascus, however, he took it upon himself to propagate his understanding of the message of Jesus.

- We have seven **Pauline letters**: Romans, 1 and 2 Corinthians, Galatians, Philippians, 1 Thessalonians, and Philemon. The other letters of the New Testament are called the **Deutero-Pauline letters**. They were written by his close associates, probably Timothy and some others, but reflect Paul's ideas closely. The letters were written in Greek and date from 15–35 years after the crucifixion.

- Paul asserted his authority as apostle to the gentiles—that is, to the non-Jews. He concluded that Jesus's message was universal. Yet, as a Pharisee Jew, he also accepted the resurrection of the flesh and the role of angels and believed in an incipient final reckoning. This explains the urgency of his mission to convert the gentiles.

- Paul was the ideal missionary for the Roman world. He sometimes referred to himself as a tent maker, which has misled some to think of him as a humble craftsman. In fact, given his education, social connections, and Roman citizenship, it is more likely that he came from a family with a military contract, making tents for the legions.

- Paul took it upon himself to preach in the synagogues of the Diaspora. He started in Antioch, the capital of Roman Syria (today part of Turkey). He reached many pagans called in the sources "Godfearers"—*theophobeis*. These pagans were familiar with Jewish monotheism, had gone to the synagogue, and may have intermarried with Jews and practiced some of the Jewish dietary laws.

Taking Sides in the Early Church

- To Paul, Jesus was the Messiah who fixed a new Torah. By the act of baptism, Jew and pagan both became Christians, a term that was first used in Antioch. Paul, ever pragmatic, also reasoned that gentiles did not need to obey the old Torah; the act of baptism was the new mark of the new Israel.

- James and members of the Jerusalem Church opposed Paul's views on this. Paul was not an original apostle, which also undermined his authority. Saint Peter seemed inclined to support Paul; but James exerted a great deal of authority, as evidenced by both the canonical texts and the apocryphal *Gospel of Saint Thomas*, written in the 2nd century A.D.

- Eventually a council was held around A.D. 48, as recorded in the Acts of the Apostles. Peter threw his support behind Paul, and as a result the Pauline converts did not have to follow the Torah if they had not originally been Jews. As a secondary result, the apostolic churches recognized themselves as part of a community.

Paul's Missions to the Roman World

- Paul, who in many ways is one of Christianity's first converts, was also the first missionary. We take the idea of proselytizing for granted, but it was a new concept in the Roman world. In the pagan traditions, despite scholars' efforts to find proselytizing by the mystery cults, it is not present. Missionary activities are something that belong to Paul.

- Paul's first mission, generally dated between A.D. 46 and 48, started in Antioch. He then took sea passage to key ports in Cyprus, then landed at Perge, Asia Minor, the center of a very important mother goddess cult. From there he went inland to Roman colonies, including Pisidian Antioch, Iconium, and Lystra.

- On that journey, he set up a number of successful house churches; that is, he converted families, and the leading members of the families made their houses available for services.

- A few years later, Paul took on a more ambitious mission back to a number of those churches, ending up at the port city of Alexandria Troas, a tacky Roman tourist center for the Trojan War. From there he visited the great cities of Greece—Thessalonica, Beroea, Athens, and Corinth—and set up more churches.

- His third mission in the early- to mid-50s took him back to Pisidian Antioch, then down the Maeander River Valley to Ephesus to the great churches of western Asia—many named in the book of Revelation as the Seven Churches of Asia—and back to the churches in Greece. Finally, he returned to the Jewish homeland via the city of Tyre.

- The most important result of Paul's journeys was the network of apostolic churches he established that became the cradle of the Christian movement. Except for Rome and Alexandria, the main centers of the Christian mission for the next 250 years were all cities where Paul established the first churches.

Who Were the First Christians?

- The definitive study of the earliest Christians is *The First Urban Christians* by Wayne Meeks. He found they were often Greek-speaking Jews or pagans familiar with monotheism. They were neither elites nor the lowly but ranked somewhere in between; they had money but not aristocratic bloodlines, and some may have been imperial freedmen.

- Whole families tended to convert together, which meant that early Christianity reflected the social hierarchy, prejudices, and assumptions of the wider Roman world. The leader of a Christian family played the role of a patron, just as he would in a pagan Roman family.

- As far as scholars can tell, the numbers of these communities were quite small. The earliest church we know about is a house church from the city of Dura-Europus, which had about 30 members. Bishops were more like today's parish priests.

- The apostolic church was not the only Christian church out there. Paul's letter to the Galatians warns the congregation not to accept teachers who teach another Christ. Scholars are not sure exactly who these people were; they are sometimes thought to be Docetists, from the Greek word *dokein*, "to seem" or "to appear." Certain people who witnessed the crucifixion believed that God could not be crucified; he only appeared to be crucified.

- Many Christians maintained the Torah and the dietary laws well into the 4th and 5th centuries A.D. The followers of John the Baptist maintained a separate identity—they are known as Mandaeans—and many of these heresies were condemned later by the more organized church, but the initial Christian message was quite diverse.

- Paul was conveyed to Rome around 66 or 67, where he was executed. Tradition states that Peter was martyred there as well. Christianity at this time was facing its first serious challenge: In

64 Emperor Nero had outlawed Christianity, and for the first time, the Roman imperial government persecuted people based on their religion. That was a major change, not only for Christians, but for the Roman world in general.

Important Terms

Deutero-Pauline letters: Letters attributed to Saint Paul that were likely written by his disciples. These are Colossians, Ephesians, 2 Thessalonians, Hebrews, 1 and 2 Timothy, and Titus.

eschaton: Greek for "last"; the ultimate reckoning by God.

Pauline letters: The seven letters of the New Testament written by Saint Paul in about A.D. 48–65: Romans, 1 and 2 Corinthians, Galatians, Philippians, 1 Thessalonians, and Philemon.

Synoptic Gospels: The Gospels of Mark, Luke, and Matthew, composed between A.D. 75 and 85, which offer a synopsis of the ministry and crucifixion of Jesus.

theophobeis: Greek for "God-fearers"; pagans who accepted Jewish monotheism without converting to Judaism.

Names to Know

Paul (a.k.a. **Paul of Tarsus**; c. 5–67): Saint and early Christian writer and missionary, born to a wealthy Pharisee family with Roman citizenship. After his conversion on the road to Damascus in about 35, Paul defined the universal message of Jesus as the conversion of the wider pagan world. He conducted three missions establishing churches in the Greek cities of Asia Minor and Greece in 46–48, 49–52, and 53–57. At the council of Jerusalem (c. 48), Peter and James the Righteous accepted Pauline converts in a compromise. Paul was arrested and imprisoned at Caesarea Maritima in 58–59. He was conveyed to Rome and martyred in the wake of the Great Fire. His seven Epistles (Romans, 1 and 2 Corinthians, Galatians, 1 Thessalonians, Philippians, and Philemon) are fundamental to Christian theology.

Hegesippus (c. 110–180): Reportedly a convert from Judaism and the earliest known Christian chronicler. His work was a major source for Eusebius's *Ecclesiastical History*, but it does not survive.

James the Righteous (d. 62) Called the brother of Jesus by Saint Paul (Galatians 1:19). He succeeded to the authority of the Jerusalem church after the crucifixion.

Suggested Reading

Brandon, *Jesus and the Zealots*.

Brown, *The Body and Society*.

Brown and Meier, *Antioch and Rome*.

Eusebius, *The History of the Church*.

Frend, *Martyrdom and Persecution in the Early Church*:

Louth and Saniforth, ed. and trans., *Early Christian Writings*.

Smith, *Jesus the Magician*.

Questions to Consider

1. What are the sources for the development of early Christian communities in the first century? What were the religious debates among early Christians? How did these debates produce different religious visions? What authority did Saint Paul claim over Saint Peter and James the Righteous?

2. How important were the missionary travels of Saint Paul? How did he turn Christianity into a world faith?

3. Who were the first urban Christians? Why did they convert, and how did they organize their congregations? What other types of Christian confessions emerged in the late 1st and early 2nd centuries?

Pagan Response—First Persecutions

Lecture 8

When we think of the persecution of Christians, it is often a Hollywood-driven image of vast numbers of martyrs thrown to the lions in the Coliseum. The truth is that for the first two centuries, there were no lions, no genocides, no systematic programs to root out and destroy Christianity in the Roman world. With a few notable exceptions, the imperial government mostly regarded Christians with baffled irritation, giving them every opportunity to recant and punishing their treasonous behavior only when compelled by law.

The First Persecution

- We have limited information on how the wider world of paganism immediately received Christianity, but we do have information as to how the Roman imperial government handled it. In the year 64, **Emperor Nero** ordered the first persecution of Christians in the city of Rome. This would have a profound influence on the Christian mission and on pagan perceptions of Christianity.

- Nero targeted the Christians as scapegoats for the Great Fire of 64. His second wife, Poppaea Sabina, who had connections in Rome's Jewish community, may have made the suggestion. Nero needed a scapegoat because he was being accused of lighting the fire himself so he could rebuild the city in his own image—the origin of the (erroneous) image of Nero fiddling while Rome burned.

- In Nero's time, the persecutions were conducted in a circus that he had specially constructed, not in the Coliseum, which was built after his death and dedicated in 80. Saints Peter and Paul were, according to tradition, executed during this persecution.

- We have an account of Nero's persecution, written by the Roman historian **Tacitus**, who was born around the year 56. He was a boy during the persecutions, but he relied on eyewitness accounts. He reports that:

Nero fastened the guilt and inflicted the most exquisite tortures upon a group hated for their abominations, whom the populous call Christians. ... Those who confessed membership were arrested. Then, on their information, great numbers were convicted not so much of guilt for the conflagration as of hatred of the human race.

Tacitus, one of Rome's great historians.

- After describing in horrifying detail the punishments Nero visited on the Christians and his own outlandish behavior, Tacitus notes, "A feeling of pity arose as people felt that [the Christians] were being sacrificed not for the public good but because of the savagery of one man."

- Tacitus's report reveals that Romans of senatorial and equestrian rank had to this point very little contact with Christians; they are not quite sure who they are.

The Confusing Rebellion of Christianity

- Tacitus's account is also verified by his contemporary **Pliny the Younger**, a distinguished government official and later governor of Bithynia-Pontus in Asia Minor. Having encountered the Christians, he wrote to Emperor Trajan because he was unsure about why they were being persecuted. He asked Trajan whether it was because of their faith or because of other crimes. Trajan's answer was evasive.

- The Romans had no real means of dealing with something like Christianity. There were no precedents to assist them. Christians did not revolt nor resort to arms, yet their faith was treason. The Romans rarely outlawed gods; therefore, they labeled

Christianity as superstition and magic, which they were more comfortable outlawing.

- One of the most significant instances of the Romans taking action against a cult was in 186 B.C. A **Senatus consultum** ("decree of the senate") took measures against devotees of Bacchus (Greek Dionysus)—not against the god. The worshipers were meeting under suspicious circumstances (the same was later said of Christians); they met at night and could therefore be a conspiracy, which could lead to social disorder.

- In Gaul and in Britain, the Romans took action against the Druids because they incited rebellion. In 70, the future emperor Titus burned down the Temple of Jerusalem not as an act of anti-Semitism but as a way of punishing the Jews for rebellion. The closest the Romans came to Christian behavior before were their dealings with Cynic philosophers, but these were usually individuals.

- The **rescript** of Nero was a legal turning point. From then on, the Christians had the unique distinction of being singled out by the imperial government as illegal. That would change the whole nature and development of the Christian message. The Christians would respond by developing institutions and means of communicating their mission in very different ways; they could no longer publicly preach.

Pliny the Younger and the Sacrifice Test

- Pliny the Younger, in his correspondence with Emperor Trajan, reveals to us he devised the sacrifice test. This was the main method the Romans used to determine whether those who were accused of Christianity really were Christians.

- Pliny set up the altars of the traditional gods of Rome or of the city, as well as a statue or icon of the emperor. Then the people denounced as Christians were brought before the statues and were told to worship the gods. That is, they had to sacrifice and eat the sacrificial meats. If they did so, they were released. If not, they were punished.

- Pliny mentioned that many people admitted they had been interested in Christianity and attended some services but had reverted to the ancestral gods. He was surprised at how many people fell into this category. Later on, in the great persecutions, these people were known as *lapsi*, people who lapsed and had sacrificed.

- Pliny continued to be perplexed by the status of Christianity in the empire. He had reports of Christians holding orgies, committing cannibalism, and committing incest; these seem to be misunderstandings based on real Christian doctrines—loving all humankind, the Eucharist, calling one another brother and sister. But all of this was based on denunciation, not evidence.

The Extent of the Early Persecutions

- What is also evident in the letter is that Pliny depended heavily on the locals to tell him who were Christians. The imperial government did not have the machinery to carry out a persecution.

- What is clear is that the persecutions are nothing like the Nazi Holocaust or the kind of ethnic cleansing that fills newspapers today. In fact, the persecution was a legal proceeding. Trajan responded to Pliny's letter about the sacrifice test with a legal argument:

  It is not possible to lay down any general rule to serve as a kind of fixed standard. ... [The Christians] are not to be sought out. If they are denounced and proved guilty, they are to be punished. ... But anonymously posted accusations ought not to have a place in any prosecution, for this is both a dangerous kind of precedent and out of keeping with the spirit of our age.

- This is an extraordinary response from an emperor: We are supposed to follow the law. Therefore, any image of the early persecution that calls to mind the Gestapo or the KGB is an inaccurate picture; there is no place for such abuse in Roman law. Even the word "martyr," attached to those Christians who died in the arena, literally means "witness," as in a legal proceeding.

- The *cognitio extra ordinem* was an extraordinary legal proceeding in which the governors could interrogate Christians, and there were many instances—even in Christian records—where the governor gave the accused every opportunity to repent and worship the Roman gods.

- Another important fact that comes out of Trajan's letter and is verified by later sources is that persecutions were local, sporadic, and short-lived. There was no concerted effort to root out Christians.

- Saint Cyprian, writing in North Africa, said there was a depressing correlation between an earthquake and a persecution. The great plague of 166–169, which swept the empire when the Roman army returned from the East, led to outbursts of persecution. So the tradition of scapegoating that began with Nero remained a part of persecutions into the 2nd century.

- But otherwise, Christians, if they avoided overt actions—if they did not proselytize or insult the gods directly—were mostly left alone. They could live inconspicuous lives and convert people through family and social networks, as long as they did not disrupt the fabric of civic life.

- The Romans never did comprehend what they were facing in Christianity. The whole idea of Christians standing in a law court, following the rules of law, and then denying the sacrifice was extraordinary. Meanwhile, the Christians themselves now had to find new ways of defining themselves, organizing their communities, and disseminating their message.

rescript: The response of a Roman emperor to a petition that had the force of law.

Senatus consultum: Decree of the Senate; a resolution by the Roman Senate that gave its backing to a proposed law.

Nero (a.k.a. **Lucius Domitius Ahenobarbus**; 37–68; r. 54–68): The last Julio-Claudian emperor. Nero was the son of Gnaeus Domitius Ahenobarbus and Agrippina the Younger (the great-granddaughter of Augustus). In 49, his mother married Claudius and secured Nero's adoption as Claudius's heir. Nero took the name Nero Claudius Caesar. In 54, Nero succeeded as emperor, but he craved popularity as an artist and therefore entrusted the affairs of state to his ministers down to 62, when he assumed direct control. By his amoral and outrageous conduct, he alienated the ruling classes and legions and thus precipitated his downfall and suicide in 68. In 64, Nero ordered the first persecution of Christians at Rome.

Pliny the Younger (a.k.a. **Caius Caeilius Plinus Secundus**; 61–112): Roman senator from northern Italy and adopted son of a famous naturalist, Pliny penned letters to Emperor Trajan that reveal the workings of civic life in Asia Minor during the Roman peace.

Tacitus (a.k.a. **Publius Cornelius Tacitus**; 56–after 120): From a northern Italian or southern Gallic provincial family, Tacitus entered a senatorial career under Vespasian. In 77, he married Julia, daughter of Gnaeus Julius Agricola. In 97, he was consul, and in 112–113, he was proconsul of Asia. He is the greatest historian of imperial Rome. He wrote *Annals* and *Histories*, covering the periods 14–68 and 68–96, respectively. He also wrote *Germania*, *Agricola*, and *Dialogus de oratoribus*. In *Annals*, Tacitus reports the persecution of Christians by Nero in 64.

Suggested Reading

de Ste Crox, "Why Were the Christians Persecuted?"

Eusebius, *The History of the Church.*

Fox, *Pagans and Christians.*

Frend, *Martyrdom and Persecution in the Early Church.*

Hopkins, "Murderous Games."

MacMullen, *Enemies of the Roman Order.*

Musurillo, ed. and trans., *Acts of the Christian Martyrs.*

Pliny the Younger, *The Letters of Pliny the Younger.*

Tacitus, *The Annals of Imperial Rome.*

Wilken, *The Christians as the Romans Saw Them.*

Questions to Consider

1. What was the impact of Nero's persecution of the Christians in 64? How did Romans view Christians in the 1st and 2nd centuries A.D.? What motivated Romans, and pagans in general, to compel Christians to sacrifice?

2. What does Pliny the Younger reveal about the imperial government's aims in persecuting Christians? Was this a priority? How does Pliny's perspective differ from that of Eusebius and the acts of the martyrs?

3. Why did the Romans fail to understand Christianity? Did they see a conflict of religion?

Christian Bishops and Apostolic Churches
Lecture 9

Before the Council of Nicaea in A.D. 325, one could not speak of a Christian Church with a capital *C* and a clear mission. But the apostolic churches of the 1st and 2nd centuries made two significant advances toward that goal: First, they developed the concept of an apostolic succession, the hierarchical structure that would become the basis of Constantine's church. Second, they rapidly created the New Testament canon that would become, with few changes, the dogma of Christianity for the next 1,500 years.

The Church in the Apostolic Heartland

- By A.D. 64 and Nero's outlawing of Christianity, the apostolic Christian heartland stretched from the imperial capital at Rome, across Greece and Asia Minor, to Antioch and Syria, down to Jerusalem, and to Alexandria in Egypt.

- Other confessions, which later Christians called heresies, existed elsewhere, but the developments in leadership and canon are peculiar to those apostolic churches in response to the fact that Christianity was now outlawed.

- There were different ways of organizing congregations before 64 and even shortly after. Most Christian churches were private property—house churches. Meetings of the faithful were comparable to reading groups. There was nothing comparable to the later basilicas and Gothic cathedrals.

- Missionary activity essentially ceased in this subapostolic era. As inefficient and limited as the imperial government was, if a missionary started preaching the way Paul did in Ephesus, he would inevitably cause a riot and be arrested.

- The only known exception is Gregory the Wonder Worker, who preached in Alexandria. A biography of Gregory written by **Gregory of Nyssa** (whose grandmother, Marciona, had been converted by Gregory the Wonder Worker) is now understood to be full of anachronisms, so we have little information about Gregory's actual doings.

The Language of Christianity

- Language also restricted Christian activity. Over half of the Roman population did not speak Latin or Greek, whereas Christians were essentially Greek speakers. There simply were no missionaries available who knew the necessary languages.

- We have no references to Coptic, Syriac, or other native language translations of the New Testament until the about the 4th century A.D., and many languages of the Roman world were never written down. Compounding this, only about 15–20 percent of the Roman population was literate, so most people had to be taught orally.

- Some missionaries converted pagans by charisma, exorcism, and miracle working, but once the missionary moved on, if there was no church to follow up, the message was essentially lost.

- What literature there was, was not written in the high literary style of the Second Sophistic movement—that is, Attic Greek; it was written in **Koine** (the vernacular). The Roman elite would therefore look upon Christian literature—if they encountered it at all—as unworthy of serious attention. To the Romans, expression and clarity of language went side by side with intellectual achievement.

- Latin did become a language of the Christians during the late 2nd century in what is today Tunisia. However, the city of Rome and much of the empire remained Greek-speaking well past the mid-3rd century.

A Small Community of Small Communities

- Christian communities were small and self-contained well into the mid-3rd century. They were very much restricted to cities.

- Christians had little money. Bishop **Cyprian of Carthage** (the second-wealthiest city of the Roman West), once raised 100,000 sestertii to ransom Christian prisoners, but a Roman senator would blow that amount of money throwing a gladiatorial game. Pope **Fabian** had about 1,500 people in his employ and living on papal charity; by comparison, the Roman emperor at the same time would hand out distributions of grain and money to 250,000 residents during a festival.

Early popes, like Pope Fabian, had little power or wealth.

The Teaching Company Collection.

- Some interesting information about early Christians comes from inscriptions on funerary monuments found in Turkey, the only early monuments we have besides the catacombs in Rome. They come from areas where there were also important Jewish communities, and the inscriptions are similar to Jewish inscriptions of the period. The symbols and information suggest that a number of these families were converts from Judaism several generations earlier and some of them were still following Jewish law.

- Many early churches were established by other churches, such as the church at Sinope on the shores of the Black Sea. The first church in Gaul, at Lugdunum (modern Lyon) was founded by Pauline Christians from either Smyrna, Ephesus, or Pergamon.

The First Authorities and the First Heresies

- In response to the threat of persecution and heresy, the monarchial bishops began to arise in the 2nd century. Bishop **Ignatius of Antioch** wrote seven letters to various churches in Asia Minor in 107. They asserted three sources of authority in the Christian community: the *episkopos*, or bishop; the evangelist, or preacher; and the prophet or prophetesses. Prophetesses still had significant respect in the early church, a holdover from Judaism.

- A generation later, Bishop **Polycarp of Smyrna**, who was martyred in 155, writes of monarchical bishops as the sole source of authority in the church. This is the beginning of the notion of apostolic succession. In particular, the bishops of Rome, Alexandria, and Antioch had special authority because of their connections to Saint Peter; Rome, as the imperial capital, had the highest position of all.

- Pope Clement I wrote a letter to the church in Corinth, just as Paul did, to settle issues around the year 95, so the pope (that is, the bishop of Rome) already had authority even with churches in the Roman East.

- One of the earliest heresies was **Montanism**, named after their leader, **Montanus**, who emerged in Asia Minor in the mid-2nd century A.D. offering what he called the New Prophecy. He was followed by two female associates, **Priscilla** and **Maximilla**, who claimed to speak in the name of the Paraclete—the Holy Spirit.

- Montanus, Priscilla, and Maximilla presented a particular challenge to the bishops because they were producing a new revelation. Polycarp would argue that revelation was over and God's message was fixed.

- The Montanists were received with skepticism. They were banished at a number of synods—local councils of bishops. In fact, the first reports of synods we have were assembled to respond to the Montanists, and the Montanists forced bishops to develop their positions.

- Developing doctrine thus became another challenge. Which texts belonged in the New Testament? By 180, there were several versions of the New Testament circulating. Some were regarded as spurious and others as genuine, but it was difficult to distinguish among them.

- The **Gnostics** were teachers, such as **Valentinus**, who took Christian notions, principles, and faith and reinterpreted them in pagan myth to create cosmic schemes of redemption. They used myth allegorically, much the way a Buddhist or Hindu teacher does. This was considered heresy and presented another problem to those who wished to establish a canon.

- **Marcion of Sinope** created his own version of the canon that rejected the entire Old Testament. He concluded that Yahweh of the Old Testament could not be the God of the New Testament, which only included the Gospel of Luke, Acts of the Apostles, and a few of Paul's letters.

- Pope Pius summoned the First Synod at Rome in 143–144 in response to Marcion's text. Marcion was excommunicated and expelled from the Roman church and—happily, it seems—went off to found his own church, which flourished in Syria. The apostolic church was forced to finally establish which texts belonged in the New Testament and how to arrange them.

- No one in the 2nd and 3rd centuries knew who would eventually end up a heretic and who would be part of the established church, despite the surety of hindsight found in Eusebius. Eusebius goes so far as to condemn the heretics as serpents planted in the bosom of mother church by Satan himself, but we must remember it was not as clear at the time.

- The pagan critic Celsus captured a sense of these Christian divisions, writing around 177. He said that the Christians were like frogs sitting around a small pond croaking about sin. Celsus understood that the Christians were divided and that division hindered proselytizing.

- Fortunately for the church, despite their divisions, the apostolic bishops were able to make two important strides toward healing their divisions during this period: They established a formal church organization, and they defined a canon of texts.

Important Terms

episkopos (pl. *episkopoi*): Greek for "overseer"; a bishop.

Gnostics: From Greek *gnostikos*, "knowledgeable"; mystics and teachers with a deeper esoteric knowledge of religious texts and therefore of the path to salvation. Many Gnostics premised their cosmology on dualist beliefs. *See* **dualism**.

Koine: From Greek *koinē*, "common"; the vernacular, simplified Greek spoken in the Hellenistic world and the Roman Empire. The books of the New Testament are written in Koine Greek rather than the archaizing literary Greek of the upper classes.

Montanism: The Christian heresy of Montanus, who in the mid 2ⁿᵈ century, proclaimed direct inspiration from the Holy Spirit. Also called the New Prophecy.

Celsus (fl. 2nd century A.D.): Pagan critic of Christianity who wrote *On the True Doctrine* in 177. His work is largely known from quotations by Origen.

Cyprian of Carthage (a.k.a. **Thasciius Caecilius Cyprianus**; d. 258): Saint and bishop (250–257) who composed in Latin numerous tracts on issues of baptism of *lapsi*, readmission of heretics into the church, and episcopal authority. He was martyred during the persecution of Valerian.

Fabian (r. 236–250): Pope respected by African and Italian bishops and credited with missions to cities in Gaul. He was martyred during the persecution of Trajan Decius on January 20, 250.

Gregory of Nyssa (335–394): Saint and bishop of Nyssa (372–394). Born at Caesarea in Cappadocia, he was the younger brother to Saint Basil of Caesarea. Gregory penned important tracts on the Trinity and the omnipotence of God, thereby rejecting the views of Origen and the pagan Neoplatonists.

Ignatius of Antioch (d. c 107): Saint and bishop. He wrote seven letters that offer the first insight into the authority and role of bishops in apostolic churches.

Marcion of Sinope (c. 85–160): Christian theologian and editor of the New Testament. In 143/4 he emigrated to Rome. He produced his own edited version of the New Testament based on the letters of Paul and the Gospel of Luke. His teachings were rejected and condemned at the first reported synod at Rome, presided over by Pope Anicetus. Marcion then founded his own church that flourished into the 5th century.

Montanus (c. 150–200): Credited with apocalyptic revelations from the Holy Spirit either in 157 or 172, Montanus and his associates, Maximilla and Priscilla, offered a so-called New Prophecy that promised redemption only to the elect. Montanus challenged the authority of bishops in apostolic churches, who condemned Montanus as a heretic and convert from paganism. Montanist churches, however, survived in Asia Minor into the 7th century.

Polycarp of Smyrna (fl. 2nd century A.D.): Saint and bishop martyred at an uncertain date during a persecution in c. 150–155. He established the role of bishops in apostolic churches and was in the forefront of fixing the Christian canon by editing the books of the New Testament.

Priscilla and **Maximilla** (fl. mid-2nd century A.D.): Prophetesses and associates of Montanus, through whom the Paraclete (Holy Spirit) was believed to have spoken.

Valentinus (c. 100–160): A noted Gnostic teacher and thinker born at Alexandria who founded school at Rome. His dualist cosmology, based on allegorical myths and middle Platonic principles, were rejected by Christians as heretical. The *Gospel of Truth*, among the texts found at Nag Hammadi, was penned by Valentinus.

Suggested Reading

Brown, *The Body and Society.*

———, *The Churches the Apostles Left Behind.*

Brown and Meier, *Antioch and Rome.*

Eusebius, *The History of the Church.*

Frend, *Martyrdom and Persecution in the Early Church.*

Grant, *Augustus to Constantine.*

———, *Formation of the New Testament.*

Harnack, *Marcion.*

Louth and Saniforth, ed. and trans., *Early Christian Writings.*

Pelikan, *The Emergence of the Catholic Tradition.*

Richardson, *The Christianity of Ignatius of Antioch.*

Richardson, ed., *Early Christian Fathers.*

Robinson, *Ignatius of Antioch and the Parting of the Ways*.

Trevett, *Montanism*.

Tyson, *Marcion and Luke-Acts*.

Questions to Consider

1. What limited the dissemination of the Christian message after the persecution of 64? What barriers did Christian missionaries face in proselytizing in the late 1st and 2nd centuries? What are the sources for determining the numbers and rank of Christians?

2. Why was the evolution of episcopal organization and canon decisive for the success of the apostolic churches? Why were alternative organization or religious authority offered?

3. What accounted for the success and long-term popularity of the confessions outside the apostolic mainstream? Were these confessions fairly condemned as heretical churches?

Pagan Critics and Christian Apologists
Lecture 10

The pagan critics of Christianity, such as Galen and Celsus, had doubts about the Christian god's power and the sanity of his worshipers. But as the apologists adopted the techniques and language of the best of classical rhetoric, Christians were finally able to explain their position to the wider Roman world. They presented themselves in very Roman terms as well: as a revival of an ancient faith, as loyal to Rome and the emperor, and as consistent with Platonic philosophy.

Who Were the Apologists?

- The **apologists** were Christian authors who wrote in defense of the faith. An apology—or *apologia* in Greek—was a formal, philosophical, and moral tract that had a long history going back to the 5th century B.C. The most famous is Plato's *Apology*, which recounts the trial of Socrates in 399 B.C.

- The need for Christians to adopt the apology was driven by pagan criticisms and Christianity's illegal status. This was the second classical literary genre the Christians had adapted for their own use, the first being the epistolary form, as in the letters of Saint Paul.

- Christians were not only answering legal charges; they were also addressing rumors like those recorded in Pliny the Younger's letters to Emperor Trajan. These charges were difficult to address because the public had no knowledge of Christian doctrines and practices.

- The apologists also had to assert over and over that they were loyal Romans, albeit in their own fashion, and should not be lumped together with social misfits like the Cynics.

The Pagan Response to Christian Apology

- The pagans, in turn, got better at criticizing Christians. The intellectual classes became increasingly aware of Christianity, and the charges leveled against Christians shifted over the course of the 3rd century toward more substantial criticisms of actual Christian doctrines. This, in turn, pushed Christian writers to become more sophisticated in explaining their faith and answering the charges.

- **Galen of Pergamon** is the first pagan whose opinions of Christianity we know in any detail. Galen is remembered as one of the great physicians of antiquity. He was a product of the Second Sophistic movement, a Platonist, and a very incisive scientist with professional connections to the imperial family.

- Galen made remarks about Christians in passing. Notably, he was not bewildered the way Pliny or Tacitus was. Rather, he was horrified by their behavior. Galen found it illogical and unreasonable that they should decide to die for their faith, especially that the men should let their wives and children die in the arena. He also opines, like many pagans, that if the god of the Christians allows so many of his people to die in the arena, he is not a very powerful god.

- Galen was perplexed by Christian doctrines such as the resurrection of the flesh because it contradicts Platonism and his own observations about the world. Platonists either believed in reincarnation or spiritual salvation. Galen, of course, was well aware of the mortality of the flesh.

- **Celsus**, mentioned in the previous lecture, was a contemporary of Galen. We know little about him; most of his writing survives as quotations in the work of the Christian writer Origen. Celsus's *On the True Doctrine* is a critique of Christianity that seems to be based on reports from Jewish informants.

- What is significant about Celsus is his approach, one that was not popular among other pagans, although many modern critics would return to it. Celsus reported that Jesus was the reputed illegitimate son of a carpenter whose mother had an affair with a Roman soldier named Panthera. He said that the adulterous couple fled to Egypt, where Jesus learned magic; calling others' religion magic or superstition was a stock insult.

- He said Jesus's followers were fishermen and tax collectors. He said it was Jesus's hysterical female followers who found the empty tomb and put out the story of his appearances. These stories are very early criticisms, probably made by the first Jews to reject Christianity. It seems Celsus went out of his way to refute Christianity on what we would call historical grounds.

- Origen went out of his way to refute Celsus's charges, and his refutation apparently was regarded as definitive. But Celsus writing reveals the important point that by the late 2nd century, pagans could distinguish Jews from Christians.

Redefining the Christian Church

- Some Christian authors actually saw Judaism as a rival. An early apologist, **Melito of Sardis**, wrote a critique of the Jews and was concerned about Christians going back to Judaism. As late as the A.D. 400, John Chrysostom, patriarch of Constantinople, told a Christian, "If you go into a building and you are not sure whether it is a synagogue or a church, ask."

- The Christian apologists helped frame the debate and elevate Christianity to the level of a philosophy rather than a superstition. Most of them drove home the fact that the Christians were loyal Romans. They cited the passages from the Synoptic Gospels where Jesus instructs his followers to "render unto Caesar his due."

- Christian apologists of the 2nd century A.D. were already framing Pontius Pilate not as an agent of Rome but as an agent of God. It was not the Romans per se who carried out the crucifixion; this was ordained, a fulfillment of prophecy.

- In paganism, new cults were never presented as new cults but the rediscovery of an old cult. To some extent, the Christians were following this notion. Christianity was a *Mos maiorum*, the custom of the ancestors, neither new nor dangerous to the Roman world.

Four Early Apologists

- **Justin the Martyr** wrote two important apologies, one addressed to the emperor Antoninus Pius, in which he stressed again the loyalty of the Christians to Rome and the second to the Roman senate.

- Justin's apologies are important because they elucidate the faith using Greek philosophical terms from Plato's *Timaeus*. While he claims that the Greek gods are false, he allows that Greek philosophers and thinkers had some glimpse of reality thanks to God's clemency and mercy. Justin thereby initiated the process of Christians appropriating the classical literary tradition.

- **Theophilus of Antioch**, writing a little bit earlier than Justin, addressed a fictional pagan friend of his named Autolycus in the work *Ad autolycum*. Not only does he use Platonism; he is the first author we know of to use the term "Trinity" and identify the three realities in Plato with the three persons of the Godhead defined at the Council of Nicaea in 325.

- Theophilus, unlike Justin, used a lot more invective and ridicule of pagan authors. He was also the first person to expound that "genesis" means "creation ex nihilo," out of nothing, not out of preexisting matter as in Platonism. This was important in moving Christian philosophy from apology to theology—that is, from defense to exposition.

- **Minucius Felix**, a Roman citizen of Carthage, wrote an important apology, *The Octavius*, in which he tried to use logic to win over a pagan. Octavius is a fictional Christian who debates with a fictional pagan called Cecilius Natalis. In the course of the debate, Octavius persuades his pagan friend of the superior revelation of Christianity.

- **Tertullian** was also a North African Roman, as well as a jurist and Stoic. Later in life, he joined the Montanists, but early on he wrote important apologies of apostolic Christianity. He was a stark rigorist, expected the incipient end of days, and had little good to say about pagan idols and traditions. He was uncompromising about the truth of Christianity; he called Rome "the whore of Babylon" and Nero "the beast of Revelation."

Tertullian was uncompromising in his theology.

Library of Congress Prints and Photographs Division, 04617v.

- Tertullian was almost too narrowly focused; the future of Latin Christianity rested with later authors such as Saint Cyprian, Saint Augustine of Hippo, and Minucius Felix, who had a broader notion of the church as the church of all sinners, set up to help us. Nonetheless, he was an important ancestor of the Latin Christian authors whose work culminated with Saint Augustine in the 5th century A.D.

Important Terms

apologist: Defender; a Christian writer who penned defenses against pagan criticism. The most important of the early apologists were Justin the Martyr (103–165), who wrote in Greek, and Tertullian (160–220), who wrote in Latin.

Mos maiorum: Latin for "custom of the ancestors"; the Roman expression for the superior authority of traditional religious and social practices.

Celsus (fl. 2nd century A.D.): Pagan critic of Christianity who wrote *On the True Doctrine* in 177. His work is largely known from quotations by Origen.

Galen of Pergamon (a.k.a. Aelius Galenus; 129–205): Physician and philosopher born of a prominent family with Roman citizenship; wrote extensively on human physiology and biology. In his writings, Galen makes a number of references to Christians and martyrdoms.

Justin the Martyr (103–165): Christian apologist who wrote (in Greek) the *First* and *Second Apologies* and *Dialogue with Typhro*.

Melito of Sardis (d. c. 180): Perhaps bishop of Sardis, he wrote an apology in Greek addressed to Emperor Marcus Aurelius. He also expressed his anxiety over Judaism and so reflected the fact that Jews occupied a favored position at Sardis.

Minucius Felix (c. 150–270): This otherwise anonymous figure wrote the earliest surviving Latin apology, *Octavius*, set as a debate between Christian Octavius and pagan Caecilius Natalis.

Tertullian (a.k.a. **Quintus Septimius Florens Tertullianus**; c. 160–c. 220): Lawyer and Christian apologist at Carthage who wrote the first major Christian works in Latin. Of foremost importance was his *Apology*, defending Christianity.

Theophilus of Antioch (d. c. 183): Bishop who wrote the apology *Ad autolycum*, in which he advanced the doctrine of creation *ex nihilo* and a doctrine of the Trinity.

Barnes, *Tertullian*.

Brown, *The Body and Society*.

Celsus, *On True Doctrine*.

Eusebius, *The History of the Church*.

Grant, *Augustus to Constantine*.

————, *Formation of the New Testament*.

Justin Martyr, *Saint Justin Martyr: The First and Second Apologies*.

Irenaeus, *Irenaeus of Lyons*.

Louth and Saniforth, ed. and trans., *Early Christian Writings*.

Parvis, *Justin Martyr and His World*.

Pelikan, *The Emergence of the Catholic Tradition*.

Richardson, ed., *Early Christian Fathers*.

Rogers, *Theophilus of Antioch*.

Theophilus of Antioch, *Ad autocylum*.

Tertulllian, *Apologia and De Spectaculis*.   Minucius Felix. *Octavius*. Translated by T. R. Glover and G. H. Rendall.

Wilken, *The Christians as the Romans Saw Them*.

————, *John Chrysostom and the Jews*.

Questions to Consider

1. How did pagan criticisms of Christianity change over the course of the 2nd and 3rd centuries? What were the most popular charges raised by pagans? What were the most damaging? What does this criticism reveal about pagan acquaintance with Christians and Christian doctrine?

2. How did apologists adapt classical genres to create defenses of the faith? Why did pagan writers so often resort to polemic? How convincing were arguments drawn from Plato and Aristotle?

3. What was the impact of the apologists on Christian self-definition? Would pagans be convinced by reading these apologies?

First Christian Theologians
Lecture 11

The important work of the Christian apologists was soon followed by the first Christian theologians, the most important of whom was Origen. Working from a deep knowledge of both Platonic philosophy and the Hebrew Old Testament, he was in the forefront of establishing the Christian canon, as well as reconciling Christian and classical philosophy. Although many of Origen's ideas were later condemned by the church, he nonetheless made important contributions to such doctrines as the nature of the Trinity and the human soul.

Christian Alexandria

- Two of the leading figures in early Christian theology, **Saint Clement** and **Origen**, lived and worked in Alexandria, and the city of Alexandria was arguably just as important for the formation of Christian theology as they were. This Greek city in Egypt, established by Alexander the Great, was home to the great library called the Mouseion.

- Alexandria was also home to many important intellectual circles in the 2nd and 3rd centuries A.D.—Christian, Jewish, pagan, and particularly Gnostic. Saint Clement refounded the Catechetical School here around 190 or 200 (the original had been disrupted by persecutions), and it became the center for Christian thinking in the Roman world.

- Alexandria was home to a Christian church of unknown origins. There is speculation that the Gospel of Matthew was composed in Alexandria at the end of the 1st century A.D. Whatever its origins, the Christian community here was serious in taking on pagan philosophers on equal terms. In this way, the Christians were heirs to the Jewish philosophical tradition in Alexandria.

Saint Clement

- Clement contributed significantly to the development of Christian theology. He wrote *Stromata*, a set of miscellaneous interpretations and observations on Christian theology. He was also convinced that the truly enlightened philosopher—one who was inspired with real knowledge (gnosis), as opposed to just technical skill—was really a Christian.

- In arguing this, Clement changed the relationship between pagans and Christians. He is saying that Christians are heirs to classical intellectual culture as much as the pagans, moving the debate away from the polemic of Tertullian's day. Christians and pagans will instead debate who has the better interpretation of Plato's vision of reality.

Origen—His Background and the Sources

- Clement's writings, as important as they were, were dwarfed by his successor and student, Origen. This name does not resonate with moderns today, in part because his writings were condemned at the Fifth Ecumenical Council in 553 by the Emperor Justinian in an effort to carry out a religious reunion within the divided imperial church.

- Origen's writings were very controversial and survive in fragments in the records of the council and a Latin rewrite by **Rufinus of Aquileia** from around 400. Rufinus actually changes Origen's text to conform to the doctrines of the early 5th century—sometimes reversing the meaning entirely.

- We also know a fair amount about his life. Origen was born into a Christian family somewhere around 185 A.D. His father was martyred in the Severan Persecution of 202–203. The family was clearly of Greek ancestry, so Origen was a speaker of Greek, but he also mastered Hebrew, one of the few church fathers who did. In some ways, he was an ascetic, and his writings are the intellectual basis for the monastic movements of the 4th century.

- Origen went on missions and was ordained a priest in Cappadocia. Origen may have been received at court in 222 by Emperor Severus Alexander. Origen eventually moved to Caesarea Maritima, founded by King Herod as his Greek capital, because it had a major library of Greek and Hebrew texts. There he wrote most of his works.

Origen's Main Works

- Origen's writings are important for several reasons. He was at the forefront of establishing the canon through his commentaries on various books of the Old Testament. His commentary on Numbers defines in middle Platonic terms what God is and defines creation as a rational act.

- Origen's *Hexapla*, or *Six Books* contains the Hebrew text, the Hebrew text transliterated into Greek letters, and then the four main Greek translations of the Hebrew Bible—including the Septuagint translation—as well as comments about how these texts relate to the New Testament. Here he created the official biblical typology (that is, the passages in the Old Testament that prefigure the New Testament) that is used to this day.

- Origen's greatest contribution to Christian theology was a work he wrote early in his career, *On First Principles*, or *Peri Archon*. It was controversial not only because of its views but also because it only exists in fragmentary form. The first three books have been reconstructed fairly accurately. The later books are more questionable.

- In this book, Origen has refined the language of analysis, which became the hallmark of Christian exegesis—the interpretation of texts. He stressed the importance of understanding the inner meaning, not just the literal meaning of the text.

- It also contains the first clear explanation of the creation of the godhead, as well as discussions of the nature of evil that borrow heavily from Plato: Evil is the absence of good. He stresses the importance of understanding free will to achieve salvation, which is the process of moving the soul back toward God.

Origens Theology

- Origen accepted the Gospel of Saint John's identification of Christ with the Logos—"the word" but more specifically the rational word of creation. The Christ Logos was eternally generated from the father—*aei gennetos*, "always generated." He seems to believe that God the father, the Christ Logos, and the Holy Spirit represent three aspects of the godhood and have a hierarchical relationship; the image uses is an eternal torch, one lighting the other.

- In the 4th century, there will be serious debate over Origen's view of the Trinity. Did he mean a hierarchy of emanations—that is, the father generated the son generated the Holy Spirit—or are they coequal and coeternal? Origen set up the intellectual debate that would occur at the Council of Nicaea and the Council of Constantinople—literally for the next century.

- Despite his dependence on Platonic thought, Origen was very much a Christian and knew his Hebrew text very well. He had a strong sense of the transcendence of God; the Christ Logos was the bridge between divinity and the material world or, in Platonic terms, from the world of being to the world of becoming.

- Souls, the *psyche*, are eternal and good, yet at the same time they possess free will. The first three books of *On First Principles* spend a great deal of time telling how souls fell away from God. They are divine, but because they have free will, they become inattentive and fall away from God like a charioteer who falls asleep at the reins— an image from Plato's *Phaedrus*.

- Some souls fell away and became angels. Others became humans and became embodied in the material world. The soul that fell the furthest was Satan. But all souls, by knowledge, can return to God.

Origen's Surprising Ideas

- At this point, Origen got himself in trouble. He thought that, if souls could fall away from God and re-attain perfection once, perhaps they could fall away again. In the next cycle, Origen suggested, perhaps Satan will play the role of Christ and Christ the role of Satan.

- This was a move away from the strong sense of linear progressive time from the Hebrew tradition and toward a Greek philosophical sense of time. Also, in this scheme, no soul need be condemned to hell for eternity; punishment is the soul contemplating and remembering with remorse its evil acts and in so doing perceiving God and attaining divinization.

- Obviously, there was a wide range of speculation available to Origen in 215 that, 100 years later, was going to be closed when decisions were made at the great councils in the 4th and 5th centuries. Later authors, including Eusebius, had great difficulty understanding how Origen could speculate so freely.

- Origen made some important contributions toward the debate between Christians and pagans. Henceforth, critics of Christianity could not resort to the stock criticisms Celsus used in the early 2nd century. Second, Origen used the language of high philosophy that the Roman elite could not dismiss. In many ways, Christian theology had now come of age.

Origen's Legacy

- Origen had gone through the Hebrew text and determined what the best Greek version of the Old Testament was. Many of the theologians and thinkers who would follow Origen did not know Hebrew; they had to depend on his work.

- One of his most important achievements was the synthesis of Platonic reasoning and philosophy with Christian doctrine. Christians were no longer as divided as they had been. They could present themselves as the heirs of Plato and claim that they had as much claim to classical tradition as the pagans did. The Christian thinkers now had a serious religious vision.

Important Terms

aei gennetos: "Eternally generated"; term used by Origen in *On First Principles* to explain the relationship between God the father and the Christ-*logos* in the Trinity.

Hexapla: Greek for "sixfold"; a set of texts complied by Origen (185–254) to establish the canonical text of the Old Testament. It comprised the Hebrew text, the Hebrew transliterated into Greek letters, and the translations in Greek of Aquila of Sinope, Symmachus the Ebionite, the Septuagint, and Theodotian.

Names to Know

Clement (c. 150–215): Saint and theologian who refounded the Catechetical School at Alexandria in about 202 and composed the *Stromata*, in which he elucidates his doctrine of salvation that influenced his most brilliant student, Origen.

Origen (185–254): Brilliant Christian theologian. Born at Alexandria of a Christian family and studied under Saint Clement, whom he succeeded as head of the Catechetical School. He was sent on a number of diplomatic missions by Bishop Demetrius of Alexandria. In 230, Origen removed himself to Caesarea Maritima because Demetrius protested Origen's ordination. Origen wrote numerous commentaries on books of the Bible and pastoral works, establishing the discipline of exegesis and typology. In 215–217, Origen composed *On First Principles*, the first serious theological work that reconciled Christian faith and Platonic philosophy. He also produced the *Hexapla*, a study of the Hebrew and Greek texts of the Old Testament. His views on cosmology and salvation were later condemned at the Fifth Ecumenical Council in 553.

Rufinus of Aquileia (c. 350–410): Roman monk who translated Greek theological and historical writings into Latin. In 372, he traveled to Alexandria and then resettled at Jerusalem, where he disputed with Saint Jerome the doctrines of Origen. In 397, Rufinus returned to Rome and translated and adapted into Latin Origen's *On First Principles*.

Suggested Reading

Bigg, *The Christian Platonists of Alexandria.*

Brown, *The Body and Society.*

Celsus, *On True Doctrine.*

Clement of Alexandria, *Works.*

Eusebius, *The History of the Church.*

Irenaeus, *Irenaeus of Lyons.*

Layton, trans. and ed., *The Gnostic Scriptures.*

MacMullen and Lane, eds., *Paganism and Christianity.*

Origen, *On First Principles.*

Pelikan, *The Emergence of the Catholic Tradition.*

Porphyry, *Against the Christians.*

Richardson, ed., *Early Christian Fathers.*

Trigg, *Origen.*

Wilken, *The Christians as the Romans Saw Them.*

1. Why was Alexandria home to so much serious intellectual debate and theology? What issues were raised by Gnostic, pagan, and Christian teachers in the city?

2. What was the impact of the Catechetical School of Alexandria? How important was Saint Clement in evolving Christian letters and thought?

3. What was the importance of *On First Principles*? What was Origen's religious vision, and how consistent was it with scripture? Why did later Christian thinkers find Origen's views heretical?

4. Why was Origen so important for Christians in evolving their doctrine? Why was this doctrine in Platonic terms acceptable to pagans? How important was Origen to the ultimate success of Christianity in the Roman world?

Imperial Crisis and Spiritual Crisis
Lecture 12

The traditional view of the so-called crisis of the 3rd century is a Roman world in complete political, economic, and spiritual breakdown, which in turn led great numbers of ordinary people to turn to Christianity. The problem with this view is that the archaeological evidence does not support it. More modern scholarship indicates that the Romans turned to Christianity for very traditional Roman reasons: because the Christian god proved himself of value to the emperor, and the emperor's faith became the faith of the elite.

The 3rd-Century Persian Wars

- The next four lectures deal with paganism in the years 235–305, which are often seen as a turning point. Roman government moved from the Principate, wherein the emperor ruled as the Princeps, or "first citizen," into the Dominate, where the emperor was an autocrat known as a *dominus noster*.

- There were several reasons for this crisis, first and foremost were military ones. The first threat came from the East: the **Sāsānid** shahs of Persia. **Ardashīr I** and **Shāpūr I** claimed the Roman eastern provinces as part of their legacy from the Persian kings of old. The Sāsānid shahs were a much more formidable foe than the Romans had fought previously.

- In 229–232 A.D., Emperor **Severus Alexander** was forced to wage the first Persian War against Ardashīr, which ended in a truce. For the first time, a Roman emperor returned from the East without a decisive victory. Severus Alexander was later assassinated by his soldiers on the Rhine.

- The next emperor to go east was **Gordian III**. He waged an expensive campaign in 242–244 and was murdered by his

Persian emperor Shāpūr I captured Emperor Valerian and subjected him to humiliations to demonstrate his power over Rome.

Praetorian prefect, Philip the Arab, who signed a treaty with the second Persian shah, Shāpūr, and promised him the equivalent of 10,000 pounds of gold.

- Two later expeditions by Emperor **Valerian** in 253–255 and 258–260 ended in an ignominious defeat. Valerian was captured and, according to Latin literary sources, used as Shāpūr's horse step.

- The frontier was stabilized by Odenathus, a merchant prince of Palmyra. He rallied the Roman armies to defeat Shāpūr in lower Iraq. However, he and his wife, Queen **Zenobia**, advanced their son as an emperor of the East, and Emperor **Aurelian** had to reconquer the East from its would-be protector.

- In 300, under Emperor **Galerius**, the Romans and Persians signed a treaty in which the strategic victory of Rome was recognized. But victory came at a high cost that forced the Romans to recognize the Persians as equals.

The Crisis on the German Frontier

- The humiliations suffered on the eastern frontier were matched by defeats and setbacks on the northern frontiers, particularly along the Rhine and the Danube. The East Germanic peoples who had arrived from Scandinavia in the mid-2nd century—Goths, Vandals, Herulians, and Gepidai—attacked Rome's borders and drove Rome's West Germanic allies into the Roman western provinces.

- In 251, Emperor **Trajan Decius** was defeated and slain by the Goths. They were checked not so much by the efforts of the central government in Rome but by a breakaway regime, the so-called Gallo-Roman emperors.

- In 260, General Postumus, commander of the Rhine armies, declared himself emperor and established a separatist Gallo-Roman state in Britain, Gaul, and Spain. His successors ruled down to 273, when the western provinces were reunited with Rome by Emperor Aurelian, the same emperor who would restore the East to central rule.

- In meeting the Germanic threat, the Roman emperors essentially had to admit that it was too big a job for any one emperor. Imperial unity briefly was compromised in meeting the multiple barbarian threats.

The Rise of the Soldier-Emperors

- More destructive than this split were the civil wars. In 40 years, there were five such major wars and a number of lesser ones, and when you pit two Roman armies against each other, they will hack each other to pieces.

- In the first half of the 3rd century, the traditional ruling aristocracy was so discredited that they were replaced by tough soldier-emperors from the Balkans. These emperors fought the foes of Rome and restored the frontiers, as well as imperial unity. They included such rulers as Aurelian, who restored the unity of the empire; Probus, who won significant victories over the Goths; and Diocletian, who reformed the state after a generation of civil war, rebellion, and foreign invasion.

- These soldier-emperors were traditional in many ways. They invoked the gods of Rome, particularly the gods of the army camp—Jupiter, Mars, and Venus Victrix. Many of them were of provincial origin and had received their citizenship through military service, but that only made them more conservative—more Roman than the Romans in some ways.

The Enigma of the 3rd Century Crisis

- Scholars of the past generation have spent an enormous amount of effort trying to make sense out of the 3rd century. There were great costs for beating back these barbarians and for ending the civil wars. First and foremost was money.

- The usual argument is that the money was rapidly debased—that is, the silver money was turned from a silver coin into a copper coin with a silver coating—sparking an inflationary spiral often compared to the Great Depression. By extension, it is argued that the savings of the Roman world were wiped out and that this hardship played to the benefit of Christianity.

- This view is overdrawn. First, the actual debasement lasted only a short time, approximately 25 years. Second, during the period of debasement, the coins were still valuable. Numerous hoards from all over the Roman Empire indicate that people were still saving these coins during the period, indicating that they still had value as money.

- Finally, in 274 and in 293, then throughout the 4th century, the soldier-emperors reformed the coinage, creating fiat money that was negotiable for a fixed amount of gold. By the 270s and 280s, prices had stabilized; the borders had restabilized; and the emperors, starting with Diocletian, had imposed reforms that brought peace and order back to the Roman world.

- There is other evidence from coins, inscriptions, and relief sculpture that indicate that the 3rd century was not as dismal as previously thought. In the cities of Italy, Africa, and Asia Minor, the ruling classes survived the crisis of the 3rd century, carrying on civic government and rallying to the soldier-emperors.

- Archaeology shows a remarkable continuity in imperial patronage to the cults of the cities and to the sanctuaries of the Roman world, as well as a loyalty expressed by the ruling elites to the Roman emperor. While invasion and civil war did bring about change, it was not a spiritual crisis.

Not Crisis but Continuity

- Romans believed in powerful ancestral traditions. Changes in perception, while important, were not revolutionary. Loyalty was now centered on the Roman emperor, not necessarily on the city of Rome or all the abstract traditions of the republic, and that resulted in the creation of a new tone of government: the Dominate, in which the emperor could rule as an autocrat.

- Rather than create disorientation or flight from public service, the religious history of the 3rd century is better understood not as a failure of nerve on the part of the ruling classes but a reaffirmation of traditional values, a move back to traditional religion and invoking of the gods of Rome as their defenders against invasion.

- We have no evidence of large numbers of Romans giving up their traditional faith for mystery cults or Christianity. We have no evidence for any new cult in the Roman Empire since Alexander of Abonouteichos created the cult of Glycon in 160, and the visual evidence indicates rebuilding of traditional cult sanctuaries during this period. That calls very much into question the idea that this was one of rapid Christianization.

- Some scholars have tried to use Christian funerary monuments of the period found in Turkey as documentation of rising numbers of Christians in the 3rd century. On closer inspection, these gravestones are simply a subset of a much larger body of gravestones, most of them pagan. Most of the monuments are very difficult to identify as Christian unless you read the inscription. They do not represent a rural Christianity on the rise.

- The problem is our preconceptions about religious change in the ancient world. In many ways, we are the heirs to the fact that the Christians won the dispute. We also are heirs to the French Revolution and the notion that a mass movement is the only significant movement in history.

- We have to divorce ourselves from both of these preconceptions when looking at the evidence of the 3rd century and remember that we are dealing with a traditional hierarchical society. Romans understood the world in terms of legal categories rather than social or economic classes.

- It was far more important that Christians converted a Roman emperor and members of the ruling aristocracy who had the means and patronage to change religion and society than to convert large numbers of pagans in the countryside.

- What came out of the 3rd century, from the pagan viewpoint, was not a social upheaval but a reaffirmation of the traditional religious values. The important change was in iconography: Henceforth, the icons placed the emperor in the company of the gods. They spoke to the gods. They had battle miracles.

- At the same time, the gods gave victory. So when Emperor Constantine invoked the Christian god and won the Battle of Milvian Bridge, that was perhaps the most powerful argument of all in favor of Christianity.

Sāsānid: The dynasty of shahs who ruled the New Persian Empire (227–642).

Ardashīr I (fl. 3rd century A.D.): Shah of Persia (224–240) who overthrew the Arsacid dynasty of Parthia and founded the Neo-Persian or Sāsānid Empire. Ardashīr waged war against Rome, proclaiming his aim to conquer the Roman East.

Aurelian (a.k.a. **Lucius Domitius Aurelianus**; c. 207–275; r. 270–275): "Restorer of the Roman world." Born of a military family in Dalmatia, Aurelian distinguished himself as a cavalry commander under Gallienus and Claudius II. In 270, the Danube army saluted Aurelian emperor, and he secured Rome after a brief civil war. Aurelian restored the political unity of the Roman Empire, defeating Zenobia of Palmyra in 272 and the Gallo-Roman emperor Tetricus in 274.

Galerius (a.k.a. **Gaius Galerius Valerius Maximianus**; c. 250–311; r. 305–311): Balkan officer created Caesar of the East in 293. He married Diocletian's daughter Galeria Valeria. In 305, Galerius succeeded Diocletian as Augustus of the East, but his political arrangements denied the succession to both Constantine and Maxentius (each the son of an emperor), so that civil war erupted after 306. Galerius was credited with the initiative for the Great Persecution in 303–313.

Gordian III (a.k.a. **Marcus Antonius Gordianus**; 225–244; r. 238–244): Grandson of Gordian I, the young Gordian III was proclaimed emperor by the Praetorian Guard and Senate at Rome in opposition to Maximinus I. His father-in-law and Praetorian prefect Gaius Furius Timisitheus directed policy after 240. In 242–244, Gordian took the field against the Persian Shah Shāpūr I. The young emperor was slain in a mutiny, staged by his prefect, Philip the Arab (who had succeeded Timistheus in 243).

Odenathus (a.k.a. **Septimius Odenathus**; r. 262–267): Merchant prince of the caravan city Palmyra, Roman senator, and Roman general (*dux*). He imposed his authority over the Roman eastern frontier after the capture of Valerian I in 260. In 262, he imposed a treaty on Shah Shāpūr I. He was murdered at Emesa.

Severus Alexander (a.k.a. **Marcus Aurelius Severus Alexander**; 208–235; r. 222–235): Son of Julia Mamaea and the senator Gessius Marcianus, he was the last Severan emperor. In 221, he was promoted to Caesar by his cousin Emperor Elagabalus (r. 218–222), whose devotion to the orgiastic rites of the Syrian sun god of Emesa compromised the dynasty. In contrast, Severus Alexander ruled judiciously under the guidance of his mother Julia Mamaea. His inconclusive wars against the Persians and Germans led to his assassination by mutinous soldiers of the Rhine army.

Shāpūr I (r. 241–272): The second Sāsānid shah of Persia, who waged three successful campaigns against the Roman Empire (242–244, 253–255, and 258–260). In 260, he captured Emperor Valerian. He sacked Antioch, the third city of the Roman Empire, in either 253 or 260. Odenathus, prince of Palmyra, compelled Shāpūr to negotiate a peace.

Trajan Decius (a.k.a. **Gaius Messius Quintus Traianus Decius**; 201–251; r. 249–251): A Pannonian provincial who attained senatorial rank under Severus Alexander and legate of Upper Pannonia, he was declared emperor by the Danube legions. He defeated and slew the emperor Philip at Verona in 249. Trajan Decius was defeated and slain by the Goths at Abrittus in Lower Moesia. He initiated the first empire-wide persecution of Christians in 250–251.

Valerian I (a.k.a. **Publius Licinius Valerianus**; c. 195–260; r. 253–260): A senator of noble origins who became legate of Raetia in the civil war of 253. He was proclaimed emperor by the Rhine legions and defeated his rival Aemilian. Valerian issued the second empire-wide persecution of Christians in 258–260. Valerian faced barbarian assaults along the northern and eastern frontiers. He waged two Persian wars (253–256 and 258–260). He was treacherously captured by Shah Shāpūr in 260 and died in captivity.

Zenobia (a.k.a. **Septimia Zenobia**; r. 267–272): The wife of Odenathus of Palmyra and mother of Vaballathus. In 267, she succeeded her husband's extraordinary position in the Roman East. Styling herself as Empress Augusta, she advanced her son Vaballathus as emperor in 270. In 270–271, Palmyrene forces occupied Asia Minor, Palestine, and Egypt. In 272, she was defeated by Aurelian and allowed to retire to a Campania villa.

Suggested Reading

Dodds, *Pagan and Christian in the Age of Anxiety.*

Harl, *Civic Coins and Civic Politics in the Roman East.*

———, *Coinage in the Roman Economy.*

MacCormack, *Art and Ceremony in Late Antiquity.*

MacMullen, *Roman Government's Response to Crisis.*

Potter, *The Roman Empire at Bay.*

Watson, *Aurelian and the Third Century.*

Questions to Consider

1. How did political and military crises transform pagan perceptions of the gods and the Roman emperor? Why would they likely not reject the ancestral gods in a crisis? Why would pagans become impatient with Christian refusal to sacrifice to the gods or the genius of the Roman emperor?

2. Why did military defeats discredit an emperor of the Severan aristocracy? What were the religious beliefs of the solider-emperors between Claudius II (268–270) and Diocletian (284–305)? Why did they allow themselves to be compared to their divine protectors? Why did Romans come to accept a certain divinity in their emperors?

3. What are the sources for arguments of spiritual crisis and a loss of faith in traditional gods after 235? What are the dangers in surmising explanations based on modern analogies?

The Great Persecutions
Lecture 13

U ntil the mid-3rd century, persecution of Christians in the Roman Empire was local, brief, and sporadic. The emperors Trajan Decius and Valerian enacted the first empire-wide persecutions, in which large numbers of Christians were actively sought out and put to the sacrifice test, then punished by public execution *ad bestias* in the amphitheaters. There is little doubt that these early martyrs helped forge the identity and strengthen the resolve of their fellow Christians; whether they played any role in converting pagans to Christianity is a matter of debate.

New Emperors, New Motives

- The Great Persecution ordered by the soldier-emperors **Trajan Decius** in 250–251 and **Valerian I** in 258–260 differed from those described previously in that they were empire wide. Residents of the entire Roman world were required to appear before altars to offer sacrifice not only to the gods, but also to the genius of the Roman emperor.

- Potentially, the imperial government could have done this at any time but had not. Previous persecutions were local, sporadic, and did not last long; they depended on the attitude of the Roman governor or local decurions toward the faith.

- The reason for these empire-wide persecutions is easily linked to the civil wars and invasions of the 3rd century and the need to win the favor of the traditional gods. Scholars have argued that the persecutions were an indication that paganism was in demise and Christianity on the rise. However, it could also be argued that the persecutions were a sign of a traditional pagan revival.

- According to pagan belief, the danger of Christians was that they denied the traditional gods their due. If you do not offer sacrifice to the gods and goddesses, they become angry and then visit communal punishment. It only took a few citizens opting out of the traditional sacrifices to bring down the wrath of the gods on everyone.

The Bureaucracy of the Persecutions

- Some scholars have suggested that tax registers were used to determine who was a Christian and who was a pagan, but imperial officials did not designate people by religious affiliation until the 4th century—that is, until the Christian emperors ruled and Christians had certain civil advantages, not disadvantages, versus pagan taxpayers.

- It is more likely that the persecutions depended on local initiative as they always had. The leading members of a city would have some sense of who the Christians were by who did not show up at the sacrifices and festivals. Eusebius says that on various occasions, especially in Asia Minor, Jews helped point out who the Christians were.

- A number of certificates—in Latin, *libellus* or *libelli*, meaning "little booklet"—have been found in Egypt that indicate that individuals appeared before the magistrates and offered sacrifice to prove their loyalty. *Libelli* were issued in enormous numbers and in some ways functioned like tax receipts. Sometimes, instead of papyrus *libelli*, these receipts were written on ostracon—potsherds, the scrap paper of the Roman world.

The Progress and Process of Persecution

- On January 1, 250, Roman officials went out to investigate and interrogate all over the empire, and governors were given wide powers to hold tribunals and determine who was a Christian and who was not, then to deal with those who failed to sacrifice. Those who failed to sacrifice could be sent to the arena for execution *ad bestias*.

- The persecution took the Christians by surprise. Pope **Fabian** was arrested and beheaded. Numerous Christians in the Church of Rome and in North Africa lapsed—that is, they sacrificed to the gods, were given certificates, and were let go.

- The Eastern churches in Asia Minor seemed to hold up much better. We know of a number of acts of Christian martyrs from Eusebius's *Ecclesiastical History*.

- The persecutions lasted for about 18 months. They came to a very abrupt end when Trajan Decius was killed by the Goths and his successor, **Trebonianus Gallus**, issued an act of clemency, in effect saying, "I have more important matters to deal with." The Christians saw the end of the persecution as an act of God.

- In 258–260, persecution resumed and raged for about two and a half years under Emperor Valerian. This one, too, abruptly stopped when the emperor was captured by an enemy—this time, the Persians.

The Effect of the Persecution on Christians

- Looking back on this era, Eusebius repeated the apologists' phrase that the blood of martyrs is the seed of the church—that is, for every Christian cut down in the arena, another pagan was moved to inquire about Christianity. This position has long been the lens through which scholars have investigated and judged religious change in the 3rd century.

- During this same period, Christians were coming to the attention of the imperial government in various other ways. Paul of Samosata, the bishop of Antioch, treated the church as his private property and tried to sell it, and his congregation asked Emperor Aurelian (r. 270–275) to adjudicate the case. Aurelian sided with the congregation, showing that Roman emperors could deal with their Christian subjects as Roman citizens.

- A second important point about those persecutions was that the Christians saw them as great tests of their faith. In Eusebius's mind, these empire-wide persecutions were the final test that led to the conversion of Constantine.

- On the whole, most Christians had stood up quite well to this test. Many bishops, like Pope Fabian, had refused to sacrifice and were martyred. This resulted in the development of two important traditions: Christians remembered the martyrs by naming their children after them, so that Christians gradually evolved their own nomenclature; and a cult of the holy dead sprang up by the end of the 3rd century.

- Among the greatest beneficiaries of these developments were the bishops. Those who stood strong against the persecutions not only increased their own fame but the fame and authority of the institution of the bishop.

- To average Christians, the empire-wide persecutions seemed like the apocalypse. This accounts in part for the popularity of the book of Revelation in this period and its addition to the New Testament.

- Martyrdom was a powerful way for Christians to define themselves as the new Israel. Christians were not supposed to offer themselves up for martyrdom like suicide victims. One was not supposed to, for example, go to a pagan festival and spit on the cult statue just to be captured and martyred; that was an act of pride. Martyrdom was carefully defined by the church fathers as an act of bravery and courage when there was no other option.

- After the persecutions, the church had to decide how to treat those who had lapsed and sacrificed but now wanted to return to the church. Should they be rebaptized? Was confession alone good enough? This division between rigorists and people with a broader notion of what the sin of sacrifice represented often split churches, particularly in North Africa. It became a major issue at the opening of the 4th century when Constantine converted.

The Christian martyrs were barely noticed by a Roman audience that was used to the violent gladiatorial games.

The Effect of the Persecution on Pagans

- Did the Great Persecution lead to large numbers of pagans being impressed by acts of martyrdom, learning about Christianity, and then converting? We have no statistical evidence for any surge in Christian numbers during the 3rd-century crisis. It is an act of faith to argue that the persecutions backfired on the imperial government.

- So, what did the persecutions and martyrdoms mean to pagans? Until very recently, it was assumed that dying in the arena would be seen as a noble act. Then Keith Hopkins, a great social historian, wrote a seminal article, "Murderous Games," in which he elucidated the pagan response to martyrdom in the broader context of Roman arena entertainment.

- Hopkins cast a great deal of doubt on claims that martyrdom converted any significant number of pagans. Romans watched many bloody spectacles. The largest building in any Roman city was an amphitheater built to house gladiatorial and animal combats, games dating back to the republic in the 3rd century B.C. that grew ever-larger throughout the centuries.

- These games were a vicarious psychological experience. They reaffirmed that the Romans were masters of the world. They also bore a message: Do not oppose the Roman order or you end up in the arena.

- One questions whether the execution of 20 or 30 Christian martyrs as an intermission during these games had much impact on the audience at all, given that the largest games might last 120 days and involve 11,000 beasts and 10,000 pairs of gladiators, not to mention the distributions of food and gifts.

- Above all, certain emperors used the gladiatorial games as a way of reinforcing the Roman social order. Romans were seated in the arena based on their ranks. The lowest of all were the criminals and outcasts on the arena floor. It is difficult to argue that the pagans in the seats would have been inclined to think that the execution of some Christians in the arena was something special.

- The persecutions and the destruction in the arena undoubtedly had a powerful impact on the Christian community, but to the Romans, they represented a traditional Roman attitude that married belief in the gods with patriotism and invoked standard punishments of invaders and outcasts. If the Christians were to make any headway, they had to demonstrate that they were Romans, too.

Names to Know

Fabian (r. 236–250): Pope respected by African and Italian bishops and credited with missions to cities in Gaul. He was martyred during the persecution of Trajan Decius on January 20, 250.

Trajan Decius (a.k.a. **Gaius Messius Quintus Traianus Decius**; 201–251; r. 249–251): A Pannonian provincial who attained senatorial rank under Severus Alexander and legate of Upper Pannonia, he was declared emperor by the Danube legions. He defeated and slew the emperor Philip at Verona in 249. Trajan Decius was defeated and slain by the Goths at Abrittus in Lower Moesia. He initiated the first empire-wide persecution of Christians in 250–251.

Trebonianus Gallus (a.k.a. **Gaius Vibius Trebonianus Gallus**; r. 251–253): A legate of Trajan Decius, he was declared emperor by the Roman army after Decius's death. Gallus faced attacks by northern barbarians and Persians. In 253, he was defeated and slain by Aemilian, governor of Moesia, whom the Danube legions had declared emperor.

Valerian I (a.k.a. **Publius Licinius Valerianus**; c. 195–260; r. 253–260): A senator of noble origins who became legate of Raetia in the civil war of 253. He was proclaimed emperor by the Rhine legions and defeated his rival Aemilian. Valerian issued the second empire-wide persecution of Christians in 258–260. Valerian faced barbarian assaults along the northern and eastern frontiers. He waged two Persian wars (253–256 and 258–260). He was treacherously captured by Shah Shāpūr in 260 and died in captivity.

Suggested Reading

Dodds, *Pagan and Christian in the Age of Anxiety.*

Eusebius, *The History of the Church: From Christ to Constantine.*

Frend, *Martyrdom and Persecution in the Early Church.*

Hopkins, "Murderous Games."

MacMullen, *Paganism in the Roman Empire.*

Nock, *Conversion.*

Potter, *The Roman Empire at Bay.*

Wilken, *The Christians as the Romans Saw Them.*

1. How did pagans and Christians view the edict of persecution issued by Trajan Decius in 250? By what means could emperors enforce empire-wide compliance of sacrificing to the gods and the spirit of the emperor?

2. How did empire-wide persecutions sharpen Christian identity and shape institutions? Why did martyrdoms fail to attract large numbers of converts?

3. What were pagan motives for empire-wide persecutions? How did they sharpen the pagan sense of piety and patriotism?

The Spirit of Late Paganism
Lecture 14

In many ways, the middle Platonic philosopher Plotinus can be seen as the pagan equivalent to his Christian contemporary, the theologian Origen. Plotinus had a mystical, henotheistic view of the *to hen*, or the One, from whom all creation descended in a Great Chain of Being, a vision that would affect Christian theologians as well. Meanwhile, on the borders of the Roman and Persian empires, the new faith of Manichaeism was rising—neither Roman nor Persian, Christian nor pagan, but a true world religion in many senses of the phrase.

The Everyday Pagan

- The majority of the residents of the Roman world during the political and military crisis, as well as the persecutions, of the 3rd century were still traditional pagans. To understand their religious attitudes, we need to look at three related but distinct issues.

    o What was happening to public pagan worship in the 3rd century?

    o What were the philosophical trends of the 3rd century?

    o How did the new faith of Manichaeism affect pagans and Christians in the empire?

- The 3rd century period is a dark period for historians because of the paucity of contemporary narrative sources. We have only the *Scriptores historiae augustae*, written at the end of the 4th century, and the Byzantine *Epitomes*, are abridgments of earlier histories created seven centuries later for Byzantine aristocrats.

- What we do have are a rising number of civic and imperial coins that provide iconography about the gods. We have a large number of inscriptions, at least to the mid-to-late 3rd century. We have archaeology, and we have enough literary sources to be able to piece together a sense of what happened to pagan worship.

- After 235, it certainly became more and more expensive to put on pagan festivals and worship. Many cities also suffered destruction at the hands of barbarians or the Persian army. Those cities that did escape destruction had to remodel themselves, even far from the frontier, constructing new walls and abandoning areas far from the city center.

What Is Civic Honor?

- More important are changes in social attitudes in the Roman world. Peter Brown expressed these as a change in the definition of honor. In the early Roman world, honor was a matter of patriotism and piety to one's city, putting on festivals and games, holding local offices and constructing civic buildings at one's own expense.

- Starting in the early 4th century, honor becomes a matter of serving the emperor by making donations and staging public and social activities that would lead to promotion within the imperial bureaucracy or army, in turn leading to privileges and exemptions from taxation for you and your family.

- That shift in honor explains, in part, some of the shifts going on in public worship. The civic elites needed assistance from the imperial government in the form of patronage and tax relief to afford these activities. Diocletian and his colleagues, as part of their reforms, supported the civic elites in restoring the cults and the cities to the way they had been before the wars.

- On the other hand, more and more of the city elite were looking at imperial service as a better option than civic service. This became a major source of tension in the 4th and 5th centuries with implications for both the pagan cults and the emerging Christian church.

The Life of Plotinus

- The philosopher **Plotinus** was one of the intellectual giants of the 3rd century. An Alexandrian born into a Greco-Egyptian family, he was very much a product of the Greek educational system. He trained with some of the city's great thinkers, including Ammonius Saccas, who may also have trained Origen.

- Plotinus was a devotee of middle Platonic text, particularly Alexander of Aphrodisias, who had reinterpreted the realities of Plato's *Timaeus*.

- Plotinus, according to the biography penned by his student **Porphyry of Tyre**, joined Gordian III in his expedition to India, where he planned to study the wisdom of the Buddhist monks and Hindu Brahmins. However, the expedition failed, and he was forced to return to Rome.

- There, he came to the attention of the emperor Gallienus, who gave him a villa in Campania, where the ruling class would visit and listen to his lectures. Plotinus popularized certain doctrines of Plato but did not write a synthetic account of his ideas; that was put together by his student Porphyry and is known as the ***Enneads***, or the *Nine Books*.

Plotinus's Godhead

- Plotinus, at the apex of more than 500 years of Platonic thought, presented a mystical, **henotheistic** vision of the divine world. He referred to glimpsing "the *to hen*, **the One**, the ultimate godhead," a single divine power manifesting itself in many ways, including the traditional gods of the Greco-Roman world.

- Plotinus godhead is an Aristotelian god of thinking on thinking. It is pure reason and rational thought detached from the material world. That intellect, which is inherently good, orders the world around it and is so full of existence that it must bubble over in **emanations**, and therefore you have an act of creation.

- The *to hen* almost unwittingly creates the world mind, which creates the world soul, which creates souls, which then create the material world and matter. A Great Chain of Being is oriented around this world soul, and the emanation scheme settles the question in Plato: How did creation take place?

- Human souls have a divine element; they are capable of rising and merging their individual souls into the godhead. Once you achieve knowledge, you are able to extinguish the individuality of your soul into the world soul. If you fail to do so, you are reincarnated and have another opportunity.

Plotinus's Legacy

- The henotheistic vision of Plotinus gains a great deal of popularity, particularly in eastern intellectual circles, and accommodated the traditional rites and gods of the Roman world. Julian the Apostate understood Plotinus's doctrines very well and would put it this way: There are many paths to the one. All are valid.

- Christians did not like Plotinus's Platonism. Origen saw it as dividing up the godhead, imposing necessity on God, and therefore limiting God. On the other hand, Origen probably liked Plotinus's eternal cycle of creations and reincarnations.

- Porphyry not only collected Plotinus's lectures; he also wrote an incisive criticism of Christian beliefs on philosophical grounds, not the crude arguments of earlier pagan critics. Porphyry's criticism is almost a compliment to Origen's work; pagan intellectuals had to take Christianity a lot more seriously.

- **Iamblichus of Chalcis** expanded on Plotinus by defining **theurgy**, an intellectual approach to the rites and traditions of the ancient gods. In *On the Mysteries* (*De mysteriis*), he wrote that having a higher knowledge of what those traditional rites and pagan worship mean was a way to achieve union with the *to hen*. Theurgy, then, becomes in some ways almost a pagan equivalent to a doctrine of grace.

- These developments were also the intellectual underpinnings of Emperor Julian II's unsuccessful attempt to reverse Constantine's conversion of the empire to Christianity and restore the pagan cults.

Mani and Manichaeism

- The religious leader **Mani** was born in a Jewish-Christian sectarian community in what we would today call Iraq. Until recently, the **Manicheans** were regarded as Christian heretics. But an important papyrus fragment from the 5th century containing a biography of Mani was recently discovered, providing new and enlightening information about the man and his followers.

- Mani was actually an inspired prophet who established a new religion that had many similarities to Christianity but also drew on the allegory and myth of the Gnostic traditions and various religions of the Near East. He received sacred books and inspiration from the son of man and the Holy Spirit, and he claimed that he was the twin brother of Jesus.

- The surviving Manichaean text are in a bewildering array of languages. They traveled from the Atlantic to China along the Silk Road. Therefore, this was a world religion from the start, and no one had as much success as the Manichaeans in carrying out missionary activities since the time of St. Paul.

- Mani taught a fundamentally dualist vision of the world. In many ways, he seems to fall into the Gnostic tradition where the material and spiritual world are in dichotomy. But Christian authors often overplay that feature. Fundamentally, Mani was an optimist who believed humans contained a spark of light and could achieve divinization with full knowledge.

- Where Mani differs from Plotinus and Origen is that he was neither pagan nor Christian. He offered an alternate vision drawing on both traditions plus traditions farther East. There are reports that he traveled to Central Asia and Northern India, and in some ways, Manichaeism in its organization is very similar to contemporary Buddhism, with a wide body of believers and an ascetic missionary monastic elect.

- Manichaeism was seen as a challenge by both pagans and Christians. Diocletian ordered the persecution of Manichaeans because he thought they were Persians loyal to the Shah. Meanwhile, the Shah was persecuting them as well.

- For the Christians, the Manichaeans posed a real challenge. They had a remarkably successful missionary tradition and won converts from the Atlantic to the borders of the Chinese Empire. To counter Manichaeism, they had to redouble their efforts at turning themselves into a Roman religion.

Important Terms

emanation: One generation of the descending levels of reality from the One in the Great Chain of Being posited by Plotinus (205–270).

Enneads: The writings of Plotinus (205–270) as collected and edited by Porphyry.

henotheism: The religious outlook regarding traditional pagan gods as aspects of a single transcendent godhead. This was the religious vision of the Neoplatonic philosopher Plotinus and the emperor Julian II.

Manichaean: A follower of the dualist faith of the prophet Mani (216–276), who taught a universal monotheism often dismissed by Christian writers as a heresy.

One, the: In Greek, "*to hen*"; term used by Plotinus (205–270) to define the ultimate, infinite divine reality that is the source of all creation by emanation.

theurgy: The esoteric practices of the enlightened Neoplatonist who understands how traditional rites have a deeper meaning to achieve mystical union with the One.

Names to Know

Iamblichus of Chalcis (c. 250–325 A.D.): Neoplatonist theurgist from Syria who studied with Porphyry at Rome. Iamblichus composed *De mysteriis* (*On the Mysteries*), an exposition of theurgy and the efficacy of sacrifice that influenced Julian and Proclus. He also composed three treatises on mathematics and a tract on the Pythagorean life.

Mani (216–276): Prophet and founder of the dualist monotheistic religion Manichaeism. Born into a community of Elcesaites, an ascetic sect of Judaizing Christians, near Ctesiphon in Babylonia, between 218 and 228, Mani experienced mystical visions, and in 240–242 he traveled to India, where he might have conversed with Buddhist monks. He returned to Persia and gained favor at the court of Shāpūr I. His teaching, however, offended Kartir and the strict Zoroastrians, who likely contrived his arrest and crucifixion by Shah Bahrām I in 276. Mani's writings, originally written in Syriac, have survived in translations.

Plotinus (205–270): Born at Lycopolis, Egypt. Plotinus gained the favor of Emperor Gallienus. He defined Neplatonism, and his disciple Porphyry compiled Plotinus's teachings into the *Enneads*. Plotinus's vision of the Great Chain of Being and synthesis of Platonic thought provided the intellectual basis for the revival of the pagan cults by Emperor Julian (360–363).

Porphyry of Tyre (c. 232–304): Greek Neoplatonic philosopher who wrote a life of his mentor, the philosopher Plotinus, a work *Against the Christians* (15 books), and a historical chronicle from the fall of Troy to about A.D. 270.

Suggested Reading

Brown, *Body and Society in Late Antiquity*.

Cox, *Biography in Late Antiquity*.

Dodds, *Pagan and Christian in the Age of Anxiety*.

Fowden, *Empire to Commonwealth*.

Frend, *Martyrdom and Persecution in the Early Church*.

Hadot, *Plotinus or the Simplicity of Vision*.

Iamblichus of Chalcis, *De mysteriis*.

Lieu, *Manichaeism in the Later Roman Empire Medieval China*.

MacMullen, *Paganism in the Roman Empire*.

Plotinus, *The Enneads*.

Potter, *The Roman Empire at Bay*.

Shaw, *Theurgy and the Soul*.

Wallis, *Neoplatonism*.

Questions to Consider

1. What are the sources for pagan religious experiences in the 3rd century? How has the paucity of sources led to scholarly misunderstanding? Why is it misleading to take a lack of sources for a lack of belief?

2. What would explain the continuity of cults and sanctuaries during the crisis of the 3rd century? How would imperial victories after 268 have altered perceptions?

3. How did the henotheism of Plotinus and Iamblichus of Chalcis create a new moral and intellectual explanation of the cults? How satisfying were their visions of the divine? How did Porphyry alter the views of pagan intellectuals towards Christianity?

4. How did Manichaeism pose a challenge to both pagans and Christians? What accounted for the remarkable success of Manichaean missionaries?

Imperial Recovery under the Tetrarchs
Lecture 15

Emperor Diocletian would revolutionize the Roman imperial military and bureaucracy through creating the tetrarchy, or "rule of four," wherein imperial authority was vested in two senior and two junior emperors. Gone was the fiction of emperor as first citizen; Diocletian's system made the emperors true autocrats, backed by an army loyal to the emperor alone. Traditional pagan worship was more important than ever to supporting this system, so empire-wide persecution of Christians returned; ironically, in about a quarter century, the first Christian emperor would use Diocletian's institutions to convert the empire to his new faith.

Diocletian Addresses the Succession

- Emperor **Diocletian** ruled from 284 to 305, a period called the **tetrarchy**, meaning "the rule of four." Diocletian chose to share his imperial power with three other colleagues and, remarkably, to step down and end a successful 20-year reign. This arrangement was a response to the military and political crisis of the 3rd century.

- The big weakness of the Roman imperial government was its lack of succession principle. The emperor did not have a real job description and was not a hereditary monarch in law, although he was in practice. When power was transferred from ruler to ruler—or dynasty to dynasty—the empire always hovered on the brink of civil war.

- It is remarkable that in the first 300 years of the empire, there were only two significant civil wars; however, between 235 and 284, there were five major civil wars and numerous invasions and usurpations; the average emperor's reign lasted about 18 months. This makes Diocletian's achievement nothing short of miraculous.

- Diocletian was a pragmatist and, contrary to opinions of earlier scholars, very much a conservative Roman. The tetrarchy made a virtue out of weakness: He had no sons and only one daughter, so he used marriage alliances and adoption to create, in effect, a new imperial family.

- Diocletian also recognized that no single emperor could meet all the threats on all the empire's frontiers as well as administer the Roman Empire at its current extent. Therefore, in 285, he elevated as his co-emperor, or Augustus, **Maximianus**, a fellow Balkan military man with a similar political outlook. Diocletian ruled the East while Maximianus ruled the West.

- In 293, Diocletian and Maximianus extended the college of rulers by creating two junior emperors, or Caesars, also from Balkan military families. The Caesar in the East was **Galerius**, who married Diocletian's daughter. The Caesar in the West was **Constantius I Chlorus**. He had a wife, Helena, and a son, Constantine; he divorced Helena and married a stepdaughter of Maximianus, so that the two Caesars were linked by marriage to the Augusti.

- Each emperor had a capital on the frontiers: Constantius at Trier, near the Rhine; Maximianus resided at Milan, the nexus of all military routes for the defense of the upper Danube; Diocletian took up residence at Nicomedia, in Asia Minor; and Galerius resided at Antioch. This provided an imperial presence at each of the four key frontiers.

- In part, the system operated so effectively because Diocletian was recognized as senior among the partners. It also allowed Diocletian and his colleagues to carry out a series of sweeping reforms.

The Failure of the Second Tetrarchy

- The arrangement worked until May 1, 305, when Diocletian, who was at that point ailing, decided to retire, and he prevailed on Maximianus to join him and make way for the Caesars. By this time,

Galerius had undue influence over Diocletian, and as a result the two new Caesars were essentially appointees of Galerius: **Severus II** in the West and **Maximinus II Daza**, Galerius's nephew, in the East.

- This second tetrarchy lasted a little over a year. It set aside the succession principles near and dear to the imperial army, cutting Maximianus's son **Maxentius** and Constantius's son Constantine out of the succession. When Constantius Chlorus was killed in York in 306, the Western army immediately declared Constantine Augustus of the West. In October, the Praetorian Guard—that is, the guard of the city of Rome—declared Maxentius Augustus of the West.

- Galerius would recognize neither of these men and elevated Caesar Severus II to Augustus of the West. Within 18 months of the abdication of Diocletian, the Roman Empire experienced a new wave of civil wars. These were significantly different from those waged in the earlier 3rd century. In effect, the empire broke up into as many as six competing states controlled by competing rulers.

Diocletian's Bureaucratic and Military Reforms

- In one way, the tetrarchy can be looked on as a failure, that it did not achieve permanent political stability. However, it gave Diocletian and his colleagues the opportunity to carry out significant reforms, among them building a new imperial army and bureaucracy beholden to the emperor alone.

- The tetrarchs dropped the fiction of ruling as a first magistrate. In the new army, the legions and cavalry bore dynastic names stressing their connection with Jupiter and Hercules. The army was reorganized on a new scale in which the cavalry was elevated to a premier military force.

- The old senatorial elite were now cut out of military commands; commands went to men who had moved up through the ranks, soldiers just like the emperors themselves. There would be further military changes under Constantine.

- The civil administration was vastly increased. Before Diocletian, Rome's civil service may have numbered 3,000 men; by our best count, the number of senior officials by Diocletian's time was 35,000. Provincial administration was divided into three levels, reflected in the later organization of the Christian church.

- These changes helped prevent civil wars and rebellion by powerful governors by dividing up the provinces and dividing the civil and military administration. That also meant the emperor no longer had to depend on the traditional elites of Rome; he was not challenged by the senators. The administration and army would follow him unquestioningly so long as they were paid.

- To play to their new servants, as well as to their subjects, the emperors created a whole new set of ceremonies to elevate themselves and enhance their divine aura. Ceremony focused power and created a barrier between the emperor and the traditional elite so they could not challenge the emperors.

- Furthermore, the emperors could now dispense with consent by the senatorial families; they did not have to mix with them as equals. They created their own civil bureaucrats, drawing heavily on the decurions of the cities, and they created a new officer corps, drawing very heavily on provincial soldiers and eventually on mercenary barbarians. This gave the tetrarchs a new position of power they could use to enforce their reforms.

- The whole tradition of honor changed. The route to advancement was now to serve one's emperor, not to serve one's city or traditional gods; not to show traditional patriotism and piety but instead to stage events in the arenas, hippodromes, or stadiums that would bring you to the attention of the emperor.

- The administration and army proved extremely expensive to fund. The emperors increased taxes, but to the credit of Diocletian and his colleagues, they also made a serious effort to roll back prices and carry out currency reforms.

The Politics of Paganism

- A keystone to this reform was winning the favor of the gods. Here, the tetrarchs took their cue from Augustus and the earlier emperors. They forged a new ideology in which the emperors were the favorites of the gods. Panegyrics—orations of praise—were delivered at imperial palaces.

- The iconography of the 3rd century culminated in a new image of the emperors and their association with the divine. Emperors were the equals or the comrades of gods. We see this with Diocletian and Jupiter, Maximianus and Hercules.

- The emperors' gods were not the gods of mystery cults nor irrational, nonclassical gods; they were the traditional gods of Rome, particularly those who had protected the armies: Sol Invictus, the Unconquerable Sun; Mars Propugnator, the conqueror; Jupiter Conservator, the preserver; and Hercules, the mortal who became a god.

- Increasingly, archaeology is revealing that in the late 3rd and early 4th centuries, there was a trend toward restoring many of the traditional shrines and sanctuaries across the Roman world. For example, the tetrarchs restored a number of temples in the city of Ephesus, including a temple to Hadrian, where four altars were added, each to one of the tetrarchs.

- All of this was part of a single policy to do homage to the traditional gods who had been the protectors of the Roman world. Diocletian's coins were stamped with the legend *GENIO POPULI ROMANI*, "to the divine spirit of the Roman people"—to all of its shrines, cults, and religious traditions. This seems a sharpened, focused, conservative revival, not the last gasp of dying paganism.

The Revival of Persecution

- These implications were not happy for the Christian community living under the tetrarchs. Back in 260 the persecutions had been halted by Gallienus. This changed abruptly in 303, when Diocletian issued the first of four edicts against the Christians. Officially, he was reacting to some Christians present at one of his public sacrifices causing ill omens.

- Additional edicts of persecution followed; these included confiscation of churches and Christian property, destruction of books, and prohibition of Christian services. One inscription from Arycanda, in Asia Minor, indicates while this was, again, an empire-wide persecution, it depended on the support of the local decurions, who call the emperors "saviors of every province and nation of mankind."

- The persecutions were not only legal; they were also in keeping with imperial policy of the tetrarchy—namely, that the spirit of the Roman people took precedence over all other religious values, and Christians and others who did not worship to the gods must be forced to conform.

- Persecutions would continue for the next 10 years, until 313. They halted because of a battle miracle, one in perfect keeping with the institutions, ceremonies, and legal positions forged by the tetrarchy in all ways but one: It was not a miracle delivered by the traditional gods of Rome but by the god of the Christians.

tetrarchy: Rule of four; the collective imperial rule established by Diocletian in 285, with two senior Augusti and two junior Caesars.

Constantius I Chlorus (a.k.a. **Flavius Valerius Constantius**; c. 250–306; r. 305–306): Born to an Illyrian military family, Constantius served under Probus and Diocletian. In 293, Maximianus adopted Constantius as his heir and appointed him Caesar. Constantius divorced his wife Helena, mother of Constantine I, and married Theodora, the stepdaughter of Maximianus. In 305, Constantius I succeeded as Augustus of the West. He died in 306, after conducting an expedition against the Picts.

Diocletian (245–316; r. 284–305): Roman emperor. A humble Dalmatian soldier declared emperor by the Eastern army, Diocletian ended the crisis of the 3rd century and retired from the throne in 305. His administrative, monetary, and fiscal reforms established the Dominate, or late Roman state. He created collegial rule, the so-called tetrarchy, whereby imperial power was shared by two senior emperors called Augusti and two junior emperors called Caesars. In 305, Diocletian retired from public life to his fortress palace of Spalato (modern Split, Croatia).

Galerius (a.k.a. **Gaius Galerius Valerius Maximianus**; c. 250–311; r. 305–311): Balkan officer created Caesar of the East in 293. He married Diocletian's daughter Galeria Valeria. In 305, Galerius succeeded Diocletian as Augustus of the East, but his political arrangements denied the succession to both Constantine and Maxentius (each the son of an emperor), so that civil war erupted after 306. Galerius was credited with the initiative for the Great Persecution in 303–313.

Maxentius (a.k.a. **Marcus Valerius Maxentius**; c. 278–312; r. 306–312): Son of Maximianus, Maxentius revolted at Rome and declared himself emperor after he had been denied the succession by Galerius. Maxentius controlled Italy and Africa. In 312, he was defeated and slain by Constantine at the Battle of Milvian Bridge.

Maximianus (a.k.a. **Marcus Aurelius Valerius Maximianus**; c. 250–310; r. 286–305): A Pannonian comrade of Diocletian, Maximianus was promoted as Augustus in the West. He abdicated in 305 but reentered politics, first as co-emperor with his son Maxentius and then with his son-in-law Constantine. He committed suicide at Massilia in 310 after he failed to raise a revolt against Constantine.

Maximinus II Daza (a.k.a. **Galerius Valerius Maximinus Daia**; c. 270–313; r. 309–313): Nephew of Galerius, he was named Caesar of the East in 305. Devoted to the old gods, Maximinus persecuted Christians. In 309, he proclaimed himself Augustus and warred against Galerius and later Licinius. In 313, defeated by Licinius, he died a refugee at Tarsus.

Severus II (a.k.a. **Flavius Valerius Severus**; c. 260–307; r. 306–307): An Illyrian officer who was created Caesar of the West by Galerius in 305. In 306, after the death of Constantius I, Galerius elevated Severus II to Augustus of the West. In 307, Severus invaded the Italian Peninsula, but his soldiers defected, and he fell into the hands of Maxentius, who executed him.

Suggested Reading

Barnes, *The New Empire of Diocletian and Constantine*.

Corcoran, *The Empire of Tetrarchs*.

Lactantius, *On the Manner in Which the Persecutors Died*.

L'Orange, *Art Forms and Civic Life in the Late Roman Empire*.

Nixon and Rodgers, *In Praise of Later Roman Emperors*.

Potter, *The Roman Empire at Bay*.

Rees, ed. and trans., *Diocletian and the Tetrarchy*.

Talbert, *Rome's World*.

1. How were Diocletian and his colleagues traditional emperors? Why did Diocletian's political solution to succession fail?

2. How did the military, administrative, and fiscal reforms of Diocletian change religious life in the Roman world? Was it possible for worship of the gods to be revived in the fashion of the Principate?

3. How conservative were tetrarchic religious policies? Why was persecution of Manichaeans and Christians part of this policy? What were the limitations of the imperial persecutors? What accounts for the acts of toleration by Galerius and Maximinus II Daza?

The Conversion of Constantine
Lecture 16

The conversion of Emperor Constantine has been a topic of debate among scholars almost since the moment it happened. But an examination of the physical evidence, much of it in the form of Constantine's coinage, makes a few things clear: Constantine understood his experience at Milvian Bridge, whatever that experience was, but he also understood the perils of imposing his minority faith on his people and was careful to introduce change gradually in the empire. Whatever the details, Constantine's conversion was indisputably a major turning point in the history of Europe.

Constantine's Conversion—Facts and Surmises

- On October 28, 312, Emperor Constantine defeated Maxentius, at the Battle of Milvian Bridge. This victory was not just a miracle; it was the Christian God who was invoked; and this battle was seen by Constantine as a justification and vindication of the power of the Christian God. From that point on, he began to identify himself with the Christian faith and, in my opinion, he converted.

- The information we have on his conversion is not nearly as good as we would like. Our two main literary accounts are written by Christian authors: **Lactantius**, who was living at the time of the battle but in far-away Nicomedia, and Eusebius, who also was not present at the battle. The fullest account comes from Eusebius's second version in his *Life of Constantine*, written almost a half a generation later.

- The conversion of Constantine has been subject to all sorts of criticisms and interpretations by both scholars and popular writers since the 4th century, and particularly since the 19th century with the advent of modern scholarship. One source neglected by most

scholars is Constantine's imperial iconography—that is, the images
and inscriptions on his coins.

- Lactantius's work, *De mortibus persecutorum* (*On the Death of the Persecutors*), includes gleeful accounts of the horrible deaths of pagan emperors who persecuted Christians. He tells us that on the eve of the battle, Constantine ordered that a symbol like the Christogram be put on the banners and shields of his soldiers. He also describes Maxentius consulting magicians and practicing black magic. These are clearly overdrawn accounts.

- Eusebius reports in his *Ecclesiastical History*, written just a couple of years after the battle but revised some 10 years later, that Constantine prayed to the Christian god and won the battle. In the *Life of Constantine*, Constantine has a succession of visions, and ultimately the entire army has a vision of the Christogram and the motto *In hoc signo victor eris*, "In this sign you will conquer."

Objections to and Support of the Contemporary Accounts

- Scholars have doubted the accuracy of the later account on various grounds. However, this account is supported by the coin evidence. In 328–329, some coins issued at Constantinople show the labarum with the Christogram. We also know in 350, a loyalist general issued coins showing the labarum, Emperor Constantius II, and the inscription *hoc signo victor eris*).

- Most scholars now believe that Eusebius did write this account, and Eusebius claims that he wrote it with the advice of the Emperor Constantine, although almost 30 years after the battle, even Constantine's memory might be subject to embroidery and elaboration.

- In the 19th century, Swiss humanist Jacob Burkhardt was the first scholar to reject Eusebius's account and generated a line of inquiry that persists down to this day, suggesting that Constantine, either before or after the battle, used Christianity as a cynical device for legitimacy, co-opting the power of the growing church and its institutions.

- This view is still held by many. However, we know that Constantine effectively created the Christian church and that the organization and even the terms such as "vicar" and "diocese" all come out of the administrative reforms of Diocletian. Also, there is little evidence for large numbers of Christians in 312. They were not represented in the Senate, the army leadership, or the Roman elite, so there was no advantage in playing to the Christians in a civil war.

- Some scholars, such as Henri Gregoire, have argued that Constantine is better understood as a syncretist. In addition to the Christian god, he worshiped the sun god, Sol Invictus; he had a vision of Apollo in 312 near Aachen; and the Christogram as described by Lactantius could be interpreted as Celtic religious symbols.

- Serious scholars still argue that perhaps Constantine fought under a variety of symbols, some of which were ambiguous and later interpreted or explained as Christian. According to legend, Bishop **Hosius of Cordoba**, whom Constantine summoned to tutor his sons in 315, had to explain to Constantine the meaning of the symbol he saw at Milvian Bridge. Perhaps Constantine crossed a bridge of solar cults from paganism to Christianity.

- That said, there is very little evidence that Constantine or his family were solar monotheists. His coinage early in his reign associates him far more with Mars; images of the sun god only occur after the conversion and after Constantine conquered the Balkan provinces, where Sol was popular among the soldiers of the Danube army.

- It seems most likely that at Milvian, Constantine knew he was fighting under a Christian symbol. He may well have had pagan symbols there, too, invoking all the gods. But there is no reason to believe that he did not know that the Christogram was the symbol of Christ. The victory likely made Constantine realize that the

Christian god was a true god, perhaps the only god, and within a few years, he came to identify himself as a Christian and monotheist.

Evidence from Coinage

- The coin evidence is significant for other reasons. Coins were disseminated in vast numbers, and repeated coinage reforms meant old money was called in and new money was issued. Iconography could change rapidly.

- There are few Christian symbols on Constantine's coins. Far more common were those continuing to invoke the pagan gods, even eight or nine years after the Battle of Milvian Bridge. Some of that is just the routine of mint masters; however, the vast majority of Constantine's subjects were pagans, and putting overt symbols of Christianity on the coins was too dangerous.

- Instead, Constantine steadily, between 313 and 324 when he reunited the Roman Empire, emptied the coinage of religious content, making himself the leading figure on the coins. He created a new portrait in which he appeared looking up to heaven. He wore the diadem, the symbol of royalty that went back to Alexander the Great. No emperor had ever worn that.

- On the reverse of the coins, where you had images of the gods traditionally, were images that celebrated the imperial family. A few divinities remained: personifications of the city of Rome or Constantinople; several personifications of the virtues. To Christians, these were classical symbols and not goddesses. Constantine was cleverly using the few religious symbols remaining on his coinage to convey ideas rather than divinities.

- By his death in 337, the coinage had been emptied of religious content and the celebration was centered on the emperor and his family—an inspired emperor who has the favor not only of the Christian god, but the pagan gods. It really was in the eye of the beholder exactly which divine power was favorable to Constantine.

- The sons of Constantine were more direct. They put the labarum on their art and coins. Emperor Magnentios, who was a rebel emperor in Gaul, actually put the Christogram on his coins. The irony is that Magnentios might have been a pagan and the symbols were being used to appeal to the army.

Constantine's Legacy

- The conversion of Constantine is significant for several reasons. One is that Constantine's conversion is the only well-documented conversion we have between Saint Paul and Saint Augustine.

- Both Paul and Augustine were intellectuals, and their conversions were based on intellectual and spiritual considerations that would appeal to the elite classes of the Roman world. Constantine was a soldier-emperor. As a pragmatic man, his conversion was much closer to the conversion experience of most of the Roman world.

- What convinced him was not the kind of subtle arguments that Augustine would make. What convinced Constantine that this god was worth invoking was that this god delivered on promises of victory.

- Eusebius plays this up in the *Life of Constantine*: Constantine's victories are cast in the traditions of the righteous kings of the Old Testament, and this is an image that will persist through the history of medieval Europe and down almost to the modern age.

- Why Constantine turned to the Christian god, we really do not know. But his conversion will be paralleled by many conversions of pagan monarchs in medieval Europe, particularly among the Scandinavian kings and the Merovingian kings of Gaul.

- On a more mundane level, the peasants and citizens of towns did not need a battle miracle from the Christian god, but there were other miracles that could be performed. One was exorcism. Other times, monks and ascetics simply defied the pagan gods, casting down their statues. When there were no consequences, that was dramatic proof to many pagans that these holy men were protected by the true god.

- Not only did Constantine convert to Christianity, but in 313 he issued the **Edict of Milan**. This not only halted the persecutions; it gave legal legitimacy to Christianity. With that decisive change, the Christians had captured the Roman monarchy.

- As the 19th-century scholar J. B. Bury put it, the conversion of Constantine is probably one of the most audacious acts carried out by an autocrat in violation of the religious opinions of the majority of his subjects. While Saint Paul gave Christianity the potential to be a world faith, Constantine, by his conversion and the institutions he forged, would make Christianity the religion of not only the Roman world, but ultimately of Europe.

Important Term

Edict of Milan: The imperial rescript issued jointly by Constantine I and Licinius I in 313 that ended the Great Persecutions and recognized Christianity as a religion.

Names to Know

Hosius (257–359): Bishop of Corduba (modern Cordova) before 300, he suffered exile during the Great Persecution of 303–305. In 313, he was invited to Treveri, where he advised the emperor Constantine on doctrinal matters. After the death of Constantine, Hosius staunchly opposed the Arian policies of Constantius II.

Lactantius (a.k.a. **Lucius Caecilius Firmianus Lactantius**; c. 240–320): Roman rhetor and tutor to Crispus, eldest son of Constantine I. Born in Roman Africa, he taught rhetoric at Nicomedia. In about 315, he composed *On the Deaths of the Persecutors* (*De mortibus persecutorum*), the prime source for and the earliest report of the conversion of Constantine in 312.

Suggested Reading

Burckhadt, *The Age of Constantine the Great.*

Drake, *Constantine and the Bishops.*

Eadie, ed. *The Conversion of Constantine.*

Eusebius, *The History of the Church from Christ to Constantine.*

———, *Life of Constantine.*

Harl, "Make Haste Slowly."

Lactantius, *On the Manner in Which the Persecutors Died.*

MacMullen, *Constantine.*

Odhal, *Constantine and the Christian Empire.*

Van Dam, *The Roman Revolution of Constantine.*

Questions to Consider

1. How trustworthy are the accounts of Lactantius and Eusebius on the conversion of Constantine? What has accounted for the debate over the conversion of Constantine?

2. Why are coins and medallions vital sources on the conversion?

3. How did Constantine view the Christian god on the eve of the Battle of Milvian Bridge? How did Constantine come to understand his new faith?

4. How did Constantine's conversion decisively change the course of the conflict between pagans and Christians?

Constantine and the Bishops
Lecture 17

Constantine's church was an imperial institution built on the bureaucracy of the tetrarchs, a dramatic change from the apostolic church that had been in existence from the time of Saint Paul. The bishops were elevated to the legal status of *honestiores*—"honorable ones"— and took on many of the duties formerly assigned to the decurions. Two events that best defined the relationship between the emperor and the church in the public's eye were the building of the Christian capital Constantinople and the First Ecumenical Council at Nicaea.

The Church and the Law

- The churches in existence at the time of Constantine's conversion were largely the apostolic churches that went back to Saint Paul and the disciples of Christ. What Constantine did, in effect, was co-opt the bishops of those churches and create a new hierarchy within the Roman imperial system.

- In early 313, Constantine and co-emperor and brother-in-law, **Licinius**, issued an imperial rescript called the Edict of Milan. It differs significantly from earlier Christian reprieves, which were acts of clemencies, or criminal pardons. This edict not only halted all persecutions but defined Christianity as a legal religion.

- The edict made all members of the Roman world free to practice the faith they wished; it halted all persecutions and declared that property of the Christians should be returned to them, that church institutions likewise should be returned to bishops, and that henceforth Christian churches and their clergy were under the legal protection of the imperial government.

- Constantine also declared that Christian bishops, under Roman law, were constituted as an **ordo** (pl. **ordines**), or legal class, with specific rights and privileges. The highest ordo in the Roman world was the senatorial order, followed by the equestrians and then the decurions. In the late empire, imperial soldiers and officials became legal classes as well. Ordos were not economic and social classes as we understand them today; class went far beyond that.

- Sometime between the 2nd and 3rd century, the traditional Roman distinction between citizen (*civis*) and noncitizen (*peregrinus*) had been replaced by **honestiores**, "those who are honored," and **humiliores**, "the humble ones." Members of the honorable ordines had many economic and legal privileges not accorded to the humble. The bishops were in one of the honored ordines, on par with imperial officials and soldiers.

Episcopal Administration in Everyday Life

- Constantine invested many powers in the bishops, so that they increasingly displaced the pagan decurion leaders in provincial cities. Over a period of 30 years, Constantine expanded the powers of the episcopal courts to include issues beyond the immediate Christian community, such as marriages, contracts, and inheritance. It was now often to the advantage of even pagan litigants to bring their cases before bishops.

- Some scholars have seen this as a loss of imperial power and the church becoming a deathless corporation, but this is really an overstatement. There was little doubt as to who was the senior partner in this arrangement. The emperor was the fount of patronage. He was turning over to the bishops the powers he did not have sufficient administrators to handle.

- The emperor used the law to convert the empire in other ways. He could legislate in favor of Christian subjects. Roman soldiers and officers who embraced the new faith were given Sundays off. Towns that converted to Christianity were given city status.

- The precise role of the emperor within the imperial church is a matter of debate. But remember that Constantine was a true Roman; he created the Christian Roman Empire the way Augustus had created the original Roman Empire. He thus had such influence, authority, charisma, and patronage that the bishops were in no position to challenge him on legal or religious matters.

Constantine as a Source of Christian Doctrine

- Shortly after Constantine's conversion, there was a schism in the North African over the status of *lapsi*—those who had lapsed into paganism and sacrificed during the persecutions of 303–312. The **Donatists**, followers of Donatus, felt *lapsi* must be rebaptized before being readmitted to the church. Followers of **Caecilian** felt that confession was sufficient.

- Representatives of each side presented letters and petitions to Constantine, and in 315 Constantine ruled in favor of the Caecilianists. Constantine exercised his legal powers as emperor to make rulings regarding Christian institutions and Christian discipline—arguably even defining dogma.

- Bishops and authors like Eusebius hailed Constantine as the equal of the apostles, comparing him to King David and Moses, a great lawgiver. Some historians have gone so far as to argue that Constantine thus understood the politics of consensus. It would be more accurate to say that Constantine was an autocratic emperor with a vast army behind him; consensus meant, "Do what I tell you, or else."

- Compare Constantine's ability to make rulings with regard to the Christian church versus the Sāsānid shah's position in relation to Zoroastrianism. The creed depended heavily on Iranian traditions, and the shah's power rested on the traditional elite. As a result of Diocletian's reforms, the Roman emperor was no longer in that position; he had his own bureaucracy and army and the means to enforce his religious decisions.

Constantinople—The New Rome

- Two other important acts of Constantine ensured the advancement of Christianity. The first of these was the creation of a new Christian capital at Constantinople. This was far more effective than any legislation he passed against the pagan cults—of which he passed little.

- The city of Rome was no longer a strategic capital; Constantinople, on the site of the former colony of Byzantium, was on an important land and sea crossroads between the Black Sea and the Aegean. Also, shifting the capital eastward reflected the shifting makeup of the senatorial class, which increasingly came from Asia Minor and Syria.

- Constantinople was founded as a Christian city. Pagan Byzantium disappeared into the new capital, which grew in less than a century from a city of 35,000 to more than 350,000 people. Constantine constructed a whole new Christian center of imperial palaces, churches, and government offices. There were villas for the senators and a hippodrome for the masses.

- Meanwhile, the senators back in Rome were delighted because these old, distinguished pagan families could ignore the Christian capital and run Rome as a pagan city well into the 5th century.

- Constantinople's churches—particularly the original Hagia Sophia (the current building is the third of that name)—became the models for Christian churches all over the empire. The standard domed basilica church represents what we believe the churches in Constantinople looked like in the early 4th century.

The Council of Nicaea

- While building a Christian capital was a significant statement, Constantine could not outlaw the pagan cults nor make Christianity the official religion of the Roman Empire—that would happen in

391–392 under Emperor Theodosius. However, in 325, Constantine presided over the Council of Nicaea, which had several profound effects on the growing church.

- The council addressed both theological and practical matters. Among the most important theological issues addressed was the nature of the Trinity. Was Christ the same substance as the father (**homoousia**) or just similar (**homoiousia**)?

- **Athanasius**, the future patriarch of Alexandria, argued for homoousia. **Arius** argued the contrary position and apparently understood it as a hierarchy, perhaps in the vein of Origen; his position was condemned. Constantine ruled in favor of the majority position on this issue. He also offered the language of similar and same substance.

- The council also determined the reckoning of the date of Easter as the first Sunday after the new moon following the spring equinox, ensuring that Easter and Passover never coincided so that Christianity and Judaism were distinct.

- The side of the Council of Nicaea that is often not noted is the impact it had on onlookers, pagans and Christians alike. A mere 12 or 13 years since the end of the persecutions, some 330 bishops from all over the Roman world, with their great retinues, were traveling to the city of Nicaea to discuss religion with the emperor. Many of these bishops had been arrested and tortured under Diocletian; now they were in Constantine's favor. It must have seemed a true miracle.

- Constantine inverted the relationship between the emperor and the gods. The pagan emperor had visited the sanctuaries; the Christian emperor summoned the bishops instead. Together, bishops and emperor ruled over the new faith and rewarded its adherents. There was now a new, fundamentally different relationship between the imperial government and its subjects. What counted in the world of Constantine was not Roman citizenship, but Christian faith.

homoiousia: From Greek for "similar substance"; the term used by Arians to define the Christ logos as inferior to the father in the Trinity.

homoousia: From Greek for "same substance"; the term used by Nicene Christians to define the Christ logos as identical in essence to the father in the Trinity.

honestiores: Latin for "more honorable ones"; an order of society in later Roman law accorded privileges and exemptions from torture in criminal proceedings.

humiliores: Latin for "more humble ones"; an order of society in later Roman law subject to direct taxation and, in criminal proceedings, to torture and corporal punishment.

ordo (pl. **ordines**): A legal class of citizens according to Roman law, or the town council of a Roman colony or municipality.

Arius (c. 250–336): Presbyter in the church of Alexandria, he argued that Christ was generated as an inferior creature from God the father. His theology, Arianism, was condemned at the First Ecumenical Council (325), but his followers converted the East Germans to the Arian confession.

Athanasius (c. 293–373): Theologian and clergyman who opposed Arius at the First Ecumenical Council of Nicaea in 325, arguing the Orthodox positions. As patriarch of Alexandria (329–373), he opposed Emperor Constantius II, a devoted Arian, and later the pagan emperor Julian II. His writings are regarded the touchstone of Orthodoxy. In about 360, he wrote the hagiography of Saint Antony of Egypt.

Licinius I (a.k.a. **Gaius Valerius Licianus Licinius**; c. 263–325; r. 308–324): A veteran officer, Licinius was elevated as Augustus of the West by Galerius after Severus II had been defeated and executed by Maxentius. In

311, Licinius succeeded to the Balkan provinces. In 313, he contracted an alliance with Constantine and married Constantine's half-sister Constantia. That same year, he defeated Maximinus II Daza and took over the eastern provinces. Twice—in 314 and 323–324—Licinius clashed with Constantine. Licinius was defeated and deposed by Constantine in 324; he was executed in 325. Licinius issued jointly with Constantine the Edict of Milan in 313. Initially tolerant of Christians, Licinius was criticized for persecution of Christians during his final war with Constantine.

Suggested Reading

Barnes, *Constantine and Eusebius.*

Drake, *Constantine and the Bishops.*

Eusebius, *The History of the Church from Christ to Constantine.*

———, *Life of Constantine.*

Garnsey, *Social Status and Legal Privilege in the Roman Empire.*

Krautheimer, *Three Christian Capitals.*

MacCormack, *Art and Ceremony in Late Antiquity.*

Odhal, *Constantine and the Christian Empire.*

Rapp, *Holy Bishops in Late Antiquity.*

Van Dam, *The Roman Revolution of Constantine.*

Questions to Consider

1. Why was the Edict of Milan such a turning point for Christianity and the Roman Empire? Why was legal status so important for the success of Christianity?

2. What was the impact of the dedication of Constantinople as a Christian capital? How did pagans react to this change? What was the opinion of the pagan senators at Rome?

3. Why would Christians and pagans alike see the Council of Nicaea as a veritable miracle? What did Constantine hope to achieve by summoning the council? What were the consequences of the council?

Christianizing the Roman World
Lecture 18

Architecture was an enormous part of how the new Christian elite asserted the new religious identity of the Roman world. Churches were sometimes newly built structures created on the basilica plan; other times, they were co-opted pagan shrines; whenever possible, they were situated for maximum effect. Bishops took over the decurions' former role in distributions, now predicated on need rather than citizenship. New centers of worship, particularly in the Holy Land, became new pilgrimage sites, and Christian identity began creating political bonds between Rome and the world beyond its borders.

The First Imperial Church Buildings

- Constantine and the bishops claimed Roman public and religious spaces for the new faith, turning the urban landscape from a pagan one into a Christian one between the 4th and 6th centuries. During this time, the **basilica** was adapted as the premier type of church building.

- There were subtle transformations of public religious spaces that varied from city to city and province to province. One example took place in Ephesus, where the Church of Mary Theotokos was built inside the temenos wall of the sanctuary to Zeus and the temple to Zeus and other public buildings were dismantled for building materials.

- Many of these very early churches only survive as foundations. Some of them can be dated based on the coin finds in or under these foundations.

- The basilica churches were constructed in prominent places: Ephesus's Church of Mary Theotokos was near the port; Hierapolis had a series of churches on the axial road running from the city gate to the cemetery. This was part of what might be called an intercept policy, diverting the crowds from the famous pagan sanctuaries in these cities.

- Another method, dictated in part by costs but also quite effective, was to convert a temple into a church. Aphrodisias, a city devoted to the worship of Aphrodite, defied the emperors and continued in pagan worship well into the 5th century. When Emperor Zeno finally brought them to heel, the Christian architects added an apse at the temple's east end and extended the rest to create a basilica layout.

- Several exceptional sanctuaries were not turned into churches, either because they were too famous and important as pagan centers or because of structural problems. The Temple of Artemis Ephesia at Ephesus is a case of both. Eventually, the sanctuary was leveled, with a single column of the original 128 left standing as a memorial to show the victory of the new faith over the old.

As the empire was converted, pagan temples were converted, too.

Episcopal Patronage

- This changing of public and religious space was paralleled by changes in social and economic life in the cities. Bishops had the patronage of the emperor; they had money, and they employed hundreds or thousands of people in constructing and decorating the new churches. This made the bishops the fount of patronage in provincial cities.

- We have a monumental inscription from Bishop Marcus Julius Eugenius of Laodicea Combusta, who boasted of turning his city Christian by architecture. The inscription is similar to those of decurions of the 1st and 2nd centuries putting up pagan and public buildings.

- Some Christians deplored these men as having lithomania—putting up buildings at random. Others saw these bishops as nourishers of the city. That meant that in addition to all this public construction, they took on the social obligations that once characterized the pagan elites.

- Pagan decurions had always given out distributions to citizens at the festivals; the higher your rank, the more you received. The Christian bishops turned this into almsgiving and reversed the precedence: The more you needed, the more you received. Its purpose was not to demonstrate the donor's honor but as an act of piety. Well-off Christian families often donated anonymously.

Christian Pilgrimage

- Pilgrimage routes changed in the Roman world from the time of Constantine on. Before Constantine, people traveled great distances to visit the oracles and the major shrines and festivals. Now, new Christian centers with little or no relationship to the old sanctuaries were emerging.

- The most obvious was the Holy Land. Saint **Helena**, Constantine's mother, made many efforts to find places associated with the early Christian traditions in the region between 326 and 328.

- Church fathers were divided on the issue. Some were avid about finding relics; others saw too much potential for fraud. But by the year 400, there was an extremely well-developed pilgrimage and trade route from the western half of the Roman Empire into the Holy Land. The region that the Romans called Palestine experienced an enormous economic boom as a result that would continue well into the early Middle Ages.

- Other sites developed along the pilgrimage routes in Italy, the Balkans, and in Asia Minor. The development of these pilgrimage routes was important in redirecting the focus of religious life in the Roman world to new locations, locations associated with the mission and crucifixion of Jesus and the early apostles.

The Revival of Missionary Activity

- Constantine initiated missionary activity outside the Roman world. This changed the diplomatic and political dimensions of Roman foreign policy on many levels.

- According to tradition, King **Tiridates III** of Armenia embraced Christianity several years before Constantine's conversion. Some historians think it is more likely the Armenians embraced Christianity because of Rome's conversion. Either way, it created a new political bond.

- The king of Axum, in northern Ethiopia, also embraced Christianity late in the reign of Constantine, as did various Arabian tribes along the frontiers between Rome and the Sāsānid Empire.

- Missions were sent to the northern peoples. The most famous of these was commissioned by Emperor Constantius II, led by **Ulfilas**. He translated the Bible into Gothic and converted the East Germanic peoples to Arian Christianity. These tribes, previously classified as barbarians, were now part of the *oikoumene*, the Christian community.

- As a result of these missions, the barriers between Rome and the outside world crossed by religious bonds. For example, Roman Emperors began intervening on Armenia's behalf against the

Persian shahs. Armenia—which in the classical age had culturally and religiously leaned toward the Iranian world—now reoriented itself toward Rome.

- Henceforth, the identity that determined one's citizenship or position in the Roman world was not "Are you a Roman citizen?" but "Are you a Christian?"

Important Terms

basilica: A Roman public building with apses at each end and a central hall, or narthex. The design was applied to a Christian church in the 4ᵗʰ century. The longitudinal axis of the basilica was distinct from the centrally planned church in the form of square with a dome at the intersection—the design favored in the middle and late Byzantine ages.

oikoumene: Greek for "inhabited"; the universal Christian world.

Names to Know

Helena (a.k.a. **Flavia Julia Helena**; c. 246–330): Saint, first wife of Constantius I, and mother of Constantine I. In about 289, Constantius divorced Helena so that he could marry Theodora, daughter of Maximianus, Augustus of the West. In 326–328, Helena traveled to Jerusalem and Bethlehem, where she reportedly found the True Cross.

Tiridates III (250–339; r. 285–339): Arsacid king of Armenia who was a loyal ally of Rome in the wars against the Persians. In 301, he reportedly converted to Christianity and was baptized by Gregory the Illuminator. There is reason to believe that Tiridates might have converted after the conversion of Emperor Constantine I.

Ulfilas (a.k.a. **Wulfila**; 311–381): Arian bishop of the Goths consecrated at the synod of Antioch in 341. As missionary to the Goths, Ulfilas adapted the Greek alphabet to Gothic and translated the Bible into Gothic in 341–343.

Suggested Reading

Atkins and Osborne, eds., *Poverty in the Roman World.*

Brown, *Poverty and Leadership in the Later Roman Empire.*

———. *Power and Persuasion in Late Antiquity.*

Dietz, *Wandering Monks, Virgins and Pilgrims.*

Drijvers, *Helena Augusta.*

Finn, *Almsgiving in the Later Roman Empire.*

Fowden, *From Empire to Commonwealth.*

Harl, "From Pagan to Christian in the Cities of Asia Minor.

Holman, *The Hungry are Dying.*

Holum, *Theodosian Empresses.*

Hunt, *Holy Land Pilgrimage in the Later Roman Empire.*

MacMullen, *The Second Church.*

van Dam, *Families and Friends in Late Roman Cappadocia.*

Questions to Consider

1. What advantages did the bishops enjoy over pagan decurions in gaining control of cities? Why were building activities so crucial for Christianizing cities?

2. How important were charity and Christian festivals in winning over city populations? How did these activities differ from earlier pagan ones?

3. What was the impact of pilgrimage in creating a wider Christian world? How did Christians view pilgrimage as an expression of faith?

4. How did Christian emperors promote missions to the peoples beyond the imperial frontiers? How did a sense of Christian commonwealth come into being? What was the historical significance of this new perception?

The Birth of Christian Aesthetics and Letters
Lecture 19

C hristians took over the cultural heritage of the pagan past and made it distinctly Christian, preserving their pagan as well as their Jewish heritage. The so-called classics became a fundamental part of the education of a Christian gentleman, particularly the high language of Platonic Greek and Ciceronian Latin. In the visual arts, Roman architectural forms were decorated with art in the classical mode—mosaics, frescoes, and relief sculpture—to deliver the Christian message through the visual language developed by paganism.

Christianizing the Basilica

- Once churches were built to claim public spaces for Christianity, the visual and decorative arts were employed to raise a sense of awe, as well as to instruct the Roman Christians in their new faith. The arts were also used to inspire and awe pagans, who might then consider converting.

- The original Roman basilicas were created in the 2nd century B.C. as administrative and law courts. When adapted for worship, a few significant changes were made. Basilica churches were always entered from one of the short ends, which faced west. The apse and altar would be on the east, where the clergy sat on a synthronum, partitioned off from the congregation.

- Sometimes a transept (a perpendicular hall) was added, as were subsidiary buildings. Light entered from windows in the upper levels. Sometimes, a dome was added where the nave and transept crossed.

- There was no mistaking that the basilica was a Roman building. However, it differed significantly from pagan temples in that it was an architecture of the interior. It was ideally suited as a place to hold worship inside.

- Another building from the Roman tradition adapted for use as a church was the dome on a square, best epitomized by the Pantheon. This type of building might be used as a mortuary church or a church to a martyr saint and was a convenient way of Christianizing a pagan sanctuary.

The 4th-Century Decorative Art Style

- To convert already existing buildings, they had to be decorated to inspire and instruct. One common technique was through typology—paired scenes from the Old and New Testament.

- In terms of style, Christians followed the aesthetic changes that characterized all arts of the later Roman world. After 235, the stress in art was on hierarchy, symmetrical presentations, and inspiring awe rather than realistic imagery. Imperial portraits, for instance, became increasingly stylized.

- In the classical period, mosaic work tended to be limited to floors, and the style was influenced by representational art. Christians, however, put mosaics on ceilings and floors, and they emphasized not realism but the message, which was highlighted by stylized artistic conventions: elongated figures with enlarged eyes that loomed impressively over the congregation.

- Most of the mosaic work was done in rough-cut stone on a gold leaf background. This was not because they could not make flatter mosaics but because these surfaces scattered light throughout the church, to impressive effect.

- Frescoes, too, were used for decoration, sometimes for financial reasons, but more often because the surface lent itself better to painting rather than mosaic. Christian artists avoided freestanding sculptures because they resembled pagan cult statues, using relief carvings instead.

- Classical art forms did not disappear. In private villas, Christian families decorated their homes with three-dimensional sculptures, floor mosaics, and decorative furniture.

The New Christian Literature

- Until Constantine's conversion, Christians had by and large been writing for other Christians. Now their writing had a much wider audience and cultural implications because increasingly the Christians were taking over the cultural leadership of the Roman world.

- Starting with Saint Paul, the Christians had perfected the epistle, or letter. Letter-writing had been the hallmark of a gentleman in both Latin and Greek; men like **Cicero** and Pliny the Younger were masters of this form.

© Hemera/Thinkstock.

Cicero's letters had been the model of Latin rhetoric for pagan gentlemen, and they became the model for Christian writers, too.

- Soon after, Christian writers came to excel at the Platonic dialogue. This form, a debate between two (but sometimes more) characters, was used by many philosophers writing both in Latin and Greek. The apologists were really the first Christians to master this form.

- Tertullian, who perfected the apology, also became skilled in the philippics (condemnation) and was one of the first Christians to attempt exegesis—that is, explaining biblical text.

- Christian letters really came of age with Saint Clement and Origen in the 4th century. They described Christian theology in a philosophical language (Atticizing Greek) that had to be read seriously by pagan critics. Latin literature did not come of age until the time of Saint Augustine, about a century later.

- New genres sprang into use by the Christians. One was the sermon, the particular genre of **John Chrysostom**, patriarch of Constantinople. Christian biography and history were both pioneered by Eusebius, who is one of our principle sources for this course. Saint Athanasius, also a patriarch of Alexandria, wrote a biography of Saint Antony that made hagiography one of the most popular genres in the Christian medieval world.

- By the opening of the 5th century, Christians had evolved a literature that was serious in intent, was written in sophisticated language (whether Latin or Greek), and could not simply be dismissed by their pagan contemporaries as ramblings of a vulgar superstition. This literature was a profound coming of age for Christian culture.

Christian Literature Looks to the Past

- In creating this literature, Christian authors drew very heavily on the classical past. If they wrote in Greek, they were trained in Homer and Plato; in the Greek historians; in Demosthenes, the famous Athenian orator of the 4th century B.C. If they wrote in Latin, they were trained in Vergil; they were trained in the writings of Cicero.

Saint Augustine was an impeccable Ciceronian, and the same was true of Saint Jerome, who translated the Bible into Latin.

- All of these Christian authors had fine classical educations; which had two long-term implications for the Roman world: First of all, it meant that the classics, these pagan literary traditions, would be preserved and transmitted to later generations. They would not be denounced, renounced, and rejected. Therefore, there was enormous cultural continuity, literary and visual, between the pagan Roman world and the Christian Roman world.

- The second important point is in preserving the visual and literary culture of the pagan world, these Christian authors, writers, and thinkers gave the Western tradition a peculiar dynamic. Thereafter, the canonical texts of the Western tradition were not only Christian, nor even a combination of Christian texts and Jewish texts translated into Greek. It also included a large body of pagan literature that had nothing to do with the Christian message.

- It is this dual tradition—the Greek and Roman pagan on the one hand and the Christian on the other—that became the basis of Western literary tradition and accounts for some of the dynamic and unusual aspects of the Western literary tradition down to this day.

Names to Know

Cicero (a.k.a. **Marcus Tullius Cicero**; 106–43 B.C.): Roman lawyer, orator, statesman, and consul of 63 B.C., Cicero was a prolific writer and master of Latin prose. He left a number of works dealing with philosophy and Roman religious practices in addition to his letters and political speeches.

John Chrysostom (349–407): Patriarch of Constantinople (398–405). A brilliant orator, he asserted the primacy of Constantinople over the Eastern churches and clashed with the emperor Arcadius.

Suggested Reading

Beckwith, *Early Christian and Byzantine Art.*

Bregman, *Synesius of Cyrene.*

Brown, *Augustine of Hippo.*

————, *The World of Late Antiquity.*

Elsner, *Imperial Rome and Christian Triumph.*

Hanfmann, *Sardis from Prehistoric to Roman Times.*

Kitzinger, *Byzantine Art in the Making.*

Krautheimer, *Early Christian Architecture.*

————, *Three Christian Capitals.*

MacCormack, *Art and Ceremony in Late Antiquity.*

Perkins, *Art of Dura-Europos.*

Rousseau, *Basil of Caesarea.*

Weitzmann, ed., *The Age of Spirituality.*

Weitzmann and Kessler, *The Frescoes of the Dura Synagogue and Christian Art.*

Questions to Consider

1. How did the Christians evolve church forms out of Roman architecture? How important were Jewish synagogues (such as the one at Sardis) as prototypes? How did Christian emperors from Constantine on contribute to this process? What were the visual and religious purposes of the basilica and centrally planned churches?

2. What were the visual and iconographic elements in Christian art in 300–450? How did Christian artists reshape classical forms to express the new faith? Did Christian art break with or transform the Greco-Roman arts? What were the elements of continuity with classical art?

3. How did Christian thinkers and writers create a distinct literature from the Greek and Latin pagan texts? What authors and genres were favored? How did this literary development ensure Christians of cultural leadership in the Roman world?

The Emperor Julian and the Pagan Reaction
Lecture 20

Julian the Apostate was the last pagan emperor of Rome. Raised a Christian but isolated from the imperial family and educated in the classics, he turned to paganism in his 20s and, on ascending the throne, attempted to re-convert the empire by turning Constantine's Christian, bureaucratic, and military institutions to his own purposes. His reign was cut short by a disastrous military expedition in Persia, but had he lived, might he have succeeded in restoring the pagan faith, or some henotheistic version of it? And how far would he have gone to accomplish his goals?

Julian's Anti-Revolution

- Emperor **Julian II** is sometimes known as Julian the Apostate or Julian the Philosopher. He is without a doubt one of the best-known figures from late antiquity. On December 11, 361, he entered Constantinople at the head of a victorious army that was supposed to fight a civil war and did not and ordered that the pagan temples immediately be reopened and the sacrifices resumed.

- This incident is a reminder that the success and triumph of Christianity was by no means inevitable after the work of Constantine and his Christian sons, who ruled between 337 and 361. Julian proved that it was by no means certain what the religious loyalties of the Roman world would be.

Who Was Julian?

- Julian was born into the imperial family. He was a nephew of the emperor Constantine. An intellectual, his native language was Greek, and from birth he was to be trained to be a theologian and bishop, probably the bishop of Constantinople.

- Julian has engendered interest from both detractors and admirers, both past and present. His foremost admirer was the historian **Ammianus Marcellinus**, who lived in the 4th century and is often called the last great imperial historian of Rome. He wrote a narrative history in Latin in which Julian's career was the centerpiece.

- Julian wrote an enormous amount in his two and a half years as emperor. He composed nine major philosophical works, plus hymns, letters, and administrative documents. One of his most important works is a critique of Christianity called *Against the Galileans*, which was so incisive that Christian students used it for centuries to hone their debate and analysis skills.

- Julian is a perplexing figure. Some see him as a hero of a lost cause; others dismiss him as an eccentric or a zealot. Still others see him as a man of great vision who could have out-Constantined Constantine had he only lived to enact his reforms.

- In September 337, Constantine died, and all potential rivals to his sons were purged from the imperial family. Constantine's youngest son, **Constantius II**, would eventually reunite the empire and rule from 337–361. He was a devout Arian Christian.

- The only males of the imperial family to survive the purge were Julian, then 6, and his half-brother Constantius Gallus, who was 12. They grew up essentially under house arrest and then, in 341, were banished to Cappadocia, in Asia Minor.

- Julian spent his formative years reading Homer and the classics, looking up at Mount Argaeus—home to the mother goddess Ma— and unsurprising by age 20, he tells us, he went back to worshiping the old gods.

Julian and the Imperial Succession

- Constantius Gallus was made Caesar and heir to Constantius II in 351 while Constantius was waging a war in the West. The

Western army was rebelling because it was mostly pagan and wanted to continue the sacrifices. However, Constantius Gallus was so incompetent and tyrannical that he was arrested and executed in 354.

- Meanwhile, Julian was allowed to return from exile to study at Constantinople, Nicomedia, Pergamon, and Ephesus. Constantius's intent was likely to make him patriarch of Constantinople—the religious counterpart to his stepbrother the emperor.

- Julian came under the influence of two middle Platonist philosophers at this time: Maximus of Ephesus and Aedistus. At this point, he secretly converted to the worship of the gods and was initiated into the Eleusinian Mysteries, keeping his true beliefs secret from the emperor.

- In 355, Julian was summoned to the imperial court. Constantius had no choice but to make Julian his heir and Caesar. Julian was sent to Gaul to command the Western army; Gaul was being overrun by German barbarians.

- Julian read up on his Julius Caesar, won brilliant victories, and re-established the frontier. The Western army came to adore their strange, bookish, Greek-speaking prince. Then the news came from Constantius of war against Persia. The emperor wanted soldiers to be transferred from the West to the East.

- This sparked a revolt in December 360. The Western army saluted Julian as emperor, and a civil war was on. Julian now publicly revealed what some of his officers already knew: He was a worshiper of the old gods.

- The Western army began to march eastward to encounter the army of Constantius II. But before the war could be fought, Constantius succumbed to illness and died in November 361. He also did something that was a blessing to the empire: He recognized Julian as his heir.

Julian the Pagan Emperor

- As recounted at the start of the lecture, Julian entered Constantinople in December 361 and immediately ordered the restoration of the gods. Between December 361 and March 363—a period of about 16 months—Julian issued sweeping legislation and administrative reforms across the Roman Empire.

- Julian attacked corruption abuses with the imperial administration, cracked down on taxes, and carried out important religious reforms. But he was not slow or cautious like his uncle, Constantine. He did not persecute the Christians, but he abruptly and completely cut off their funding. He proclaimed religious toleration and then allowed the Arians and the Nicenes, who were divided over the issue of the Trinity, sue each over who had control of which bishopric.

- Julian also began to organize a pagan counterchurch. They were to take over all the charitable actions of the Christian bishops and therefore win over the poor in the cities. At the same time, he remitted taxes to cities. He passed legislation in favor of the pagan decurions. He understood that the restoration of the pagan cults depended on promoting this new imperial religious hierarchy and the decurion pagan families in the provincial cities.

- Julian's paganism was not the traditional restoration of the cults, but a new faith he called Hellenism. It involved study of philosophy as well as the worship and veneration of the cults, all subsidized by the imperial state and supported by the bureaucracy that Constantine had built up for the Christian church. This was perplexing to pagans, who never in their traditions had anything like this type of state organization.

- This leads to debates about what Julian really intended in the long run. Some scholars even argue that, once the Persian threat had been put down, Julian would have begun persecuting the Christians.

- The idea of a Julian persecution is borne out by several of his writings, the most peculiar one called the ***Misopogon*** (*Beard Hater*), a strange piece of satire in which he indulges in a fair amount of self-criticism, then turns the criticism back on his Christian critics. It suggests a nervous, zealous, and impatient personality that might have turned to violence, given the chance. Other scholars argue that Julian had a much more tolerant nature.

- Several important reforms went in tandem with restoring the pagan gods and switching patronage from the Christian church to the pagan cults. One regarded with the greatest bitterness by his Christian opponents was a law requiring that teachers only teach what they believe in and that students read texts that they believed in. This prevented Christian scholars from teaching the classics and Christian students from reading them, relegating them to second-class status in intellectual circles.

- Julian also supported the Jews and attempted to rebuild Jerusalem; that is, Julian upheld the validity of the Old Israel against the New Israel. In *Against the Galileans*, he wrote some incisive biblical criticism, particularly on the apocalyptic literature of the Old Testament.

The Death of Julian

- The war against Persia and Shah Shāpūr II had a religious dimension for Julian. As he left Constantinople and made his way east, he visited the various cult centers to win the favor of the traditional gods. This was in the tradition of pagan emperors who had battled the Iranian foe for centuries.

- The attack on the Persian capital city of Ctesiphon went badly awry, whether due to Julian's mistakes or the quality of the Roman army is debated by many scholars. The army arrived in Mesopotamia at the height of the blazing summer. Provisions were not delivered on time, and Julian had to order a retreat.

- On retreat, Julian was mortally wounded in a skirmish. In the Middle Ages, the story would be elaborated to say he was killed by a Christian in the employ of a Persian shah.

- That evening, as Julian lay dying, the senior officers met in the imperial tent. They turned to the pagan Praetorian Prefect, Salutius, and asked him to become emperor. He refused. Then they turned to the second in command, a Nicene Christian named Jovian, and offered him the throne.

- Jovian was nervous. He reminded them that he was a Christian. The officers replied, "Tonight in this tent, we are all Christians. Get us out of Persia." Jovian accepted the emperorship. He signed an ignominious peace where he gave up strategic provinces, but got the army back to the Roman Empire.

- The campaign was disastrous for the pagan cause. To the Christians, it was a vindication of their faith. The death of Julian meant the end of his reforms, and the Christians would assume their cultural and political dominance in the Roman world.

Important Term

Misopogon: "Beard Hater"; the satirical tract written by the pagan emperor Julian to refute his Christian detractors at Antioch in 362. Julian was jeered at for sporting the long beard of a pagan philosopher.

Names to Know

Ammianus Marcellinus (330–395): Soldier and last great pagan historian of Rome. Born in Antioch, Ammianus served under emperors from Constantius II (r. 337–361) to Theodosius I (r. 379–395). He composed a history in 31 books (of which books 1–12 are lost) covering Roman history from A.D. 96 to 378. Ammianus displays exceptional objectivity in discussing the pagan revival by Emperor Julian (r. 360–363), so that his account is fundamental to the religious history of the 4th century.

Constantius II (a.k.a. **Flavius Julius Constantius**; 317–361; r. 337–361): Son of Constantine I and Fausta, Constantius II was proclaimed Caesar in 324 and succeeded jointly as Augustus with his brothers Constantine II and Constans in 337. Constantius ruled in the East, waging a war against the Persians. He crushed the rebellion by Magnentius and the Western army in 350–353. In 361, Constantius died of illness while en route to face his cousin Julian, who had been declared emperor by the Western army. An Arian Christian, Constantius sponsored Ulfilas, the so-called apostle to the Goths.

Julian II (a.k.a. **Julian the Apostate** or **Flavius Claudius Julianus**; 332–363; r. 360–363): Nephew of the first Christian emperor, Constantine I, he survived the purge of 337 and was raised and educated in the wastes of Cappadocia. Devoted to the classics, Julian secretly renounced his Christianity in 351. Promoted to Caesar in 355, Julian brilliantly cleared Gaul of Germanic invaders, and he was proclaimed emperor by the Western army. His brief reign saw the restoration of paganism to civic life; his reforms were cut short by his untimely death while on campaign in Persia. His works include orations, philosophical tracts, hymns to Helios and Magna Mater, and critiques on Christian dogma.

Suggested Reading

Ammianus Marcellinus, *The Later Roman Empire*.

———, *Roman History*.

Athanassadi-Fowden, *Julian and Hellenism*.

Barnes, *Athanasius and Constantius*.

Bowersock, *Julian the Apostate*.

Browing, *The Emperor Julian*.

Chuvin, *A Chronicle of the Last Pagans*.

Dill, *Roman Society in the Last Century of the Western Empire*.

Julian, *Works*.

Tougher, trans. and ed., *Julian the Apostate*.

Trombley, *Hellenic Religion and Christianization*.

Vidal, *Julian*.

Zosimus, *New History*.

Questions to Consider

1. What led Julian to return to the worship of the gods? How was Julian both intellectual and mystic? How important were the pagan classics, notably Homer and Plato, in leading Julian back to paganism?

2. Was Julian's Hellenism a plausible counter to the Christian church created by Constantine? Why would many pagans not understand Julian's Hellenism? What were the long-term prospects of Julian's laws if he had won in Persia and ruled for 30 years? Was Julian the hero of a lost cause?

3. How was Julian's mystical henotheism typical of many pagan intellectuals? What was the role of theurgy?

4. Why did pagan officers elect Jovian as Julian's successor? What were the consequences of the pagans' failure to find a pagan successor to Julian?

Struggle over Faith and Culture
Lecture 21

After the death of Emperor Julian II, the pagan elite, particularly in Rome, Athens, and Alexandria, were not so certain Christianity had won the battle for Roman culture. A new pagan literature developed to defend the old faith, some of it in imitation of Christian literary forms. But lacking a leader like Julian and with an essentially conservative outlook, they were unable to mount an effective counter-revolution to restore their faith, and by the middle of the 5th century, the intellectual and cultural leadership of the Roman world was decisively Christian.

Julian's Successors

- In the generation or so after the death of Julian the Apostate, the question was reopened: Which religion was going to take charge of the Roman world? It quickly became clear that the pagans were in no position to re-establish the leadership. Even if they had a pagan emperor, they had no one with Julian's vision.

- On the other hand, Emperor Jovian, although a Christian, turned out to be a feckless ruler. He was found dead under mysterious circumstances in February 364; two senior army officers, the brothers **Valentinian I** and **Valens**, were proclaimed the next emperors. Neither was a man of first-rate ability, although they were respected by the army at the time.

- Valentinian and Valens were provincials of barbarian origin. Both Arian Christians at their accession, Valentinian converted to Nicene Christianity when he took over the western half of the Roman world, while Valens remained an Arian and ruled in the eastern half, reflecting the religious sentiments of each region.

- Because they were not connected to the imperial family of Constantine, they had to establish the second Christian dynasty of Rome. At first, they tried to cloak themselves in the symbols of Constantine: Coins, medallions, and public arts all featured the labarum with the Christogram.

- The brothers did get rid of some of Julian's laws— the law on education and imperial funding of the cults, for example—they did not outlaw the sacrifices or ban the traditional rites; they had to take a moderate position because the pagans had regained ground under Julian. Many army officers and soldiers were still pagans, and many of the provincial cities were in the hands of a pagan elite.

Hypatia of Alexandria was murdered by Christian monks.

- Until 391–392, the pagans found themselves in a position somewhat analogous to the early years of Constantine: Christianity was the favored faith; yet the old gods had not been outlawed. This ambiguous situation meant the pagans were caught off guard when Emperor Theodosius I eventually outlawed the cults.

- Furthermore, Valens and Valentinian did not inherit a united imperial church; Christianity was still divided between the Arians and Nicenes over the Trinitarian issue. That, too, would change with Theodosius, who would come down decisively on the side of the Nicene Creed.

The State of Pagan Culture after Julian

- Archaeologists have documented that the shrines and temples continued to operate throughout the 4th century and into the

5th century, some of them even after Theodosius I outlawed the sacrifices.

- There was a resurgence in Neoplatonic thought in Athens; one outstanding figure in the movement was **Proclus**, who wrote in the 5th century. At Alexandria, the great school continued to flourish. One of its most controversial figures was the mathematician **Hypatia**; she was hacked to death by a crowd of Christian monks in 414, as dramatized in the film *Agora*, but little of her work survives and her exact positions are unknown.

- Philosophers writing in Athens and Alexandria continued to articulate the Great Chain of Being of Plotinus and fostered the traditions of theurgy. These philosophers also evolved the doctrine sometimes proxy sacrifice: the learned philosopher can offer up sacrifices, knowing the intellectual meaning of these rites, on behalf of the entire community and can win the favor of the gods for the entire Roman world.

- There was enormous literary output by pagan authors. This included histories, such as that of Ammianus Marcellinus. Most literary production came from Rome in the West or Athens, Alexandria, and Antioch in the East.

The City of Rome in the Late Empire

- The administration of the city of Rome fell to the great senatorial families, who had never abandoned the goddess Roma or the traditional gods of Rome. They had enough wealth, power, and distance to ignore the upstart Christian emperors in Constantinople, and they essentially did as they wished. That included holding old offices of the city of Rome, conducting pagan ceremonies and sacrifices, and engaging in literary production.

- A number of individuals from this late senatorial aristocracy were great patrons of the gods and also edited the works of Vergil and of Cicero. One was Vettius Agorius Praetextatus; he and his wife epitomized pagan patronage, putting on festivals that lasted weeks. By one calculation, two-thirds of the calendar year in the city of Rome was engaged in pagan holidays.

- Another illustrious Roman was **Symmachus**, the leading pagan of the 4th century. Christian emperors had to pay attention to him; he was urban prefect of the city and governor of Africa. He alone could fund a remarkable circle of literati who edited text and carried out pagan festivals.

- The letters of Symmachus are not only in Ciceronian Latin; they contain no references to Christianity or Constantine and his successors whatsoever. They contain no references to the pope, who happened to be right on the other side of the Tiber River at the Ianiculum, which will eventually become Vatican City. This illustrates how difficult it sometimes is to date religious change in the Roman world.

- Only during the pontificate of Pope Leo I, in the mid-5th century, did the Roman aristocracy finally come over to Christianity.

The Great Eastern Cities in the Late Empire

- In the East, the picture was much the same as in Rome. Athens remained a pagan city into the 5th century. Alexandria was divided between pagans and Christians, and when the laws of 391–392 outlawed the cults, there were riots and demonstrations. The **Serapeum** and the Mouseion (the Library of Alexandria) were destroyed, as also dramatized in the film *Agora*.

- In the late 4th and early 5th centuries, a significant amount of pagan literature was composed in Greek, which became the final blossoming of pagan literature. Most classicists do not bother reading it. It is generally written in a high-blown style, particularly the epic poetry.

- **Quintus of Smyrna** wrote what is probably the longest written work in all antiquity; at more than 20,000 verses, it is longer than the *Iliad* and the *Odyssey* combined. The poem is interesting only to specialists today, but it demonstrates that it was by no means assured, at least in the minds of these pagans, that they had lost the struggle for Roman cultural dominance.

- A new brand of pagan history was produced. Most of these works have only survived in fragments. One that has come down to us intact is **Zosimus**'s *New History*. It is a continuous, linear narrative in the Greek and Roman tradition. But it is also a new kind of pagan apologetic literature: Zosimus argues that the reason the Roman Empire was suffering military reverses on the frontier was because the Christian emperors had abandoned the worship of the traditional gods.

- Orators operated in the same light. **Themistius of Constantinople** and **Libanius of Antioch**, who both knew Julian, continued to write into the reign of Theodosius I. They composed traditional panegyrics to the emperor and trained students in letters and the classics. They devised with new forms of oratory to appeal to Christian emperors for toleration of pagans, modeled on arguments the Christians had made in the 2nd century: We are loyal Roman citizens following Roman traditions. You Christian emperors should tolerate us.

- A similar type of literature was penned by Symmachus. He wrote a series of letters to the Christian emperors Gratian and Valentinian II arguing that the Altar of Victory in the Roman senate house, which was removed as offensive on orders of Valentinian I—should be restored.

The Ultimate Failure of the Pagan Resurgence

- This literature is indicative of the mixed religious situation after Julian and of one other point: The pagans never understood that there was a religious conflict. They did not understand that what was at stake was which religious system would control the destinies of the Roman world and eventually the cultural future of the Western tradition.

- The pagans never had a coherent thought of proselytizing. Part of this was in the nature of the pagan religious outlook; but also, this was because the pagan leaders of the Roman world were essentially a Mandarin elite. They were social conservatives, wary of defying the emperor openly. To defy the emperor would invite civil war. Civil war would invite revolution and social change, something that none of the pagan literati wanted.

- The pagans never had a coherent sense of how to win the emperor back to the old gods. They lacked the leadership and vision to mount a coherent effort. As a result, many pagans, particularly of the upper classes, eventually crossed over to Christianity, particularly via the philosophical and aesthetic bridge of Neoplatonism.

Important Term

Serapeum (a.k.a. **Serapeion**): A temple of Serapis, the Hellenized Osiris who was the tutelary god of Alexandria, Egypt. The destruction of the Serapeum of Alexandria by Christians in 391 marked a major defeat for paganism.

Names to Know

Hypatia (c. 360–415): Daughter of the mathematician Theon (c. 335–405) who taught mathematics and astronomy at Alexandria. She succeeded to the head of the pagan philosophical school at Alexandria in 400 and so was perceived as a threat by Patriarch Cyril. In 415, she was assaulted and hacked to pieces by a crowd of monks. Her works do not survive, but she apparently wrote commentaries on philosophy and astronomy.

Libanius of Antioch (314–394): Pagan rhetorician and sophist of Antioch who trained talented young men, pagan and Christian, destined for imperial service. He was a friend to the emperor Julian II, and yet he was allowed to present an oration protesting the desecration of temples in 383–388 to Theodosius I. Sixty-four orations of Libanius—along with commentaries, rhetorical exercises, and over 1,500 letters—have survived.

Proclus (c. 410–485): Brilliant Neoplatonic thinker and theurgist who was born of a wealthy family in Lycia but studied in Athens under Syrianus and succeeded the latter as head of the Academy in Athens. His *Elements of Theology, Platonic Theology*, and *Elements of Physics* are the climax of Greek philosophical thinking. He composed commentaries on Plato's *Timaeus* and *Alcibiades I*, as well as religious hymns.

Quintus of Smyrna (fl. 4th century A.D.): Pagan poet who composed the epic *Posthomerica*, a work of more than 20,000 lines (twice the length of the *Iliad* and the *Odyssey* combined), which told of events at Troy after Homer's epic leaves off.

Symmachus (a.k.a. **Quintus Aurelius Symmachus**; c. 340–402): The most distinguished Roman pagan senator of the 4th century and an accomplished man of letters. He served as proconsul of Africa (373), urban prefect (384–385), and consul (391). He presided over the pagan cultural and literary revival of Rome. In a series of orations (*relationes*), he pleaded for the restoration of the Altar of Victory to the Senate house (*Curia*) in 382–390. He supported Magnus Maximus in 387–388, but Theodosius pardoned him, and he retired from public life after 391.

Themistius of Constantinople (317–391): Pagan rhetorician and philosopher born of a noble family in Asia Minor, he was a loyal servant at Constantinople to successive emperors between Constantius II (r. 337–361) and Theodosius I (r. 379–395). Constantius II elected Themisitius, although a pagan, into the Christian senate of Constantinople (355). Themistius served as proconsul (358) and urban prefect (359–360). He favored Julian II, but he was respected as the senior pagan senator by Julian's Christian successors. Thirty-six orations of Themistius have survived, but his philosophical works and commentaries survive only in fragments.

171

Valens (a.k.a. **Flavius Valens**; c. 328–378; r. 364–378): Born of a military family in Pannonia, he served under Julian and Jovian. In 364, his brother Valentinian I created Valens emperor of the East. A devoted Arian Christian, Valens faced opposition from the Nicene bishops. His Persian war was inconclusive. In 378, he was decisively defeated and slain by the Goths at Adrianople.

Valentinian I (a.k.a. **Flavius Valentinianus**; 321–375; r. 364–375): Born to a Pannonian military family, he was a senior officer acclaimed emperor by the Eastern army after the death of Jovian. Valentinian appointed his brother Valens emperor of the East and campaigned against the Germans on the Rhine and Upper Danube, where he strengthened fortifications. He was succeeded by his two sons, Gratian (r. 367–383) and Valentinian II (r. 375–392).

Zosimus (c. 480–515): Greek historian who wrote *New History*, in which he attributes the decline of Roman power to the rejection of the gods in favor of Christianity.

Suggested Reading

Alföldi, *A Conflict of Ideas in the Late Roman Empire*.

Ammianus Marcellinus, *The Later Roman Empire*.

———, *Roman History*.

Bregman, *Synesius of Cyrene*.

Brown, *Augustine of Hippo*.

Barnes, *Athanasius and Constantius*.

Barrow, Prefect and Emperor.

Chauvin, *A Chronicle of the Last Pagans*.

Dill, *Roman Society in the Last Century of the Western Empire*.

Green, *The City of the Moon*.

Harl, "Sacrifice and Pagan Belief in Fifth- and Sixth-Century Byzantium."

Lenski, *Failure of Empire*.

Matthews, *Western Aristocracies and the Imperial Court*.

Saltzman, *The Making of a Christian Aristocracy*.

Segal, *Edessa, the Blessed City*.

Trombley, *Hellenic Religion and Christianization*.

Zosimus, *New History*.

Questions to Consider

1. How did pagans and Christians view the failure of Julian? How could pagans maintain their roles as cultural leaders and the validity of the gods in the later 4th and 5th centuries?

2. How conscious were pagan writers of representing an older order being replaced by a Christian one? How could the senators at Rome ignore the Christian world into the 5th century? How was the flowering of Greek pagan literature after Julian II the Indian summer of the classical world?

3. How did Christian prelates and writers accommodate the pagan literary heritage as a means to win converts? How typical was the conversion of Synesius of Cyrene? Why did Roman senators convert in the early 5th century?

New Christian Warriors—Ascetics and Monks
Lecture 22

W hile the emperor and the bishops presided over Christian life in the cities, a separate and parallel source of Christian authority was developing in the countryside: the ascetics. They did not arise out of the classical or Jewish intellectual traditions but were a unique development that arose from an attempt to live like Christ. These hermits and monks became the Christian warriors of the post-persecution world: performing miracles, attacking pagan shrines, and affecting mass conversions through inspiration and, occasionally, fear.

The Ascetic Precedent

- What we know about the first Christian ascetics, often collectively known as the friends of God, comes from the literature of the 4th, 5th, and 6th centuries. These are hagiographies, the lives of particular ascetics who were later declared saints, rather than examinations of how these figures fit into the wider picture of religious change in the Roman world.

- Many of Julian's reforms addressed the institutional church created by Constantine, but the ascetics were a popular tradition that stood in many ways outside the control of both the emperor and the bishops. Had Julian lived to push through his reforms, they might have presented a real challenge to him and might have significantly limited his success.

- Asceticism was not new to the Mediterranean world, but among the pagans, particularly followers of the various Greek philosophical traditions, asceticism was an individual choice usually associated with an intellectual effort to focus on a problem.

- Perhaps the only exceptions to this rule were the Cynic philosophers, who rejected the traditional Greco-Roman world, often with a great deal of panache and ostentatious display. But they were essentially perceived as a fringe group of troublemakers, and the number of cynics who took this stance were very few, as far as we know.

- Some Egyptian cults had ascetic traditions, usually associated with ritual purity. Priests who undertook ascetic discipline were often called the *katochoi*, a term used by later Christian authors, meaning someone who is possessed with the gods.

- There were some Jewish ascetics; we have references to them in the writings of Philo of Alexandria and Flavius Josephus. In Egypt, they were known as the Therapeutae. The Essenes lived in Roman Palestine; scholars traditionally connected them with the Dead Sea Scrolls, although that view has now been called into question.

- These Jewish sects were seen later by Christian authors, particularly Eusebius, as prototypes for the Christian monk and the Christian hermit, but these communities were not on the scale of the Christian communities in the 4th century.

Christian Asceticism

- From Christianity's earliest days, all the way back to the New Testament text, sexual renunciation and withdrawal from the world were the hallmarks of holiness. In the early 2nd century, Christians agreed that, to paraphrase Saint **Cyprian**, those who had chosen the path of virginity were the most pious and holy of the Christian flock.

- This was quite different from pagan philosophy terms, or even the early Christian philosophy of Origen or Saint Clement, who would argue that the true Christian is the true intellectual. Asceticism was the popular vision of Christianity: Those who gave up the material world, who left their own people and registered themselves in the citizenship in heaven, those were the true Christians.

- Two events crystallized the emergence of an organized ascetic movement, first among hermits and then in communal organizations. The first was the end of the persecutions, which meant the end of martyrdom. Martyrs had been regarded as Christian heroes. Ascetics succeeded to that role. In some ways, they were seen as greater heroes because their sacrifice was a perpetual one.

- The second development, less well studied, was the challenge presented by Manichaeism. The Manichaeans had an organized elect, called the Hearers, organized along the lines of ascetic cells. Some have seen comparisons between the Hearers and the Jewish ascetic traditions; others see them as a version of Buddhist monastic traditions. Either way, Christian monasticism, consciously or unconsciously, was also a response to this Manichean threat.

Antony and Pachomius—Defining Christian Monasticism

- Saint **Antony of Egypt** was born to a Greco-Egyptian family of some wealth and distinction in the city of Alexandria sometime in the mid-3rd century. Around the age of 20, he decided to imitate the life of Christ. He gave away his possessions, put his sister in a proto-convent, and went to study asceticism with Christian hermits living in the Libyan Desert, the Wadi el-Natrun.

- Antony had to learn discipline very quickly: how to live on very little food and water and concentrate on the oneness of God. Above all, he had to learn to resist temptation and madness. Several times, he went alone into the desert and had to be rescued from his own excesses.

- Eventually, he developed a serenity and a union with God that awed all who saw him. He had achieved detachment—which to pagan philosophers would be the apathy of the Stoics or the union with the One of Plotinus. It was hailed a triumph.

- Saint Augustine claims in his *Confessions* that reading the life of Antony is what finally brought him back to Christianity. The role

Antony played in inspiring others to embrace the ascetic tradition cannot be underestimated.

- Saint **Pachomius** was a near contemporary of Antony. A Roman Egyptian, he had been forcefully drafted into a Roman civil war, possibly by Maximinus of Gaza. Each night, his commanders locked him and his fellow soldiers up to prevent desertion, and he was impressed by the Christians who fed these imprisoned recruits. He thus converted to Christianity.

- In 323, shortly before Constantine reunited the Roman world, Pachomius established the first monastic community at Tabennisi in Upper Egypt that became the prototype for the medieval monastery. It was the first community devoted to what Antony did on his own.

- Pachomius established what is called in Greek a cenobium, or a common living. It was walled off from the outside world. Each member was assigned tasks, and they were supervised by an abbot—"father" in the Coptic language. Activities were therefore divided between religious devotions and duties necessary to support the self-sustaining community.

Monasticism in the Wider Roman World

- Pachomius's monastic community was an instant success. By the time Julian was proclaimed emperor in December 360, by one count there were more than 7,000 monasteries in the Nile Valley alone. At the start of the 6th century, the city of Constantinople proper had something like 60–70 known monasteries; there were 40 or 50 more in the surrounding cities.

- Monastic communities became the characteristic form of late antique Christianity and the touchstone of medieval Christianity. They emerged outside the control of the imperial government and largely outside of the control of the bishops.

- Monasticism was a popular movement, with its own institutions and its own traditions in which the celibate life and the pious life were fused as the supreme expression of Christianity. Ascetics may have constituted a tiny minority of the Roman world, but to the Christians, they were the most important and notably pious members of the Christian community.

- Given this position, they had a number of important roles to play in popular Christianity. They acted as arbiters for Christian peasants and as a link between the bishops of the city and the peasants of the countryside.

- Ascetics were Christian warriors who promoted conversion. This happened in several ways. Often they simply built monasteries in desolate areas and acted as an example of the Christian way of life to the pagan locals.

- The ascetics also succeeded to the role of the prophets of the Old Testament. The hagiographies repeatedly compare them to Elijah and Elisha. They cast down pagan idols and cult statues. They performed exorcisms and miracles.

- Several monks epitomized the image of the Christian warriors; one was **Barsuma**, an Aramaic-speaking peasant. He had a beard down to his toes, wore an old Roman breastplate, ran around barefoot, and carried a cudgel. He and his similarly clad followers went from village to village in Syria, challenging the cult statues and throwing priests in the fire. There are reports that when Barsuma showed up, whole villages would convert on the spot.

- Among so-called pillar saints of Syria and in southeastern Turkey, the most famous was Saint **Symeon Stylites**. He performed remarkable feats, usually standing in the form of a cross on top of his pillar. Every morning he touched his toes 1,244 times as an act of devotion.

- When Emperor Theodosius II wanted to rescind some of the legislation of his grandfather, Theodosius I, who had outlawed paganism, Symeon Stylites thundered Theodosius II, calling down the wrath of God. The emperor withdrew his acts of toleration.

- The power of these saints and ascetics was well beyond any kind of definable organization. They were the revered holy ones of popular Christianity.

Names to Know

Antony of Egypt (c. 260–357): Early Christian monastic and saint. Born of a wealthy Greco-Egyptian family, Antony embraced an ascetic life in the Libyan desert from c. 280. His example inspired many Christians to embrace the ascetic life. In about 360, Patriarch Athanasius of Alexandria wrote a life of Antony, which served as the model for all later hagiographies.

Barsuma (fl. c. 380–440): Fierce Syrian ascetic who converted pagan villages in the style of the prophets of Israel.

Cyprian of Carthage (a.k.a. **Thasciius Caecilius Cyprianus**; d. 258): Saint and bishop (250–257) who composed in Latin numerous tracts on issues of baptism of *lapsi*, readmission of heretics into the church, and episcopal authority. He was martyred during the persecution of Valerian.

Pachomius (c. 290–346): Saint and pagan convert to Christianity who undertook an ascetic life, founding the first monastery at Tabennesi in Upper Egypt in 323.

Symeon Stylites (c. 390–459): Christian ascetic who followed the example of Saint Antony. During his last 37 years, he spent his life atop a pillar east of Antioch as a symbol of his withdrawal from the world. He was hailed as the most pious saint of the Roman East, respected by the emperors Theodosius II and Marcian.

Suggested Reading

Athanasius, *The Life of Saint Antony and the Letter to Marcellinus*.

Brown, *The Cult of Saints*.

———, "The Rise and Function of the Holy Man in Late Antiquity."

Chitty, *The Desert, A City*.

Dawes and Baynes, trans., *Three Byzantine Saints*.

Hirschfeld, *The Judaean Desert Monasteries in the Judaean Period*.

MacMullen, *The Second Church*.

Rousseau, *Pachomius*.

Waddell, *The Desert Fathers*.

Questions to Consider

1. What were the sources for Christian asceticism? In what ways did Christian ascetics differ from those of paganism and Judaism? What led to the spread of ascetic ideals from the late 3rd century on?

2. Why did the example of Saint Antony inspire imitation or pilgrimage by so many Christians? Why was hagiography so popular?

3. What was the impact of Saint Pachomius on Christian asceticism? Why did monasticism come to define medieval Christianity? What were the cultural and economic impacts of monasteries?

4. How did monks see themselves as the heirs to the prophets of Israel? Why were they the most effective warriors against paganism?

Turning Point—Theodosius I

Lecture 23

The reign of Emperor Theodosius I was the final crucial turning point for the development of Christianity in the Roman world. He enacted legislation—backed up with force—that ended once and for all the open practice of traditional pagan worship in the Roman world. Nicene Christianity was established as the empire's official faith, and religion, not legal class, became the ultimate token of citizenship. In many ways, Theodosius's reign marks the birth of medieval Europe.

The End of Pagan Alexandria

- In 391, shortly after Emperor Theodosius passed the laws that outlawed sacrifice, and therefore pagan worship, the patriarch of Alexandria released his monks to attack the pagans who occupied the Serapeum and Mouseion. The excuse was that the pagans were secretly worshiping in underground sanctuaries.

- The pagans objected; they occupied both the Serapeum and Mouseion to protect them, and the monks and a large Christian crowd—really a rabble—stormed the buildings, smashed the statues, and destroyed papyrus scrolls. The fighting spread across Alexandria. The imperial army did nothing. Classical Alexandria was destroyed, and Christian Alexandria emerged.

- Scholars and popular writers have viewed this destruction as a turning point—for good reason. The pagans who witnessed this destruction were absolutely intimidated. There are reports of conversions on the spot. In addition, the entire action, while not ordered by the imperial government, was certainly approved of by the emperor, the logical result of his legislation.

Christianity Divided

- In 363, when Emperor Julian died, there was a strong chance of another civil war between the largely Christian Eastern army and the largely pagan Western army. Valentinian and Valens, as Christian emperors, were in a very uncertain position.

- Valentinian and Valens were very suspicious of the ruling classes, Christian and pagan both. They held a series of treason trials in which officials and officers were removed, in part to get rid of Julian's appointees, but also because they did not trust the polished elite.

- In addition, they lacked legitimacy. Valentinian had two sons by different marriages, an older son, **Gratian**, and a younger son, **Valentinian II**, who later married the surviving granddaughter of Constantine in an attempt to make a dynastic connection.

- Under Julian, all the Christian confessions were recognized because Julian's official policy was toleration. As a result, the Nicene bishops had brought many suits against the Arians, declaring their version of the Trinity as official imperial

Valentinian II came to the throne as a child in a dangerous time.

church policy. The Arian position had gained favor in the later days of Constantine's reign; in fact, Constantine was formally baptized by an Arian bishop, and his sons were devoted Arians.

- Valentinian I, as western emperor, was astute enough to realize that he had to court the Nicene bishops in the Western provinces.

Valens, reigning in the East, remained an ardent Arian. He faced opposition in Egypt and division in the Balkans and Asia Minor. As a result, there was no united Christian policy, and by default the pagans were tolerated.

- In the big cities with a lot of imperial patronage, Christianity reigned, and powerful intellects came up with theology to counter the Arians. Rome, on the other hand, was largely in the hands of the pagans, as was Athens and the lesser cities of Gaul, northern Italy, Britain, and Spain.

Valentinian's Sons and Civil War in the West

- Valentinian proved to be an extremely able emperor, but he died suddenly in 375 and left his two young sons in control of the Western Empire. Gratian, the older, ruled over the Rhine frontier, Gaul, and Britain. Valentinian II, the younger, with his mother Empress Justina, ruled from Milan. Bishop **Ambrose of Milan** exercised a powerful control over this young emperor.

- The brothers did not get along, but they did agree that they should rule as Nicene Christians. They passed tentative legislation to cut back on pagan toleration. Gratian, for instance imposed some liabilities on pagan priests. They also removed the Altar of Victory—removed by their father but restored in the interim—from the Roman senate house again.

- The Western army did not take well to this legislation. In the 350s and 360s, the emperors had begun building their armies mostly from barbarian tribal regiments known as federates. These were usually Germanic peoples; if they were Christian, they were only Christian in name. Between the legislation and Gratian's fecklessness—he spent most of his time drinking and never led an army into battle— the Western army was sparked into rebellion.

- In 383, the army in Britain declared their commander, **Magnus Maximus**, emperor of the West. That army invaded Gaul and was received by the army in the Rhine. Gratian was deserted, captured, and executed.

- Magnus Maximus was willing, at this point, to cut a deal with Valentinian II, but Valentinian refused. Magnus Maximus invaded Italy and drove Valentinian II and his mother east to Constantinople.

Theodosius Outlaws Paganism

- At that point, **Theodosius I** was emperor in the East, having been elevated in 379. Theodosius had been married into the imperial family and been commissioned to take charge of the Roman East after the disaster of the Battle of Adrianople, where Emperor Valens was killed by the Goths.

- Theodosius was a devoted Nicene Christian. He was also a tough general who commanded the respect of the various German federate regiments. When the imperial family fled from Milan to Constantinople, Theodosius immediately mounted an attack against Magnus Maximus; and in 388, somewhere on the Sava River, defeated the Western army and killed Magnus Maximus.

- It looked as if the toleration of pagans was going to end. Theodosius outlawed Manichaeism and initiated a wave of persecution. He did not immediately move against the pagan cults, but he turned a blind eye to his administrators, particularly **Maternus Cynegius**, who was the prefect of the Roman East, when he and a cadre of monks attacked the pagan shrines.

- Learned pagans reacted as you would expect: with prose. Libanius wrote *On the Temples*—an oration arguing that it was unseemly to attack the great temples that were part of the classical tradition. Theodosius, of course, ignored these arguments.

- Theodosius was able to move against the gods in a way that the emperor Constantine had never dared to do for several reasons. One was his success as a general. But he also summoned, in 381, the Second Ecumenical Council at Constantinople, which enacted several important changes that unified the church and solidified his position. Theodosius presided over this council just as Constantine had presided over the first.

- The council reinstated all of the canons at the Council of Nicaea and declared Constantinople a **Petrine See**—that is, a see equivalent to that of Rome. It also proscribed Arianism and made the imperial church officially Nicene.

- In 391–392, Theodosius issued a series of three laws banning public sacrifice throughout the Roman world and declared that the only religion in the Roman Empire with any legitimacy was Nicene Christianity.

- Think about how dramatically the situation has changed in the 350 years covered in this course. Henceforth, the definition of a Roman would be based on religious affiliation. This would not only affect the pagans; it would eventually affect the Jews and so-called heretics as well.

- Inevitably, there were reactions, particularly in Alexandria and in the West. At the time of the promulgation of these laws, there was a Frankish general named **Arbogast**, who held the position of *magister militum*, or master of the soldiers, in the Western field army. Arbogast seems to have been behind the murder of Valentinian II in 392.

The Last Rebellion

- After Valentinian's murder, a grammarian named **Eugenius** was proclaimed emperor by the Western army of the Rhine. Eugenius, while technically a Christian, openly tolerated the sacrifices to the gods. Theodosius now faced yet another Western army—

the fourth in that century—of pagan soldiers rebelling against pro-Christian policies.

- For the first time, the Roman senators reacted and they proclaimed their loyalty to the Western usurper. Theodosius marched west, and a major battle was fought on September 5–6, 394—the **Battle of the Frigidus**.

- Eugenius was captured and executed; Arbogast committed suicide. The Roman senators—who had not fought, of course, but had written letters of support—were embarrassed and surrendered unconditionally. The result was a second miraculous victory for a Christian emperor, another Milvian Bridge.

- Fortunately for the pagans, Theodosius died suddenly on January 17, 395, before he could pass any more legislation. He was succeeded by his incompetent sons, Arcadius and Honorius, and so began the rapid collapse of the Western Empire, which disintegrated by 476.

- Christian monarchy was never again in question in the empire. The pagans were barred from all public worship. Increasingly, the word "pagan" came to denote a barbarian; the educated pagans began to disappear. By the early 5th century, many had converted to Christianity.

- Above all, Theodosius had defined Roman citizenship and Roman identity, by religion, not by legal rights; and those who did not follow were subject to the full punishment of Roman law. Theodosius had taken the first step to creating the persecuting society of medieval Europe.

Important Terms

Frigidus, Battle of: The victory of Theodosius I over the rebel Western army of Eugenius and the magister militum Arbogast on September 5–6, 394. It was hailed as a victory of Christianity over paganism.

Petrine Sees: The five great apostolic sees founded by Peter or his disciples. The order was fixed at the Fourth Ecumenical Council as Rome, Constantinople, Alexandria, Antioch, and Jerusalem. Rome claims primacy and Constantinople claims equality with Rome.

Names to Know

Ambrose of MIlan (a.k.a. **Aurelius Ambrosius**; 337–397): Saint and staunch opponent of Arianism who was elected bishop of Milan in 374. He was mentor to the young Emperor Valentinian II (r. 375–392) and advocated measures against pagan worship. In 390, he compelled Emperor Theodosius I to seek penance for permitting the massacre of citizens of Thessalonica by Gothic soldiers. Ambrose was also patron to Augustine of Hippo.

Arbogast (c. 360–394): A Frankish officer under Gratian (r. 367–383) who rose to *magister militum* of the West in 388. In 392, he advanced as Emperor Eugenius (r. 392–394) in a pagan revolt against Theodosius I. The Western army was defeated at the Battle of Frigidus (394), and Arbogast committed suicide.

Eugenius (a.k.a. **Flavius Eugenius**; r. 392–394): Grammarian elevated as Western emperor by Arbogast, *magister militum* of the Western army, and backed by the Senate. He was defeated, captured, and executed after his defeat at the Battle of Frigidus on September 6, 394.

Gratian (a.k.a. **Flavius Gratianus**; 359–383; r. 367–383): The elder son of Valentinian I, he made his court at Treveri. Gratian pursed antipagan measures and promoted Nicene Christianity. In 383, he was betrayed and murdered near Lugdunum (Lyon) by supporters of Magnus Maximus, who had been proclaimed emperor by the army of Britain.

Magnus Maximus (a.k.a. **Flavius Magnus Maximus**; c. 335–388; r. 383–388): Soldier who rose in the service of Count Theodosius and then Emperor Gratian. In 380, he succeeded to the command of the army of Britain. In response to the antipagan laws, in 383, Magnus Maximus rebelled and invaded Gaul. Gratian was deserted and murdered. In 387, Magnus Maximus invaded the Italian Peninsula so that Valentinian II fled to Constantinople. In

388, Theodosius I defeated Magnus Maximus at the Battle on the Save. He fled to Aquileia, surrendered, and was executed.

Maternus Cynegius (d. 388): Christian from Spain who rose in the service of Theodosius I. As prefect of the East (384–388), he initiated riots by monks against pagan temples and synagogues. In protest, the pagan rhetorician Libanius wrote his *Pro templis* (*On the Temples*), an oration delivered to Theodosius I.

Theodosius I (a.k.a. **Theodosius the Great**; c. 346–395; r. 379–395): The son of Count Theodosius, a leading general of Valentinian I, Theodosius rose to high command under Gratian. In 379, as Augustus of the East, Theodosius restored order in the Roman East. In 387, he married Galla, sister of Valentinian II (r. 375–392). In return, Theodosius defeated the usurper Magnus Maximus (r. 383–388), who had overthrown the Western emperor Gratian. A devout Nicene Christian, Theodosius summoned the Second Ecumenical Council in 381 and outlawed pagan sacrifices in 391–392. He faced a revolt of the Western army in 392–394. By the victory at Frigidus (394), Theodoius crushed the rebels and reunited the Roman Empire.

Valentinian II (a.k.a. **Flavius Valentinianus**; 371–392; r. 375–392): The son of Valentinian and Justinia and half-brother of Gratian. In 375, he was declared joint emperor and resided at Mediolaunum (Milan) under the influence of his mother and Bishop Ambrose of Milan. Reared as a staunch Nicene, Valentinian supported antipagan measures that precipitated the revolt of Magnus Maximus. In 387, he fled to Constantinople and allied with Theodosius I against Magnus Maximus. In 388–392, Valentinian was restored as emperor of the West, and he was murdered on the orders of Arbogast.

Suggested Reading

Alföldi, *A Conflict of Ideas in the Late Roman Empire*.

Ammianus Marcellinus, *The Later Roman Empire*.

———, *Roman History*.

Barnes, *Athanasius and Constantius.*

Barrow, *Prefect and Emperor.*

Brown, *Power and Persuasion in Late Antiquity.*

Dill, *Roman Society in the Last Century of the Western Empire.*

Holum, *Theodosian Empresses.*

Kaegi, *Byzantium and the Decline of Rome.*

King, *The Emperor Theodosius and the Establishment of Christianity.*

Lenski, *The Crisis of the Roman Empire.*

MacMullen, *Christianizing the Roman Empire.*

Matthews, *Western Aristocracies and the Imperial Court.*

Trombley, *Hellenic Religion and Christianization.*

Zosimus, *New History.*

Questions to Consider

1. Why were Christian emperors cautious in their religious policy in 363–379? What were the limits of imperial power in enforcing religious conformity?

2. How powerful were bishops in their cities by 395? How did the failure of Julian and his institutional paganism (Hellenism) contribute to the rise of bishops? What factors were necessary for cities to remain faithful to the ancestral gods after 363?

3. How could Theodosius I mount such effective attacks against pagan cults? What accounted for the failure of pagans to rally against imperial coercion? Did the pagan senators who backed Eugenius and Arbogast have a coherent policy to restore the gods?

4. Why did pagans, given their numbers, fail to take action after 395? How does the reign of Theodosius I represent a turning point?

Justinian and the Demise of Paganism
Lecture 24

O ver a century passed between the reigns of Theodosius I and Justinian, but the latter emperor completed the logic of the former's laws, ensuring that Theodosius's world became the world of medieval Europe. Justinian extended the persecution and suppression of pagans to Jews and heretics. He called ecumenical councils to condemn not only contemporary non-mainstream thinking but unconventional writings of long-dead theologians. His building programs created a Christian skyline that circled the Mediterranean. To some, he is a hero of the faith; to others, he is the father of medieval persecution.

Justinian against the Apostates

- Theodosius outlawed the pagan cults, and he redefined Roman identity along religious lines. But the majority of the Roman population was still by no means Christian. Most scholars agree that, during his reign, the pagan population of the empire was certainly over 50 percent.

- **Justinian I**, in effect, completed the logic of Theodosius's laws of 391–392. He conducted a number of important changes, reforms, and measures that insured that, by the time he died in 565, the Roman world was essentially Christian both in numbers and outlook.

- Justinian operated within a framework of legal precedents to crack down on the crypto-pagans. These were individuals who were outwardly Christians but privately sacrificing to the pagan gods. These included many high-ranking Roman officials, including a powerful prefect named Phocas.

- In 529, Justinian ordered a crackdown in his administration. The crypto-pagan officials were given the opportunity to renounce what Justinian regarded as black magic and to reaffirm their faith as Christians.

- In 546, after a plague and some unsuccessful attempts to recapture the Roman West, Justinian conducted another crackdown and many of the same officials were caught again, including Phocas. Phocas was executed, and his body was mutilated as a warning to others.

- To Justinian, the crypto-pagan problem was more than simple apostasy. Many Christians saw the old gods as demons. The crypto-pagans were not expressing innocent, private belief; they were in league with the devil himself, which could account for the empire's various setbacks.

- It should be noted that these pagans' faith was as genuine as Justinian's. They continued to sacrifice in defiance of the laws because they believed. Some of them were theurgists; others believed in proxy sacrifice for the good of the empire.

Justinian's Christian Army

- The imperial army was now definitively Christian, fighting under the banners of the cross or the crucifix, not the Christogram, which could be misinterpreted as the talisman of the family of Constantine. Military saints emerged as important figures as well.

- All battles were preceded with sermons by priests, who accompanied the armies. The victories won by Justinian's commanders took place where the imperial army had not won battles since the Battle of Adrianople almost 150 years earlier. All of that confirmed that God was favorable to a Roman Christian army.

Converting the Countryside

- Justinian made a concerted effort to spread the faith to the lesser cities and the countryside of the Roman Empire. He appointed very able bishops in the cities of the Roman East to carry out aggressive proselytizing, especially in the villages, towns, and satellite communities their cities administered.

- **John of Amida** was consecrated as bishop of Ephesus around 535. He spent a generation proselytizing in the countryside around Ephesus, and most scholars believe that this was one of the most Christianized areas of the Roman world in the time of Justinian.

- John's biographer claims John was personally responsible for converting 80,000 pagans. John razed temples and ordered the construction of 12 monasteries and 96 churches. He also brought in tough monks from Syria, like Barsuma, to aid in these efforts.

Justinian Architecture

- Justinian was responsible for a whole new wave of building, particularly the construction of impressive cathedral churches. The most famous of these by far is the current church of Hagia Sophia, but many similar structures are being uncovered by archaeologists, especially in cities in Asia Minor.

- These domed basilican cathedral churches came to dominate the skyline of the cities of the Roman world under Justinian. That included the eastern half of the Empire and a good deal of the western: the provinces in Africa, the provinces in Italy, parts of Spain, and the western provinces lost in the 5th century to the Germanic peoples and reconquered by Justinian's armies.

The Other Non-Christians

- The word "Hellene" had come to designate a pagan, a nonbeliever; "pagan" came to designate, by Justinian's time, someone one step away from the barbarians—the equivalent of the English word "heathen."

- By the end of Justinian's reign, there were no longer any pagan intellectuals. The Academy at Athens came to an end. The patriarchs of Alexandria were essentially Christian pharaohs; there was no intellectual life in Alexandria that was not Christian. This became increasingly the case across the Roman world, whether under the direct rule of the Roman emperor or under the various Germanic kings who ruled the West in the 5th century.

- Less palatable in any number of ways were Justinian's efforts to achieve religious unity through converting the Jews and the Samaritans. Justinian ordered the first forced baptisms of Jews on record, beginning a dreary record of anti-Semitism that continued throughout the Middle Ages and into the modern age.

- Justinian's less brutal methods of conversion included forbidding the Jews to read the Torah in Hebrew; they had to use the Septuagint, the logic being that if they read Greek, maybe they would eventually convert to Christianity.

- The image of Jews as living in ghettos—that is, in distinct communities—in the Middle Ages and into the modern age had now come about in the 6th century, thanks to Justinian's attempts at conversion.

- Justinian also made a concerted effort to convert peoples beyond the imperial frontier. Various Roman allies, particularly along the eastern frontiers, were now classified as Christians and members of the Roman community. These included the Armenians; the various Georgian peoples of Transcaucasia; some Arabian tribes; a few cities on the western shores of India; Axum; Yemen; Nubia; parts of Persia; and several Germanic tribes.

- Justinian often moved against cult centers that were perceived as particularly important on these frontiers. Even strategic locations where emperors had previously turned a blind eye were Christianized.

- Justinian made a concerted effort to remove cult statues not only from these frontier areas but also from the great sanctuaries such as Olympia, Delphi, and Athens bring them to Constantinople, where they were turned into park elements. In doing so, he announced the victory of Christianity, emptied the statues of their religious content, and deprived the pagans of their focus of worship.

Justinian's Ecumenical Council

- The Council of Ephesus in 431 and the Council of Chalcedon in 451 had built upon the rulings of Nicaea and defined the nature of Christ as it is now accepted by most Christians: the nature of Christ is human and divine, comingled, and distinct.

- One of the most important losing positions at Chalcedon was the Monophysite (from Greek *monophysis*) position that argued that Christ was essentially divine—that is, he has a single nature. This issue was a sharp divisor of Justinian's empire.

- To heal the divide and persuade all Christians to accept the ruling of Chalcedon, Justinian targeted a common enemy by persecuting Jews, pagans, and heretics. In addition, Justinian tried to target the writings of Origen and three **Nestorian** heretic writers from the 5th century.

- In 553, Justinian summoned the Fifth Ecumenical Council to condemn these writings. With this act, he effectively created medieval censorship: In all previous councils, the losing side was given the chance to present its case. Here, the writings of men long deceased and who had died in communion with the then-Christian church were posthumously condemned and sent into the flames.

The World Justinian Made

- Justinian's empire would disintegrate within two generations of his death. Europe became the heir to classical Rome. The classical arts and writing survived, but in a Christian world, a world that reckoned time by the birth of Christ and saw Jerusalem as the center of the Earth.

- This world was rather parochial in its views: The pagan gods were demons and utterly intolerable. There was an immense gap between the divine and the mundane that could only be crossed by the holy ones. As Iamblichus of Chalcis once said, "You Christians have emptied the world of gods, and you have made it a lonely place."

- For the next 12 centuries, a civilized individual in the West was one who was a Christian, who was an heir to the imperial church of Constantine, Theodosius, and Justinian. For the next 12 centuries, the notions of the divine and of ethics came out of the age of Justinian. His world was the basis for the religious and ethical values of the West down to this day.

Important Terms

monophysis: Greek for "single nature"; The doctrine stressing the single, divine nature of Christ from which the Monophysites got their name. This became the doctrine of the Egyptian, Armenian, Syriac, and Ethiopian churches.

Nestorianism: The followers of Nestorius, patriarch of Constantinople from 429 to 431, who argued that Mary was the mother of Christ the human (Christotokos), rather than mother of Christ the God (Theotokos). Nestorius's views were rejected at the Third Ecumenical Council at Ephesus in 431. *See* **Theotokos**.

Names to Know

John of Amida (c. 507–585): A Monophysite ascetic trained in the Syrian tradition. As bishop of Ephesus (535–575), he carried out aggressive efforts to convert pagans in Western Asia Minor.

Justinian I (a.k.a. **Justinian the Great**; 483–565; r. 527–565): Byzantine (Eastern Roman) emperor. Justinian succeeded his uncle and adoptive father Justin I as a mature, experienced ruler of 46. The greatest emperor since Constantine, he restored imperial rule in the Italian Peninsula and Africa. His most enduring achievements are Hagia Sophia and the *Corpus Iuris Civilis*.

Suggested Reading

Brown, *The Body and Society*.

Browning, *Justinian and Theodora*.

Cameron, *The Mediterranean World in Late Antiquity*.

Dawes and Baynes, *Three Byzantine Saints*.

Fowden, *Empire to Commonwealth*.

Kitzinger, *Byzantine Art in the Making*.

Harl, "Sacrifice and Pagan Belief in Fifth- and Sixth-Century Byzantium."

Frend, *The Rise of the Monophysite Movement*.

Mainestone, *Hagia Sophia*.

Meyendorff, *Imperial Unity, Christian Divisions*.

Moorhead, *Justinian*.

Procopius, *The Secret History*.

———, *Works*.

Rosen, *Justinian's Flea*.

Trombley, *Hellenic Religion and Christianization*.

von Simson, *Sacred Fortress*.

Questions to Consider

1. How ruthless was Justinian in imposing religious uniformity on his subjects? Why did he remove pagans from imperial administration? Why did he move to close temples and remove cult statues? How important was Justinian in the demise of paganism?

2. What were the respective roles of bishops and monks in converting cities and the countryside in the era of Justinian? Why did these later pagans fail to oppose Justinian? How did the nature of pagan worship contribute to the demise of paganism?

3. How important was Justinian in promoting the spread of Christianity beyond the empire? What was the impact of the theological debates within the imperial church in defining doctrine and spreading Christianity? How did Justinian use architecture and arts to uphold and spread the Christian message?

4. In what ways was Christianity, by the death of Justinian, medieval and quite different from that of the high Roman Empire?

Timeline

B.C.

167 .... Hellenization measures of the
Seleucid king Antiochus IV.

167–161 .... Revolt of the Maccabees.

164 .... Recovery and rededication of the
Temple of Jerusalem; Foundation
of Hasmonaean kingdom.

164–161 .... Judas Maccabaeus serves as high priest.

161 .... Friendship (*amicitia*) established
between Rome and Judaea.

142/1 .... Consolidation of Hasmonaean
power; withdrawal of Seleucid
garrisons in Judaea.

142–135/4 .... Simon serves as high
priest and ethnarch.

67–63 .... Civil war in the Hasmonaean
house between John Hyrcanus
II and Aristobulus II.

63 .... Intervention of Pompey the Great
(Gnaeus Pompeius Magnus); Roman
siege and capture of Jerusalem; John
Hyrcanus II imposed as high priest.

62–40 .... Continual civil war and instability
in the Hasmonaean kingdom.

40	Parthian invasion; flight of Herod the Great to Rome; Rome recognizes Herod as king of the Jews.
37	Herod the Great captures Jerusalem; Mark Antony confirms Herod as king of the Jews.
37–4	Reign of Herod the Great.
31	Battle of Actium; Octavian (Augustus) reorganizes the Roman East; Herod's kingship is reconfirmed; first abandonment of Qumran by the Essenes due to earthquake.
27	Octavian is acclaimed as Augustus, Emperor of Rome.
27 B.C.–14 A.D.	Reign of Augustus.
20	Construction of the Second Temple commenced by Herod.
c. 10	Birth of Marcus Julius Agrippa, later King Herod Agrippa I of Judaea.
c. 6?	Birth of Jesus Christ (Joshua bar Joseph).
4	Death of Herod the Great; division of the Herodian kingdom.
4 B.C. –6 A.D.	Archelaus serves as ethnarch of Judaea.
4 B.C. –34 A.D.	Philip serves as tetrarch of Iturea.

4 B.C. –39 A.D. .... Herod Antipas serves as
tetrarch of Galilee.

A.D.

6 .... Rome annexes Judaea;
deposition of Archelaus.

6–9 .... Coponius serves as Roman
procurator of Judaea.

14–37 .... Reign of Emperor Tiberius.

18–37 .... Caiaphas serves as high
priest of Jerusalem.

19 .... Expulsion of the Jews from Rome.

c. 26 .... Ministry of John the Baptist.

26–36 .... Pontius Pilate serves as
procurator of Judaea.

c. 27–30 .... Ministry of Jesus Christ.

c. 30 .... Crucifixion of Jesus Christ.

c. 35 .... Martyrdom of Stephen; conversion of
Paul of Tarsus outside of Damascus.

36 .... Recall and prosecution of Pontius
Pilate for maladministration.

37 .... Deposition of Caiaphas; birth of
the historian Flavius Josephus.

37–41.. Reign of Emperor Caligula (Gaius); anti-Jewish policy of Caligula provokes unrest in Jerusalem and Judaea.

38.. Anti-Jewish riot in Alexandria, Egypt.

c. 40–45.. Heretic Simon Magus *flourit* in Samaria.

41.. Jewish embassy to Claudius in Rome; accession of Herod Agrippa I as king of Judaea and Samaria; end of direct Roman rule in Judaea.

41–54.. Reign of Emperor Claudius.

42.. Martyrdom of James.

44.. Death of Herod Agrippa I; Rome annexes Judaea again.

46–48.. First Missionary Journey of Paul and Barnabas; churches founded in Cyprus, Galatia, and Pisidia.

48.. Council of Jerusalem accepts the mission to preach to gentiles.

c. 48–62.. Composition of the Pauline Epistles (Romans, Philippians, Galatians, 1 and 2 Corinthians, 1 Thessalonians, and Philemon).

49.. Expulsion of the Jews from Rome.

49–52	Second missionary journey of Paul and Barnabas; churches are founded in cities of Asia and Bithynia; first missions to Greece (Philippi, Beroea, Athens, and Corinth).
c. 50	Compilation of the *First Book of Enoch* (Jewish apocalyptic literature).
52–60	Antonius Felix serves as procurator in Judaea.
53–56	Paul**'s mission** at Ephesus; organization of churches in the Maeander Valley, including Colossae and perhaps Laodicea ad Lycum.
54–68	Reign of Emperor Nero.
56–57	Paul's tour of inspection of Corinth, Philippi, Thessalonica, Troas, and the Aegean islands.
58	Departure of Paul from Miletus to Jerusalem; arrest and imprisonment of Paul at Jerusalem.
59–60	Paul's journey to Rome.
60	End of the Christian Jewish community in Jerusalem (according to Eusebius).
60–62	Paul in Rome.
c. 60	Gnostic thinker Menander *flourit*.
c. 63	Arrival of Peter in Rome.

64	Great Fire in Rome; Neronian persecution of Christians.
c. 65–80	Composition of the pastoral Epistles.
66–74	First Jewish Revolt.
68	Suicide of Nero; civil war in the Roman Empire; Qumran destroyed.
68–69	Year of the Four Emperors.
69–79	Reign of Emperor Vespasian.
70	Fall of Jerusalem to Titus; end of serious Jewish resistance in Palestine.
73	Fall of Masada.
c. 75	Flavius Josephus writes *History of the Jewish War*.
79–81	Reign of Emperor Titus.
c. 80–100	Synoptic Gospels (Mark, Luke, and Matthew) take on their final form.
81–96	Reign of Emperor Domitian.
c. 95–100	Composition of the book of Revelation, the Letter to the Hebrews, and the Catholic Epistles.
c. 93	Flavius Josephus writes *The Antiquities of the Jews*.
96–98	Reign of Emperor Nerva.

98–117 .... Reign of Emperor Trajan.

c. 100 .... Death of Flavius Josephus;
First Letter of Clement written;
composition of the *Didachē* (in
Syria) and the Gospel of Thomas.

c. 100–120 .... Gospel of John takes on its final form;
composition of the Johannine Epistles;
Second Letter of Peter written.

c. 107 .... Seven letters of Ignatius of
Antioch composed; monarchical
bishop evident in Antioch.

c. 108 .... *Letter to the Philippians*
written by Polycarp.

112–113 .... Pliny the Younger, governor of
Bithynia, corresponds with Trajan
regarding Christians and makes the first
report of the use of the sacrifice test.

114–117 .... Trajan's Parthian War.

115–117 .... Jewish Uprisings in Cyprus, Egypt,
Cyrenaica, and Mesopotamia.

117–138 .... Reign of Emperor Hadrian.

c. 120 .... Composition of *Shepherd of Hermas*.

124 .... Issuance of Hadrian's Rescript to
Minucius Fundanus, proconsul of Asia,
concerning toleration of Christians.

c. 125	Quadratus composes the first work of Christian apologetics; Hadrian creates the Panhellenion, the league of Greek cities with great sanctuaries and games throughout the Roman world.
c. 130	Conversion of Justin the Martyr; composition of the *Letter of Barnabas*; date of the oldest known papyri fragments of the Gospels and the works of Papias; beginning of the Gnostic schools of Alexandria and Rome; Basilides *flourit*; first Gnostic Gospel composed in Egypt.
132–135	Second Jewish Revolt (Bar Kochba War)
135	Destruction of the Temple of Jerusalem; Jerusalem is turned into the Roman colony of Aelia Capitolina
138–161	Reign of Emperor Antoninus Pius.
c. 140–160	Marcion of Pontus edits the Gospel of Luke and the Pauline letters, founding his own church at Rome; Valentinus is active at Rome, applying Gnostic-style interpretation to scripture; school of Valentinus emerges; imperial rescripts are issued concerning treatment of Christians in Macedonia and Achaea.
c. 143	Marcion writes *Contradictions*.

144	Marcion is expelled from the Roman church by a synod called by Pope Pius I; Marcionite missions are sent to Asia Minor, Syria, and Mesopotamia.
c. 150	*Letter of Diognetus* written.
154–155	Bishop Polycarp of Smyrna visits Rome.
c. 155	Justin the Martyr composes *First Apology*; martyrdom of Polycarp.
c. 160	Justin the Martyr composes *Second Apology*; activities of Alexander of Abonouteichos and the creation of cult of Glycon (160–180).
c. 160–200	Galen of Pergamon *flourit*; criticism of Christians.
161–180	Marcus Aurelius, Emperor of Rome
161–166	Parthian War of Marcus Aurelius.
165	Martyrdom of Justin the Martyr; outbreak of plague in the Roman Empire.
c. 165–175	Sporadic persecutions of Christians in the cities of western Asia Minor.
167–180	Marcomannic and Quadic Wars on the Danube River; first signs of stress on the northern frontier of the Roman Empire; Marcus Aurelius writes *Meditations*.

172 .... Montanus proclaims his mission and the New Prophecy in Phrygia; rise of the Montanist heresy in Asia Minor.

175 .... Gnostic Heracleon *flourit*; Hegesippus (anti-Gnostic historian and source of Eusebius) active; writer Tatian *flourit*.

177 .... Persecution of Christians at Lugdunum (Lyon); Athenagoras writes his apology *Supplication for the Christians*.

178 .... Celsus writes *True Reason*, a critique of Christianity; Irenaeus becomes Bishop of Lyon.

c. 180 .... Scillian Martyrs at Carthage; Theophilus of Antioch writes his apology *Against Autolycus*; Apollinaris and Miltiades write anti-Montanist tracts; Bishop Avircus Marcellus of Hierapolis takes measures against the Montanists; Catechetical School established at Alexandria; Clement of Alexandria active.

180–192 .... Reign of Emperor Commodus.

185 .... Birth of Origen; Irenaeus writes *Against Heresies*.

189–199 .... Pope Victor becomes the first Latin-speaking pope.

190–200 .... The first catacombs are constructed in Rome.

193–211 .... Reign of Emperor Septimius Severus.

193–197 .... Roman civil war over
succession to Commodus.

c. 195 .... Conversion of Tertullian to Christianity.

195–197 .... First Parthian War of Septimius Severus.

197 .... Tertullian writes *Apology*; local
persecutions in Africa.

199–200 .... Second Parthian War of
Septimius Severus.

c. 202–206 .... Persecutions in North Africa;
Tertullian writes tracts against
Gnostics and Marcionites.

203 .... Origen succeeds Clement at the
Catechetical School at Alexandria.

205 .... Birth of Plotinus, the
Neoplatonic philosopher.

c. 207 .... Tertullian converts to Montanism
(a.k.a. the Cataphrygian heresy).

208–211 .... British campaign of Septimius Severus.

211–217 .... Reign of Emperor Caracalla.

212 .... *Constitutio Antoniniana* extends
Roman citizenship to all free
residents of the empire.

213.. Tertullian writes *Against Praxeas* criticizing the Monarchians.

c. 215.. Philostratus writes *Life of Apollonius of Tyana*.

215–217.. Parthian War of Caracalla.

215–219.. Origen withdraws from Alexandria.

216.. Birth of Mani.

217–218.. Reign of Emperor Macrinus.

218–222.. Reign of Emperor Elagabalus; introduction of Baal of Emesa (sun god) at Rome.

c. 220–230...................................... Apologist Marcus Minucius Felix *flourit*; Lucius Cassius Dio writes *Roman History*.

222–235.. Reign of Emperor Severus Alexander.

c. 229–230...................................... Origen composes *On First Principles*.

230–233.. Persian War of Severus Alexander.

c. 230.. Origen departs from Alexandria for Caesarea in Palestine; the heretic Artemon *flourit*.

c. 230–240...................................... Synods of Iconium and Synnada on rebaptism of heretics and schismatics.

232.. Birth of Porphyry of Tyre, disciple of Plotinus and critic of Christians.

233–244.. Plotinus visits Alexandria.

233–235.. German War of Severus Alexander.

235.. Assassination of Severus Alexander
at Mainz; beginning of political
instability in the empire; outbreak of
persecutions of Christian leaders.

235–238.. Reign of Emperor Maximinus Thrax.

236.. Persecutions in Cappadocia; deaths of
Pontian and Hippolytus; Elevation of
Pope Fabius; development of Roman
diaconate and the catacombs; Origen
writes *Exhortation to Martyrdom*.

238.. Maximinus Thrax wages war against
Goths and Carpi on the Danube River;
outbreak of Roman civil war; the
two Gordiani brothers declared joint
emperors in North Africa, then Pupienus
Maximus and Balbinus in Rome.

238–244.. Reign of Emperor Gordian III.

240.. Mani begins his mission in Persia;
Origen writes tracts against
the Monarchian heretics.

240–325.. Construction of phanero-Christian
tombs in central and eastern Phrygia.

242–244.. Persian War of Gordian III.

243–260 .... Missionary activities of Gregory
Thaumaturgus (the Wonderworker)
in Pontus and Cappadocia.

244–249 .... Reign of Emperor Philip I "the
Arab"; toleration of Christianity
in the empire begins.

248 .... Millennian Games of Rome celebrated;
Origen writes *Against Celsus*; anti-
Christian pogroms in Alexandria; first
major Gothic incursions in the Balkans.

248–300 .... "Christians for Christians" funerary
monuments in northwest Phrygia.

249–251 .... Reign of Emperor Decius.

250–251 .... Decian persecution begins as general
orders for sacrifice are circulated
throughout the empire and Christian
leaders are arrested; Cyprian flees
Carthage; Dionysius flees Alexandria;
Pope Fabian is arrested and executed.

251 .... Cyprian reasserts his authority over
the African church by council and
writes *On the Unity of the Catholic
Church*, the first defense of papal
leadership; Novatian Schism; defeat
and death of Decius at the hands
of the Goths ends the persecution;
Cornelius is elected pope.

251–253 .... Reign of emperors Trebonianus
Gallus and Volusian.

252... Outbreak of the Persian War; Shah
Shāpūr I of Persia invades Armenia.

253–260...................................... Reign of emperors Valerian
I and Gallienus.

254–256...................................... First Persian expedition of Valerian.

254... Death of Origen at Tyre; Stephen I
becomes pope; Spanish congregations
appeal to Cyprian, bishop of Carthage.

255–257...................................... Rebaptism controversy.

256... Fall of Dura-Europos to the Persians;
Council of 97 Bishops at Carthage.

257–260...................................... Valerianic Persecution; execution of
Pope Sixtus III, Cyprian, and Laurence;
Second Persian expedition of Valerian

260... Defeat and capture of Valerian I by
Shāpūr I near Edessa; Postumus is
declared emperor of the Rhine legions;
formation of the Gallo-Roman Empire;
Great Eastern Revolt of Quietus and
Macrianus II; Gallienus publishes
an edict of toleration of Christianity,
ending the Valerianic persecution and
starting "the Peace of the Church."

260–268...................................... Gallienus reigns as sole emperor
of Rome; Plotinus teaches at Rome
under imperial patronage.

260–274...................................... Debasement of imperial
currency and inflation.

261–272... Paul of Samosata serves as
bishop of Antioch.

262–272... Eastern Roman provinces fall
under the sway of Odenathus
and then Zenobia of Palmyra.

262.. Goths invade the Aegean world
and Asia Minor, burning the
Artemision of Ephesus.

c. 263.. Porphyry visits Rome.

264–268... Council of Antioch issues three
condemnations of Paul of Samosata.

268–270... Reign of Claudius II Gothicus;
beginning of imperial recovery.

269.. Claudius defeats the Goths
at Naissus (Nish).

270.. Outbreak of plague; death of
Plotinus in Rome; Saint Antony
of Egypt withdraws into the
desert; Felix I becomes pope.

270–275... Reign of Emperor Aurelian.

272.. Aurelian recovers the eastern
provinces from Zenobia; church of
Antioch appeals to Aurelian against
Paul of Samosata; first imperial
intervention in church affairs.

273..Aurelian recovers the western provinces; restoration of the Roman Empire; Aurelian promotes the cult of Sol Invictus as his comrade (*comes*).

c. 275...Porphyry writes *Against the Christians*.

276–282...Reign of Emperor Probus.

276..Mani is executed by King Bahram II of Persia; Manichaean missions spread across the Persian and Roman empires.

c. 280...Commodian and Anatolius *flourit*.

282–283 ....Reign of Emperor Carus.

283–284..Reign of Emperor Carinus.

284–305..Reign of Emperor Diocletian; restoration of imperial order.

285..Maximian is elevated to Augustus of the West by Diocletian.

293..Galerius and Constantius I Chlorus elevated as Caesars of East and West, respectively; formation of the first Roman tetrarchy is complete.

296–299..Persian War of Galerius.

296–304..Marcellinus serves as pope.

297..Diocletian issues an edict of persecution of Manicheans.

298–302 .... Christians are forced to resign from the Roman army and administration.

c. 300 .... Reputed conversion of the royal family of Armenia by Gregory the Illuminator.

c. 300–318 .... Lactantius *flourit*

301 .... Diocletian issues the Edict of Maximum Prices.

303 .... Diocletian issues three edicts of persecution of Christians, initiating the Great Persecution.

304 .... Diocletian's fourth edict of persecution is issued, ordering general sacrifice; apostasy of Pope Marcellinus.

305 .... Abdications of Diocletian and Maximianus; accession of Galerius and Constantius I as Augusti; accession of Severus II as Caesar in the West and Maximinus II Daza as Caesar in the East.

306 .... Fifth edict of persecution is issued in the East; Maximinus II reorganizes pagan cults in the East; Constantius I orders toleration for Christians in Rome and Africa; death of Constantius I; Western army proclaims Constantine I "the Great" emperor while Maxentius is proclaimed emperor at Rome; civil war breaks out.

306–312 .... Reign of Emperor Maxentius.

306–324.. Civil war.

306–337.. Reign of Emperor
Constantine the Great.

308.. Conference of Carnuntum to regulate
the imperial succession fails; Sixth edict
of persecution in the East; outbreak of
the Meletian Schism; confusion between
the Roman and African churches.

311.. Galerius issues an edict of toleration;
death of Galerius; election of Caecilian
as bishop of Carthage; outbreak of the
Donatist Schism; Rigorous persecutions
by Maximinus in the East; Eusebius
of Caesarea composes *Historia
Ecclesiastica*; Miltiades is elected pope.

312.. Anti-Caecilianist Council in Africa;
defeat and death of Maxentius at the
Battle of Milvian Bridge; conversion
of Constantine to Christianity.

313.. Edict of Milan by Constantine and
Licinius proclaims toleration of
Christianity; anti-Caecilianists appeal
to Constantine; Lactantius composes
Divine Institutes; Licinius conquers
the East; death of Maximinus II; end
of the Great Persecution; Council
of Rome vindicates Caecilian.

314.. Councils of Arles and Ancyra;
Lactantius writes *On the
Deaths of the Persecutors*.

316... Constantine acquits Caecilian; Donatist opposition forms in North Africa.

c. 318.. Outbreak of Arian Controversy.

321–324.. Persecution of Christians by Licinius in the East.

323... Pachomius organizes the first ascetic community at Tabennisi in Upper Egypt; growth of cenobitism.

324... Battle of Chrysopolis marks the final victory of Constantine in the East; Eusebius revises his *Historia ecclesiastica.*

325... Council of Nicaea condemns Arius.

329–373.. Athanasius becomes patriarch of Alexandria.

330... Dedication of Constantinople, the "New Rome," as the Christian capital; Athanasius moves against the Meletians.

330–337.. Constantine issues edicts against certain pagan practices.

335... Council of Tyre condemns Athanasius; exile of Athanasius to Treveri (Trier); Constantine accepts Arian views; Constantine celebrates *tricennalia* in Jerusalem.

336... Eusebius writes *Tricennial Oration*;
Donatus holds a council on rebaptism.

337... Baptism of Constantine I by an Arian
bishop; death of Constantine; mass
executions within the imperial family
leave only Julian and Constantius
Gallus standing; Arianism gains
favor at imperial courts; Athanasius
Returns from his first exile to
Alexandria; outbreak of persecutions
of Christians in Persian Empire.

337–340.................................... Reign of Emperor Constantine II.

337–345.................................... Persian War against Shah Shāpūr II.

337–350.................................... Reign of Emperor Constans.

337–361.................................... Reign of Constantius II.

c. 338...................................... Eusebius composes *Life of Constantine*.

339... Roman Council under Pope Julius I
vindicates Athanasius and Marcellus
of Ancyra; second exile of Athanasius;
Eusebius of Nicomedia ordains Ulfilas
(Wulfila) as missionary to the Goths.

340... Pachomian foundation at
Panopolis expands the monastic
movement in Egypt.

342	Imperial prohibition of pagan sacrifices; at the Arian Council of Sardica, Arian missionaries are promoted within and beyond the Roman Empire; Ulfilas translates the Bible into Gothic; conversion of the Goths, Gepidae, and Vandals to Arian Christianity.
344–46	Julian studies at Marcellum.
346	Return of Athanasius to Alexandria; death of Pachomius and spread of the monastic movement; Julian commences study at Nicomedia.
348	Council of Carthage; "Catholic" ascendency in North Africa.
350	Usurpation of Magnentius in the West; death of Constans.
351	Constantius II defeats Magnentius at the Battle of Mursa and reoccupies the Italian Peninsula; Constantius Gallus becomes Caesar in the East; Julian studies with Maximus at Ephesus; final conversion of Julian to paganism.
353	Final defeat and death of Magnentius; reunification of the Roman Empire under Constantius II.
354	Birth of Augustine.
354–358	Germanic invasions of Gaul.

355...Julian is created Caesar of the
West; death of Donatus in exile.

356...Constantius II prohibits public
pagan worship on pain of death;
death of Antony in Egypt; third
exile of Athanasius begins.

357...Julian defeats the Alemanni at the
Battle of Argentorate (Strasburg)
and restores the Rhine *limes*;
Constantius II visits Rome.

359...Siege and fall of Amida; outbreak
of Second Persian War against
Shāpūr II; Council of Ariminum.

360...Julian II "the Apostate" **is** proclaimed
Augustus by the Western army; civil
war breaks out between Julian II
and Constantius II; dedication of the
Hagia Sophia in Constantinople.

361...Death of Constantius II; reunification
of the Roman Empire under Julian
II; Julian restores worship of the
pagan gods and enacts legislation
to restore cults and cities.

362...Julian's edict on education; Athanasius
returns to Alexandria; restoration
of the Orthodox Party in Egypt;
Donatists return from exile; election
of Parmenian Donatist bishop of
Carthage; fourth exile of Athanasius;
Julian winters at Antioch and
clashes with the city's Christians.

363.. Publication of *Misopogon*; failure of
the Roman offensive against Ctesiphon;
retreat and death of Julian II; peace
with Persia; Romans surrender Nisibis.

363–364... Reign of Emperor Jovian,
a Nicene Christian.

364–366... Return and fifth exile of Athanasius.

364–375... Reign of Emperor Valentinian
I, a Nicene, in the West.

364–378... Reign of Emperor Valens,
an Arian, in the East.

366–367... Usurpation of the imperial
throne by Procopius.

366–384... Pontificate of Damasus.

367.. Elevation of Gratian as Augustus;
Ausonius becomes tutor of Gratian.

c. 370–79.. Basil of Caesarea *flourit*.

373.. Consecration of Ambrose as bishop
of Milan; death of Athanasius;
consecration of Gregory of
Nazianzus as bishop of Sasima.

374.. Jerome retires to the desert
of Chalcis; consecration of
Gregory as bishop of Nyssa.

375... Death of Valentinian I; Latin and
pagan literary revival at Rome under
the circle of Symmachus; outbreak
of Priscillianism dispute in Spain.

375–392.. Reigns of emperors Gratian and
Valentinian II in the West.

378... Defeat and death of Valens by
the Visigoths at the Battle of
Adrianople; crisis in the Balkans.

379... Elevation of Theodosius I "the
Great" as Augustus;   Theodosius
restores *limes* on the Lower Danube
River; recruitment and promotion
of Germans in the Roman Army.

380... Imperial laws are issued
against heresies.

381... Second Ecumenical Council of
Constantinople upholds the Nicene
Creed and condemns Arianism.

382... Theodosius I proclaims Nicene
Christianity the official state
religion of the empire; dispute
over the Altar of Victory begins.

383... Jerome translates the Bible into
Latin; death of Gratian.

383–388.. Imperial usurpation of
Magnus Maximus.

384... Conflict between Valentinian
II and Ambrose.

384–387.. Augustine at Milan.

385... Condemnation and execution of
Priscillian; Jerome arrives in Bethlehem.

386... Augustine returns to
Catholic Christianity.

388... Defeat and death of Magnus
Maximus; restoration of legitimate
imperial rule in the West.

390... Massacre at Thessalonica; Ambrose
forces the penance of Theodosius I

391... Edict of Theodosius I closes
the pagan temples and outlaws
sacrifices; Christian riots destroy
the Serapeum in Alexandria.

392... Revolt of Eugenius in the West begins,
backed by the Western army and
pagan Roman senators; renewed anti-
pagan and anti-heretical legislation
is issued by Theodosius I; Theodore
is made bishop of Mopsuestia.

394... Battle of the Frigidus ends the
revolt in the West; Theodosius
I reunites the Roman Empire;
Donatist Council at Bagai.

395... Death of Theodosius I; division
of Roman Empire.

395–408... Reign of Emperor Arcadius in the East.

395–423... Reign of Emperor Honorius
in the West; disintegration of
imperial rule in the West.

396–397... Augustine writes *Confessions*.

398.. John Chyrsostom is consecrated
as patriarch of Constantinople.

399.. Augustine initiates an anti-Donatist
campaign in North Africa.

400.. Alaric and the Visigoths migrate west,
Stilicho defends the Italian Peninsula.

406.. Great Germanic invasion of
Gaul; collapse of imperial rule in
northwestern Europe; execution of
Stilicho triggers a political crisis
in the West; death of Arcadius.

408–450... Reign of Theodosius II in the East.

409–410... Roman forces depart from Britain.

409–415... Synesius becomes bishop of
Ptolemais in Cyrene.

410.. Alaric sacks Rome.

411.. Augustine commences writing *City
of God*; outbreak of the Pelagian
Controversy; Ataulf leads the
Visigoths into southern Gaul.

412.. Consecration of Cyril as patriarch of
Alexandria; emergence of Alexandria
as the leading see of the East.

413.. Beginning of construction of the
land walls of Constantinople.

415.. Constantius, *magister militum*
of the West, campaigns in Gaul;
murder of Hypatia in Alexandria;
imperial edict bars pagans from
military and civil positions.

415–421... Stabilization of the Western Empire.

416–418... Visigoths invade Spain

c. 420–440?...................................... Anglo-Saxon migrations
into Britain begin.

423.. Death of Honorius; accession
of Usurper John; political
crisis in the West.

425.. Valentinian III is placed on the Western
throne by the Eastern Roman army.

428.. Consecration of Nestorius as
patriarch of Constantinople.

429.. Germanus visits Britain; Gaiseric and
the Vandals conquer North Africa;
Nestorius and Cyril**'s** debate over
Christology leads to the outbreak
of the Nestorian Controversy.

430...Death of Augustine; Vincent of
Lerins and ecclesiastical historians
Socrates and Sozomen *flourit*.

431...Third Ecumenical Council at Ephesus
condemns and deposes Nestorius.

432...Patrick's mission to Ireland.

433...Formula of Reunion; accession
of Attila as king of the Huns.

435–458...Theodoret of Cyrrhus *flourit*.

438...Publication of the *Codex Theodosianus*.

439...Vandals capture Carthage.

440–461...Pontificate of Leo I "The Great."

442–447...Attila ravages the Balkans.

444...Death of Cyril; consecration
of Dioscurus as Patriarch
of Constantinople.

446...Dispute between Patriarch Flavian
of Constantinople and Eutyches;
Dioscurus supports Eutyches; renewal
of the Christological Controversy.

448...Condemnation of Eutyches
by Home Synod.

449... Dioscurus proclaims the Monophysite Christology during the Latrocinium ("Robber Council") of Ephesus; deposition of Flavian; Pope Leo I writes his *Tome* in support of Flavian.

450... Death of Theodosius II; accession of Marcian as emperor in the East; Attila delivers ultimatum to Court of Ravenna.

451... Aetius checks Attila's invasion of Gaul at the Battle of Chalons; Orthodox Christology of Two Natures is proclaimed at the Fourth Ecumenical Council at Chalcedon; deposition of Dioscorus; Jerusalem is raised to Patriarchical status; Constantinople is recognized as the "New Rome"; anti-Chalcedonian riots in Syria and Egypt.

452... Attila and the Huns invade the Italian Peninsula; embassy of Pope Leo I to Attila; withdrawal of the Hun army from the peninsula; Leo rejects Canon 28 of Chalcedon; Death of Attila and the collapse of Hun Empire.

455... Death of Valentinian III leads to dynastic and political confusion in the Western Empire; Vandals sack Rome; Avitus becomes emperor in the West; Ricimer, *magister militum*, manipulates the imperial throne.

457–461... Reign of Emperor Majorian in the West.

457–473... Reign of Emperor Leo I in the East.

460–482.. Timothy "Wobble Cap" becomes
patriarch of Alexandria.

461–465.. Reign of Emperor Severus
III in the West.

466–484.. Euric and the Visigoths conquer Spain
and advance Arian Christianity.

467–472.. Reign of Emperor
Anthemius in the West.

468.. Abortive naval expedition
against the Vandals.

471.. Acacius becomes patriarch
of Constantinople.

472–473.. Olybrius becomes emperor of
the West; death of Ricimer.

473–474.. Reign of Emperor Leo II in the East.

473–474.. Reign of Emperor Glycerius
in the West.

474–475.. Reign of Emperor Julius
Nepos in the West.

474–491.. Reign of Emperor Zeno in the East.

475–476.. Reign of Emperor Romulus
Augustulus in the West.

476.. Odoacer deposes Romulus
Augustus and recognizes Zeno
as the sole emperor; end of the
Western Roman Empire.

482.. Zeno proclaims the Henoticon;
Monophysite Peter Mongo becomes
patriarch of Alexandria.

483.. Consecration of Pope Felix III; Vandals
persecute Orthodox Christians.

484.. Felix condemns the Henoticon
and excommunicates Acacius;
Acacius excommunicates Felix III;
Zeno moves toward reconciliation
with the Monophysites.

484–488.. Revolt of Leontius and
Illus in Asia Minor.

484–519.. Acacian Schism.

489–491.. Theodoric and the Ostrogoths
conquer the Italian Peninsula.

491–518.. Reign of Emperor Anastasius I.

496–498.. Failure of Anastasius to end
the Acacian Schism.

c. 498.. Conversion of Clovis and the
Franks to Catholic Christianity.

502.. Mission of the nine saints to Ethiopia.

505–516.. John Nikiou serves as patriarch of Alexandria.

512–518.. Severus serves as patriarch of Antioch.

513.. Revolt of Vitalian and anti-Monophysite rising against Anastasius I.

514–523.. Pontificate of Hormisdas.

518–527.. Reign of Emperor Justin I.

519.. Justin rescinds the Henoticon and ends the Acacian Schism; acceptance of the Chalcedonian creed in the East; Severus of Antioch organizes Monophysite counterchurch and monasteries.

519–523.. Persecution of the Monophysites.

523–526.. Pontificate of John II.

525.. Death of Theoderic.

527.. Outbreak of First Persian War; death of Justin I.

527–565.. Reign of Emperor Justinian I.

528–529.. Justinian purges the Roman administration of pagans.

529.. Benedict founds the monastery of Monte Cassino; end of the Academy at Athens; publication of the first edition of the *Codex Justinianus'* Justinian proposes the Theopaschite theology.

530... Belisarius defeats the Persians
at the Battle of Daras.

532... Nika Revolt and the destruction of
Hagia Sophia; "Perpetual Peace" is
concluded with Shah Chosroes I;
abortive conference with Monophysite
leaders at Constantinople.

533... Belisarius retakes North Africa from
the Vandals; publication of *Digest*.

534... Publication of the revised
Codex Justinianus.

535... Belisarius invades Sicily; imperial
laws against are declared against
heretics in North Africa.

536... Belisarius invades the Italian
Peninsula and reoccupies Rome;
outbreak of the Great Mutiny
in North Africa; Goths depose
Theodahad and elect Wittigis king.

537... Deposition of Pope Silverius
by Belisarius; election of Pope
Vigilius; dedication of Hagia
Sophia; Gothic siege of Rome.

538–540... Renewed imperial offensive
in the Italian Peninsula.

540... Belisarius captures Ravenna;
outbreak of the Second Persian
War; Persians sack Antioch.

542	Mission of John of Ephesus in Asia Minor; Mission of Julian to Nubia; mission of James Baradaeus and growth of the Syrian Monophysite (Jacobite) Church; Totila, king of the Goths, recovers the Italian Peninsula.
545–546	Totila besieges and captures Rome; collapse of Byzantine position in the Italian Peninsula.
546	Justinian condemns the Three Chapters; Justinian seeks reconciliation with moderate Monophysites; second purge of pagans from Justinian's administration.
547	Belisarius retakes Rome; death of Benedict of Nursia; dedication of the Church of San Vitale in Ravenna; Pope Vigilius arrives in Constantinople; dispute between Vigilius and Justinian over the Three Chapters.
548	Death of the Empress Theodora; recall of Belisarius from the Italian Peninsula; Vigilius issues *Judicatum*; John Troglita pacifies North Africa.
549–550	Totila besieges and captures Rome.
552	Narses defeats Totila at the Battle of Busta Gallorum; Imperial reconquest of the Italian Peninsula commences.

553 .... Fifth Ecumenical Council at
Constantinople; condemnation
of the Three Chapters; arrest and
imprisonment of Vigilius; imperial
forces recover southern Spain.

554 .... Narses issues the Pragmatic
Sanction; reorganization of the Italian
Peninsula; Vigilius's *Constitutum*
and exile; alienation of Western
and Monophysite churches.

555–561 .... Pontificate of Pelagius I.

558 .... Replacement of the Great
Dome of Hagia Sophia; raids
of Kotrigurs in the Balkans.

562 .... Justinian and Chosroes I conclude the
Fifty-Year Peace; third purge of pagans
from Justinian's administration.

565 .... Initiation of new discussions
with Monophysites; Justinian
proposes the Apthartodocetist
doctrine; death of Justinian.

565–578 .... Reign of Emperor Justin II.

Glossary

acropolis: A Greek city's citadel and location of its main temples.

adventus: "Arrival"; the ceremony of official welcome extended by a provincial city to the Roman emperor between the 2nd and 4th centuries A.D. The cult statues of the leading civic gods were often presented on the emperor's arrival.

aei gennetos: "Eternally generated"; term used by Origen in *On First Principles* to explain the relationship between God the father and the Christ-*logos* in the Trinity.

agora: The market and public center of a Greek city, equivalent to a Roman forum.

amphitheater: A freestanding Roman structure built for spectacles, notably gladiatorial and animal combats. It is the largest building in any Roman city. The Colosseum (Flavian Amphitheater) at Rome, dedicated in 80 A.D., is the largest example.

aniconic: An outlook rejecting the representation of the divine by images.

apatheia: Apathy; detachment from emotions, the highest state of enlightenment for a Stoic. *See* **Stoicism**.

apocalypse: "Revealing what is hidden"; in Jewish and Christian literature and thought, the final reckoning of God. The book of Revelation is a prophecy of the apocalypse.

apologist: Defender; a Christian writer who penned defenses against pagan criticism. The most important of the early apologists were Justin the Martyr (103–165), who wrote in Greek, and Tertullian (160–220), who wrote in Latin.

apostate: "One standing apart"; one who has renounced his or her original faith. The emperor Julian (360–363), for example, was born and baptized a Christian but is called the Apostate because he renounced Christianity and embraced the pagan gods.

apostle: From Greek *apostolos*, *stello* meaning "sending away" in the diplomatic or military sense. Christians used the term to denote the original followers of Jesus who established the first churches.

archbishop: The highest bishop of the metropolis of a Roman (and therefore ecclesiastical) province with authority over bishops in the dioceses of his province. Called a metropolitan in Orthodox Christianity.

Arianism: The doctrine of Arius (c. 250–336) that maintains Christ is lesser in substance to God the father. The doctrine was rejected at the First Ecumenical Council in 325 and again at the Second Ecumenical Council in 381.

Artemision: A temple of Artemis, more specifically the one near Ephesus considered one of the Seven Wonders of the Ancient World.

Asclepieion: A sanctuary to Asclepius, god of healing; the most celebrated ones were at Epidaurus, on the island of Cos, and outside of Pergamon.

atheism: "Denying gods"; term applied by pagans to Christians who denied the ancestral gods.

Avesta: The liturgical texts of Zoroastrianism that survive in later, redacted versions from between the 3rd and 9th centuries A.D. The oldest hymns of the Avesta, the Gathas, are believed to have been composed by Zoroaster in the 6th century B.C.

Baal: "Lord"; the pious title of respect accorded to a city's leading god in the Semitic-speaking provinces of the Roman Empire.

baetyl: An aniconic representation of a god (*baal*) in the Semitic-speaking provinces of the Roman Empire.

basilica: A Roman public building with apses at each end and a central hall, or narthex. The design was applied to a Christian church in the 4th century. The longitudinal axis of the basilica was distinct from the centrally planned church in the form of square with a dome at the intersection—the design favored in the middle and late Byzantine ages.

bishop: The ordained leader of the church of a diocese. The first known bishop is Ignatius of Antioch (d. A.D. 107). The bishops of Rome, Alexandria, and Antioch claimed an apostolic succession to Saint Peter, and so their dioceses were recognized as Petrine Sees at the Second Ecumenical Council of Constantinople in 381.

boule (pl. *boulai*): Council, either elected or chosen by lot, that summoned the assembly of citizens and supervised officials.

bouleuterion: A council hall.

Byzantine: Of the Eastern Roman Empire.

Byzantium: The name of the Greek colony founded on the site of modern Istanbul in 668 B.C. In A.D. 330, Emperor Constantine the Great refounded the city as Constantinople, or New Rome. Byzantium is applied to the Eastern Roman civilization of the 4th through 15th centuries to distinguish it from the parent state of Rome.

canon: From Greek *kanon*, "a rod," hence a measuring stick; those Christian books of supreme authority in which dogma is revealed.

Catechetical School: Founded at Alexandria, Egypt, c. 190, the first Christian school to train theologians and clergy.

Catholic: "Universal"; term used to designate the Western medieval Latin-speaking church that accepted the doctrines of the Fourth Ecumenical Council (451) and the primacy of the pope at Rome. *See also* **Orthodox**.

Cenobium: "Living together"; the first communal centers of ascetics organized by Saint Pachomius (280–346) in Egypt.

Chaldaean Oracles: An allegorical poem in Greek hexameter, this inspired revelation was attributed to Julianus the Chaldaean, who was reputed to have lived in the time of Marcus Aurelius (r. 161–180). Neoplatonists from Porphyry on considered a sacred book of theurgy. The poem was apparently penned by Neoplatonists influenced by Syrian solar cults, middle Platonic theurgy, and even contemporary Jewish ideas.

Christogram: The combined Greek letters chi and rho, the first two letters of *Christos*. Before the Battle of Milvian Bridge, Constantine applied this symbol to his military standard (vexillum) and so created a Christian banner, or labarum.

Christology: The theology of the two natures (human and divine) of Christ.

collegium (pl. **collegia**): A Roman burial society to which members contribute and celebrate rites with ritual meals.

commune: From Greek *koinon*, a league of cities with a province devoted to the worship of the Roman imperial family.

consecratio: Consecration; the rite of deifying a deceased emperor.

Constitutio Antoniniana de Civitate: Edict of A.D. 212 issued by Emperor Caracalla extending Roman citizenship to all free residents of the empire.

consul: One of two annually elected senior officials of the Roman Republic with the right to command an army (imperium). A consul became a proconsul whenever his term of office was prorogued or extended. *See also* **proconsul**.

Corinthian order: The most ornate classical architectural order favored by the Romans.

cosmology: From Greek *kosmos*, "ordering"; the study or theology of the creation and operation of the universe.

council: A meeting of prelates and theologians to determine dogma. *See* **ecumenical council**.

Cybele (a.k.a. **Kubaba**): The great mother goddess of Anatolia, whose principal shrine was at Pessinus. She was known to the Romans as the Great Mother (Magna Mater).

cynicism: From *cynos*, "dog"; the Greek philosophy of Diogenes of Sinope (c. 412–323 B.C.) that rejected the material world.

deacon: From Greek *diakonos*; an assistant, lay or ordained, to the clergy in the Roman world.

decurions: The landed civic elites defined as capable of holding municipal office with wealth assessed in excess of 25,000 denarii or one-tenth the property qualification of a Roman senator.

Demiurge: "Craftsman"; the term used by Plato in his dialogue *Timaeus* (c. 360 B.C.) to describe the creator God.

Deutero-Pauline letters: Letters attributed to Saint Paul that were likely written by his disciples. These are Colossians, Ephesians, 2 Thessalonians, Hebrews, 1 and 2 Timothy, and Titus.

Diaspora: "Scattering"; the settlements of Jews living outside the homeland in the Hellenistic and Roman ages.

Diatessaron: The Syriac translation of the four canonical Gospels into a single, reconciled narrative by Tatian (c. 120–180).

Didachē: From Greek, "instruction"; a treatise of the early 2nd century, probably written in Syria, dealing with ritual and discipline within the early church.

dike: "Justice"; first expressed in the poems of Hesiod (c. 700 B.C.). It is the rule of law in a *polis*, and the virtue was personified as a goddess.

divus/diva (m. pl. ***divi***; fem. pl. ***divae***): Latin for "defied one"; the spirit (*genius*) of an emperor or member of the imperial family that was, on his funeral pyre, taken to join the gods. This deification was confirmed by a decree of the Senate.

Docetists: From Greek *dokein*, "to seem"; Christian heretics who maintained that the physical body of Jesus only appeared to have been crucified. This view is often regarded as Gnostic because it is premised on a material view of evil. *See* **dualism**.

dogma: Greek for "that which is surmised"; a religion's established beliefs.

Dominate: The late Roman Empire (284–476), in which the emperor ruled as an autocrat or lord (dominus). The designation is used in contrast to the Principate (27 B.C.–A.D. 284), when emperors ruled like magistrates of a Roman Republic. *See* **Principate**.

Donatists: Followers of Donatus, the bishop of Carthage in Roman North Africa, who maintained that Christians who lapsed and sacrificed to pagan gods during the persecution of 303–313 must be re-baptized.

Doric order: The austere architectural order used for Greek temples and favored in the Peloponnese.

dualist: One who believes in a stark division between a good spiritual world and an evil physical or material world. Gnostic teachers were apparently dualists in their cosmology. Zoroastrianism is premised on a dualist view of an eternal conflict between the creator god of good, Ahura Mazdā, and the evil destructive spirit Ahriman.

ecumenical council: A world council summoned by the Roman emperor to determine Christian dogma. The First Ecumenical Council at Nicaea (325) and the Second at Constantinople (381) proclaimed the Trinity and rejected Arianism. The Third Ecumenical Council at Ephesus (431) proclaimed the Virgin Mary as the mother of God (Theotokos) and rejected Nestorianism. The Fourth Ecumenical Council at Chalcedon (451) defined the two natures of Christ and rejected Monophysitism.

Edict of Milan: The imperial rescript issued jointly by Constantine I and Licinius I in 313 that ended the Great Persecutions and recognized Christianity as a religion.

ekkesia: An assembly of all citizens of a *polis* with the right to vote for laws and elect magistrates. Christians adapted the word to designate a church or congregation.

emanation: One generation of the descending levels of reality from the One in the great chain of being posited by Plotinus (205–270).

Enneads: The writings of Plotinus (205–270) as collected and edited by Porphyry of Tyre.

epibatereion: Greek for "the boarding"; the spring ceremony to Isis at the start of the sailing season.

epigraphy: The scholarly study of inscriptions.

epiphany: From Greek *epiphanein*, "to appear"; the appearance of a divinity within its cult statue when sacrifices and prayers were offered.

Episcopal: Matters concerning a bishop.

episkopos (pl. *episkopoi*): Greek for "overseer"; a bishop.

equestrian: The landed property class of Roman citizens (assessed at 100,000 denarii) who stood below the senatorial order in the Principate. They provided the jurists, officials, and army officers of the imperial government.

eschaton: Greek for "last"; the ultimate reckoning by God.

Essenes: Members of an ascetic Jewish sect, called a "philosophy" by Josephus, from the 2nd century B.C. to 1st century A.D. Some scholars have attributed the composition of the Dead Sea Scrolls to the Essenes.

evangelist: From Greek *eu anglein*, "well-bringer," or bringer of good news; bringer of the faith of Christ.

evocatio: Latin for "calling out"; the Roman ceremony of winning over the gods of a foe with promises of temples and votive offerings. The ceremony was performed by a magistrate with imperium—the right to command an army.

Frigidus, Battle of: The victory of Theodosius I over the rebel Western army of Eugenius and the magister militum Arbogast on September 5–6, 394. It was hailed as a victory of Christianity over paganism.

genius: Latin for "spirit"; The spirit of each man. The genius of the emperor may be defied upon his death and consecration. Juno is the spirit of each woman. *See* **divus**.

Gnostics: From Greek *gnostikos*, "knowledgeable"; mystics and teachers with a deeper esoteric knowledge of religious texts and therefore of the path to salvation. Many Gnostics premised their cosmology on dualist beliefs. *See* **dualism**.

Great Persecution: The empire-wide persecutions of Christians ordered by Emperor Decius in 250–251, Valerian in 258–260, and the tetrarchs in 303–313.

gymnosophist: Greek for "naked wise men"; the classical name for the holy men of India, particularly Buddhist ascetics.

Hasmonaean: The royal dynasty of Judaea, founded by Simon Maccabaeus in 165 B.C. and ruling until 37 B.C. when Herod the Great seized power in the Jewish homeland.

Hellene, **Hellenic**: The name Greeks apply to themselves.

Hellenistic: Greek-like; the period between the death of Alexander the Great and the Battle of Actium (i.e., 323–31 B.C.). It also denotes the civilization of this period, which was fusion of Hellenic and Near Eastern traditions.

henotheism: The religious outlook regarding traditional pagan gods as aspects of a single transcendent godhead. This was the religious vision of the Neoplatonic philosopher Plotinus and the emperor Julian II.

heresiarch: The leader of a heretical sect of Christians.

heresiologist: A Christian author who writes about and refutes heresies.

heresy: From Greek *hairere*, "to choose"; a doctrine condemned by formal council as outside accepted Christian theology and teachings.

Hexapla: Greek for "sixfold"; a set of texts complied by Origen (185–254) to establish the canonical text of the Old Testament. It comprised the Hebrew text, the Hebrew transliterated into Greek letters, and the translations in Greek of Aquila of Sinope, Symmachus the Ebionite, the Septuagint, and Theodotian.

hippodrome: A stadium for chariot races.

hodēgētria: Any icon of Mary Theotokos (Mary, mother of God), but it referred to the icon reputedly painted by Saint Luke that was the palladium of Constantinople from 626 on.

homoiousia: From Greek for "similar substance"; the term used by Arians to define the Christ logos as inferior to the father in the Trinity.

homoousia: From Greek for "same substance"; the term used by Nicene Christians to define the Christ logos as identical in essence to the father in the Trinity.

honestiores: Latin for "more honorable ones"; an order of society in later Roman law accorded privileges and exemptions from torture in criminal proceedings.

humiliores: Latin for "more humble ones" an order of society in later Roman law subject to direct taxation and, in criminal proceedings, to torture and corporal punishment.

icon: The depiction of Christ, Mary Theotokos, or a saint on perishable material to which believer prays for intercession before God.

iconoclast: "Destroyer of icons"; those who argued that icons were idols and should be removed from Christian worship, particularly in the years 726–843.

iconodule: "Servant of icons"; those favoring the use of icons as means of intercession.

interpretatio Graeca: The identification of a local god with a Greek equivalent.

interpertatio Romana: The assimilation of a local god into the Roman equivalent.

Ionic order: Architectural order favored by Greek cities of Asia Minor.

kairos: To the pagan Greeks, an opportune moment, believed to be the gift of the gods. For Christian writers, the period of the ministry and crucifixion of Jesus that transcends strict linear time (*chronos*).

Koine: From Greek *koinē*, "common"; the vernacular, simplified Greek spoken in the Hellenistic world and the Roman Empire. The books of the New Testament are written in Koine Greek rather than the archaizing literary Greek of the upper classes.

labarum: The Roman military banner (vexillum) carrying the Christogram. Constantine ordered its creation before the Battle of Milvian Bridge in 312.

lapsus (pl. *lapsi*): Latin for "lapsed"; Christians who sacrificed to pagan gods during the persecutions.

Lares: The guardian spirits of Roman homes, settlements, and roads. *See also* **penates.**

legion: The main formation of the army of the Roman Republic and Principate. Each legion (of 5,400 men) comprised professional swordsmen and specialists, all Roman citizens. The auxiliaries (*auxilia*) were provincial units providing cavalry, archers, and light armed infantry.

liturgy: From Greek *leitourgia* (in Latin, *munera*), "service for the people"; a civic or religious obligation assumed by citizens out of patriotism. For Christians, denotes the pattern of worship. *See **philotimia** and **philopatris**.*

Logos: Greek for "word"; in Stoic philosophy, the divine active intelligence of the universe. Christians (based on John 1:1) applied the term to Christ as the second person of the Trinity.

Manichaean: A follower of the dualist faith of the prophet Mani (216–276) who taught a universal monotheism often dismissed by Christian writers as a heresy.

martyr: Greek for "witness"; a Christian who refused to sacrifice to the gods and renounce Christianity in a Roman legal proceeding. The martyr was consigned to the arena.

Messiah: Hebrew for "anointed one"; in Jewish Apocalyptic literature, the Messiah is a descendant of King David who will restore Israel. The Greek equivalent is *Christos*.

metropolitan: The equivalent of an archbishop in the Orthodox Church.

Milvian Bridge, Battle of: The victory of Constantine the Great over his rival Maxentius north of Rome on October 28, 312. Constantine credited his victory to the Christian God.

Misopogon: "Beard Hater"; the satirical tract written by the pagan emperor Julian to refute his Christian detractors at Antioch in 362. Julian was jeered at for sporting the long beard of a pagan philosopher.

mission: From Latin *mittere*, "one having been sent," especially in a diplomatic or military sense; the term was adapted by Christians to denote preaching the faith.

Mithraism: The Roman cult of the god Mithras, originally a Persian god of oaths. The cult was popular among Roman soldiers and customs officials in the 1st–4th centuries A.D.

monophysis: Greek for "single nature"; The doctrine stressing the single, divine nature of Christ from which the Monophysites got their name. This became the doctrine of the Egyptian, Armenian, Syriac, and Ethiopian churches.

Mos maiorum: Latin for "custom of the ancestors"; the Roman expression for the superior authority of traditional religious and social practices.

Montanism: The Christian heresy of Montanus, who in 157 or 172, proclaimed direct inspiration from the Holy Spirit. Also called the New Prophecy.

mystery cults: In older scholarship, this name was given to certain pagan sects seen as ecstatic, irrational cults that displaced traditional worship in anticipation of Christianity. Mystery cults had initiation rites and conformed to general pagan expectations of piety.

necropolis: Greek for "city of the dead"; cemeteries outside the walls of a Greek or Roman city. This was intended to prevent ritual pollution of the living.

neokoros: Greek for "temple-warden"; A Greek city possessed of a temple dedicated to the Roman emperor.

Neoplatonism: The Platonic philosophical doctrines as interpreted by Plotinus (205–270) and later philosophers.

Nestorianism: The followers of Nestorius, patriarch of Constantinople from 429 to 431, who argued that Mary was the mother of Christ the human (Christotokos), rather than mother of Christ the God (Theotokos). Nestorius's views were rejected at the Third Ecumenical Council at Ephesus in 431. *See* **Theotokos**.

New Prophecy: *See* **Montanism**.

nous: Greek for "mind"; The second level of reality—rational intelligence—in middle Platonic and Neoplatonic philosophy.

numismatics: The scholarly study of coins.

oikoumene: Greek for "inhabited"; the universal Christian world.

One, the: In Greek, **"*to hen*"**; term used by Plotinus (205–270) to define the ultimate, infinite divine reality that is the source of all creation by emanation.

ordo (pl. **ordines**): A legal class of citizens according to Roman law, or the town council of a Roman colony or municipality.

Orthodox: Greek for "correct"; the term used to designate the primarily Greek-speaking church of the Byzantine Empire that accepted the doctrines of the Council of Chalcedon (451). It was extended to include those Slavic and other churches that acknowledged the spiritual authority of the patriarch of Constantinople.

pagan: From Latin *pagus* (pl. *pagi*), "a rural district"; a worshiper of the ancestral gods.

Panhellenion: The religious league of Greek sanctuaries founded by Emperor Hadrian (r. 117–138).

patriarch: Greek for "paternal ruler"; the Greek equivalent of the Latin pope (from *papa*, "father"). The patriarch of Constantinople is the head of the Orthodox Church.

Pauline letters: The seven letters of the New Testament written by Saint Paul in about A.D. 48–65: Romans, 1 and 2 Corinthians, Galatians, Philippians, 1 Thessalonians, and Philemon. *See also* **Deutero-Pauline letters**.

Peace of the Church: The period between the persecution of Valerian and that of the tetrarchs (260–303). It is regarded as the golden age by Christian writers.

penates: Roman guardian spirits of the hearth. *See also* **Lares**.

Petrine Sees: The five great apostolic sees founded by Peter or his disciples. The order was fixed at the Fourth Ecumenical Council as Rome, Constantinople, Alexandria, Antioch, and Jerusalem. Rome claims primacy, and Constantinople claims equality with Rome.

Pharisees: Jewish teachers and moral leaders who interpreted the Torah more broadly and dominated the synagogues of the Diaspora from the 2nd century B.C. onward. Pharisee Judaism became the basis for Rabbinical Judaism after A.D. 70.

philotimia and ***philopatris***: The prized public virtues of a *polis*—love of honor and love of country that motivated public gift giving and service.

polis (pl. ***poleis***): City-state; the Greek political community that permitted citizens to live according to the rule of law and so distinguished Greeks from other peoples.

presbyter: From Greek *presbyteros*, "elder"; often used in classical Greek for an ambassador. It was a term used in synagogues and early churches to denote a senior minister.

Principate: The Early Roman Empire (27 B.C.–A.D. 284), when the emperor, styled as the princeps ("prince"), ruled as the first citizen of a republic. *See* **Dominate**.

psyche: Greek for "soul"; the Greek philosophical term for the eternal soul. In middle Platonic and Neoplatonic cosmology, the world soul is the third reality below the divine mind (nous).

rescript: The response of a Roman emperor to a petition that had the force of law.

rigorist: A Jewish or Christian sectarian who argues for strict adherence to doctrine as the only path to salvation or enlightenment.

sacramentum: Latin for "oath," particularly the annual oath sworn by Roman army to the emperor.

Sadducees: Members of the Jewish upper classes from the mid-2nd century B.C. through the late 1st century A.D. who practiced strict ritual purity, maintenance of the sacrifices at the temple, and adherence to the Torah.

Sanhedrin: The governing religious council at Jerusalem first reported in the reign of the Hasmonaean king Alexander Jannaeus (103–76 B.C.).

Sāsānid: The dynasty of shahs who ruled the New Persian Empire (227–642).

schism: From Greek for "cutting"; a dispute resulting in mutual excommunication that arose over matters of church discipline or organization rather than theology. *See* **heresy**.

Second Sophistic movement: Late 1st century A.D. cultural movement among the Greek elite classes of the Roman Empire to revive Attic Greek and classical arts and aesthetics.

senator: A member of the aristocratic families of Rome of the highest property qualification (250,000 denarii) who sat in the Senate and served in the high offices of state.

Senatus consultum: Decree of the Senate; a resolution by the Roman Senate that gave its backing to a proposed law.

Septuagint: Greek for 70; the earliest translation of the Hebrew Bible into Koine Greek, created during the 3rd century B.C. It was produced at Alexandria and by 70 interpreters—hence the name.

Serapeum (a.k.a. **Serapeion**): A temple of Serapis, the Hellenized Osiris who was the tutelary god of Alexandria, Egypt. The destruction of the Serapeum of Alexandria by Christians in 391 marked a major defeat for paganism.

Shepherd of Hermas: A Christian tract written in Greek in the early 2nd century A.D. that reports the visions of Hermas, a freedman and brother of Bishop Pius of Rome.

sophist: Greek for "wise one"; a learned writer and thinker of the Greek elite classes in the Roman Eastern provinces. Sophists promoted the Second Sophistic movement.

sortition: The selection of officials by lot, characteristic of Greek constitutions.

Stoicism: The philosophical doctrines of Zeno of Citium (334–262 B.C.). Zeno could not afford a school, so he taught under the public stoas—hence the name of the philosophy.

strategos (pl. **strategoi**): Greek for "general"; the leading magistrate of a Greek city, annually elected.

synagogue: From Greek *synagoge*, "gathering together"; a consecrated prayer space in Judaism. The synagogue did not replace the Temple of Jerusalem.

syncretism: From Greek for "mixing with"; the identification of one's national gods with their counterparts of other peoples, so that Roman Jupiter was equated with Greek Zeus, Syrian Baal, and Egyptian Amon, for example. Such an outlook encouraged diversity in pagan worship rather than an incipient monotheism.

synnaos: Greek for "temple sharing"; the placement of a cult statue of the Roman emperor within a temple of a city god.

synod: From Greek *synodos*, "sitting around"); a regional council of bishops.

synoecism: A union of villages and towns to form a single *polis*.

Synoptic Gospels: The Gospels of Mark, Luke, and Matthew, composed between A.D. 75 and 85, which offer a synopsis of the ministry and crucifixion of Jesus.

taurobolium: A votive sacrifice of a bull or pig to the goddess Cybele; it was misrepresented by the Christian critic Prudentius, writing around A.D. 400, as distorted blood baptism.

tetrarchy: Rule of four; the collective imperial rule established by Diocletian in 285, with two senior Augusti and two junior Caesars.

theophobeis: Greek for "God-fearers"; pagans who accepted Jewish monotheism without converting to Judaism.

theos (pl. ***theoi***) Greek for "god"; used as hyperbole to describe the Roman emperor. It is often used to designate Zeus or the principal god of a city without implying monotheism.

Theotokos: Greek for "mother of God"; title designating Mary as the mother of the human and divine natures of Christ, accepted at the Third Ecumenical Council (431).

theurgy: The esoteric practices of the enlightened Neoplatonist who understands how traditional rites have a deeper meaning to achieve mystical union with the One.

Three Chapters: Select passages from the works of Theodore of Mopsuestia, Theodoret of Cyrrhus, and Ibas of Edessa that were condemned as Nestorian at the Fifth Ecumenical Council in 553. Emperor Justinian (527–565) had hoped to use this issue as a means to win over the Monophysites to the imperial church.

Torah: The five books of the Bible that constitute the Law of Moses (Genesis, Exodus, Leviticus, Numbers, and Deuteronomy). Known in Greek as the Pentateuch.

votive offerings: Gifts promised to the gods in return for the granting of a favor expressed in a prayer.

Vulgate: The Latin translation of the Bible by Saint Jerome (347–420) that was used in the medieval West.

Yahweh: The Hebrew name for God, often written as four consonants (the Tetragrammaton) and not pronounced aloud when reading the Torah.

Zealot: From Greek *zelotes*, "emulator"; a member of a Jewish sect promoting rebellion against Rome to bring about the restoration of Israel under a messiah.

Zoroastrianism: The universal monotheism of Iran attributed to the teacher Zoroaster, who lived in the 6th century B.C. and reformed as the state religion of the Sāsānid Empire (227–642). *See also* **Avesta**.

Biographical Notes

Aelia Pulcheria (399–453): Sister of Emperor Theodosius II (r. 408–450) and wife of Emperor Marcian (r. 450–457); she defined the role of a Christian empress. Created Augusta in 414, she directed policy for her weak-willed brother and upheld Orthodox positions at Ephesus (431) and Chalcedon (451).

Aelius Aristides (117–180): Greek rhetorician, orator, and stylist of the Second Sophistic movement. Born at Hadriani, Mysia, in northwestern Asia Minor. After traveling widely, including a visit to Rome, he settled at Smyrna. His poor health turned him into a hypochondriac so that he was devoted to Serapis and the healing god Asclepius. His surviving works include speeches on religious and political life, his *Sacred Tales*, and poems. Foremost of his orations are *Panatheneia* and *To Rome*.

Alexander of Abonouteichos (c. 105–c. 170): Charlatan philosopher who founded the cult of the serpent god Glycon in northern Asia Minor. He gained the patronage of Emperor Marcus Aurelius and the contempt of Lucian, who wrote a satirical critique of Alexander and the cult of Glycon.

Alexander the Great (356–323 B.C.; r. 336–323 B.C.): King of Macedon and captain general of the Hellenic League; conquered the Persian Empire in 334–324 B.C. and so founded the Hellenistic world. In about 324 B.C., Greek cities offered divine honors to Alexander and so created the ruler cults of the Hellenistic world.

Ambrose of Milan (a.k.a. **Aurelius Ambrosius**; 337–397): Saint and staunch opponent of Arianism who was elected bishop of Milan in 374. He was mentor to the young Emperor Valentinian II (r. 375–392) and advocated measures against pagan worship. In 390, he compelled Emperor Theodosius I to seek penance for permitting the massacre of citizens of Thessalonica by Gothic soldiers. Ambrose was also patron to Augustine of Hippo.

Ammianus Marcellinus (330–395): Soldier and last great pagan historian of Rome. Born in Antioch, Ammianus served under emperors from Constantius II (r. 337-361) to Theodosius I (r. 379–395). He composed a history in 31 books (of which books 1–12 are lost) covering Roman history from A.D. 96 to 378. Ammianus displays exceptional objectivity in discussing the pagan revival by Emperor Julian (r. 360–363), so that his account is fundamental to the religious history of the 4th century.

Anicetus (fl. 2nd century A.D.): Pope (r. 150–167) who summoned the first reported synod of the Roman church to condemn Marcion and Montanists.

Antony of Egypt (c. 260–357): Early Christian monastic and saint. Born of a wealthy Greco-Egyptian family, Antony embraced an ascetic life in the Libyan desert from c. 280. His example inspired many Christians to embrace the ascetic life. In about 360, Patriarch Athanasius of Alexandria wrote a life of Antony, which served as the model for all later hagiographies.

Apollonius of Rhodes (c. 300–250 B.C.): Composer of a learned epic about Jason and the Argonauts (*Argonautica*) typical of the Hellenistic age.

Apollonius of Tyana (c. 15–100): Sophist and Neopythagorean philosopher whose legendary travels and exploits were recorded in a biography written by Philostratus. Apollonius was hailed as archetypical pagan sage.

Apuleius (a.k.a. **Lucius Apuleius**; fl. 2nd century A.D.): Latin rhetorician and priest. Born at Madaura in North Africa, he was educated at Carthage and Rome. Apuleius composed *Metamorphoses* (*Golden Ass*)—a romantic novel of the amazing adventures of Lucius, who is turned into an ass and is eventually restored by the Egyptian goddess Isis.

Arbogast (c. 360–394): A Frankish officer under Gratian (r. 367–383) who rose to *magister militum* of the West in 388. In 392, he advanced as Emperor Eugenius (r. 392–394) in a pagan revolt against Theodosius I. The Western army was defeated at the Battle of Frigidus (394), and Arbogast committed suicide.

Arcadius (377–408; r. 395–408): The weak-willed elder son of Theodosius I and Aelia Flaccilla. He was proclaimed Augustus in 383 and in 395 succeeded to the Eastern Roman throne. He was dominated by his ministers, who averted the crisis posed by Alaric and the Visigoths.

Archelaus (23 B.C.–A.D. 18; r. 4 B.C.–A.D. 6): Son of Herod the Great and Malthace who succeeded his father as ethnarch of Judaea and Samaria. He was deposed for tyrannical rule and replaced by Roman procurators.

Ardashīr I (fl. 3rd century A.D.): Shah of Persia (224–240 who verthrew the Arsacid dynasty of Parthia and founded the Neo-Persian or Sāsānid Empire. Ardashīr waged war against Rome, proclaiming his aim to conquer the Roman East.

Aristotle (384–322 B.C.): Greek philosopher who studied at Plato's Academy in Athens from 366 to 347 B.C. and then became tutor to Alexander the Great between 343 and 341 B.C. In 335 B.C., Aristotle settled once more in Athens, establishing his school, the Lyceum. He wrote on a vast array of subjects (philosophy, natural sciences, mathematics, morality, logic, and politics). His critique on Plato's cosmology and conception of a rational creator god influenced middle Platonic and Neoplatonic writers.

Arius (c. 250–336): Presbyter in the church of Alexandria, he argued that Christ was generated as an inferior creature from God the father. His theology, Arianism, was condemned at the First Ecumenical Council (325), but his followers converted the East Germans to the Arian confession.

Athanasius (c. 293–373): Theologian and clergyman who opposed Arius at the First Ecumenical Council of Nicaea in 325, arguing the Orthodox positions. As patriarch of Alexandria (329–373), he opposed Emperor Constantius II, a devoted Arian, and later the pagan emperor Julian II. His writings are regarded the touchstone of Orthodoxy. In about 360, he wrote the hagiography of Saint Antony of Egypt.

Augustine (354–430): Saint and bishop of Hippo Regius (395–430). Born at Thagaste, Africa, Augustine mastered rhetoric and philosophy, gaining powerful patrons at Rome and Milan. In his beliefs, he progressed from a pagan Platonist to Platonized Christian. His voluminous writings, notably *City of God* and *Confessions*, defined Western Christianity in the Middle Ages.

Augustus (a.k.a. **Gaius Julius Caesar Octavianus**; 63 B.C.–A.D. 14; r. 27 B.C.–A.D. 14): First Roman emperor, or princeps, and grand-nephew and adopted son of the dictator Gaius Julius Caesar. Called by convention Octavian, 43 B.C., he allied with Mark Antony and Marcus Aemilius Lepidus in the Second Triumvirate to defeat the Liberators. Octavian secured the Italian Peninsula, while Antony ordered the Roman East. In 31 B.C., Octavian defeated Antony and his unpopular consort Cleopatra VII, queen of Ptolemaic Egypt, at Actium. The suicides of Antony and Cleopatra left Octavian master of the Roman world. In 27 B.C., Octavian relinquished his extraordinary powers as triumvir. The Senate voted Octavian tribunician power, proconsular imperium, and the name Augustus. Henceforth, Octavian ruled as emperor. As emperor, he restored peace and prosperity for 45 years, doubled the size of the Roman Empire, and founded the institutions of the Principate.

Aurelian (a.k.a. **Lucius Domitius Aurelianus**; c. 207–275; r. 270–275): "Restorer of the Roman world." Born of a military family in Dalmatia, Aurelian distinguished himself as a cavalry commander under Gallienus and Claudius II. In 270, the Danube army saluted Aurelian emperor, and he secured Rome after a brief civil war. Aurelian restored the political unity of the Roman Empire, defeating Zenobia of Palmyra in 272 and the Gallo-Roman emperor Tetricus in 274.

Barnabas (fl. early 1st century A.D.): An early Levite convert and Christian teacher of Antioch who accompanied Saint Paul on his first trip to Asia Minor (Acts 13:14) in about 45–47. He attended the council of Jerusalem in about 48.

Barsuma (fl. c. 380–440): Fierce Syrian ascetic who converted pagan villages in the style of the prophets of Israel.

Basil of Caesarea (a.k.a. **Basil the Great**; 330–379): Christian saint, theologian, and bishop of Caesarea (370–379) who wrote refutations of Arian theology and the monastic rule *Ascetica*, which still governs Orthodox monasteries. He was brother to Gregory of Nyssa.

Basilides (fl. c. 117–138): Gnostic thinker and teacher at Alexandria who founded a distinct school of Gnosticism based on his (now lost) commentaries on the Gospels.

Benedict of Nursia (480–547): Saint and monastic who founded the monastery of Monte Cassino in 529 and composed *Opus Dei*, the rule for Benedictine monks.

Caligula (a.k.a. **Gaius Julius Caesar**; 12–41; r. 37–41): Roman emperor, son of Germanicus and Agrippina the Elder nicknamed Caligula ("little boots") by the Rhine legions. He succeeded his uncle Tiberius as a popular ruler of Julian descent, but his arbitrary and savage rule, aggravated by madness and divine pretensions, led to his assassination by officers of the Praetorian Guard.

Caracalla (a.k.a. **Marcus Aurelius Severus Antoninus**; 188–217; r. 198–217): The savage son of Septimius Severus and Julia Domna nicknamed Caracalla after his favorite Gallic cloak. He was created co-emperor by his father in 198 and succeeded as joint ruler with his brother Geta in 211. In 212, he ordered the murder of Geta and issued the *Constitutio Antoniniana*. He was murdered by his Praetorian prefect Macrinus during the Parthian expedition (214–217). Carcalla patronized the sanctuaries of Asia Minor, notably the Asclepieion of Pergamon.

Carus (a.k.a. **Marcus Aurelius Carus**; r. 282–283): Praetorian Prefect of Probus who was declared emperor by the Eastern legions. He elevated his sons Carinus (r. 283–285) and Numerian (r. 283–284) as co-emperors. He invaded Mesopotamia, defeating the Persian army, but was killed by lightning near Ctesiphon.

Cato the Elder (a.k.a. **Marcus Porcius Cato Maior**; 234–149 B.C.): Roman conservative statesman and spokesmen for ancestral custom (*mos maiorum*). Elected consul in 195 B.C., Cato waged a campaign in Nearer Spain and gained a triumph. He is known for his practical writings and stern measures when censor in 184–183 B.C.

Catullus (a.k.a. **Gaius Valerius Catulus**; c. 84–54 B.C.): Born at Verona, he is the brilliant lyric poet of the late Roman Republic. Over 100 of his poems survive, including 63 which deal with the cult of Cybele and Attis, the Phrygian fertility divinities of Asia Minor.

Celsus (fl. 2ⁿᵈ century A.D.): Pagan critic of Chrsitianity who wrote *On the True Doctrine* in 177. His work is largely known from quotations by Origen.

Chrysippus (c. 280–207 B.C.): Native of Soli in Cilicia and a leading Stoic philosopher who taught at Athens, perfecting Stoic physics and logic.

Cicero (a.k.a. **Marcus Tullius Cicero**; 106–43 B.C.): Roman lawyer, orator, statesman, and consul of 63 B.C., Cicero was a prolific writer and master of Latin prose. He left a number of works dealing with philosophy and Roman religious practices in addition to his letters and political speeches.

Claudius (a.k.a. **Tiberius Claudius Drusus**; 10 B.C.–A.D. 54; r. A.D. 41–54): The second son of Drusus and Antonia Minor. Claudius received no political training because he was assumed to be weak minded due to his grotesque appearance—a result of infantile paralysis and a stutter. In A.D. 41, after the assassination of Caligula, the Praetorian Guard declared Claudius emperor. He proved an able administrator, and in 43, led the invasion of Britain. He is believed to have been murdered by his fourth wife and niece, Agrippina the Younger, in the interests of her son, Nero.

Claudius II Gothicus (c. 215–270; r. 268–270): An Illyrian provincial, Claudius rose through the ranks to become a senior officer of Gallienus. He participated in the murder of Gallienus and ascended the throne as the first soldier-emperor. In 269, he defeated a major Gothic force at Naissus in Upper Moesia (modern Niš, Serbia), and was hailed Gothicus. He died of plague early in 270.

Clement (c. 150–215): Saint and theologian who refounded the Catechetical School at Alexandria in about 202 and composed the *Stromata*, in which he elucidates his doctrine of salvation that influenced his most brilliant student, Origen.

Cleopatra VII (r. 51–30 B.C.): Ptolemaic queen of Egypt who established liaisons with Julius Caesar and then Marc Antony to secure the independence of her kingdom.

Commodus (a.k.a. **Marcus Aelius Aurelius Commodus**; 161–192; r. 177–192): The only surviving son of Marcus Aurelius and Faustina II. In 177, Commodus was made co-emperor by his father, and in 180, on the death of Marcus Aurelius, he abruptly ended the German campaign to return to Rome. Lazy and savage by nature, Commodus devoted his genius to the arena, fighting as a gladiator to the outrage of the ruling classes. In 189, after a mental collapse, he believed he was Hercules reincarnated, so that his increasingly arbitrary rule resulted in his assassination.

Constantine I (a.k.a. **Constantine the Great**; after 280–337; r. 306–337): Emperor who first legalized Christianity in the Roman Empire. Declared emperor by the Western army, Constantine reunited the empire in 324. In 312, after the Battle of Milvian Bridge, he was convinced his victory was the gift of the Christian God and converted to Christianity. The first Christian emperor, he created the imperial church. In 325, he summoned and presided over the First Ecumenical Council at Nicaea that declared heretical the views of Arius. In his later years, Constantine was won over by the Arians, so that on his deathbed he was baptized by an Arian bishop. He built a new Christian capital at Constantinople on the site of Byzantium in 330.

Constantius I Chlorus (a.k.a. **Flavius Valerius Constantius**; c. 250–306; r. 305–306): Born to an Illyrian military family, Constantius served under Probus and Diocletian. In 293, Maximianus adopted Constantius as his heir and appointed him Caesar. Constantius divorced his wife Helena, mother of Constantine I, and married Theodora, the stepdaughter of Maximianus. In 305, Constantius I succeeded as Augustus of the West. He died in 306, after conducting an expedition against the Picts.

Constantius II (a.k.a. **Flavius Julius Constantius**; 317–361; r. 337–361): Son of Constantine I and Fausta, Constantius II was proclaimed Caesar in 324 and succeeded jointly as Augustus with his brothers Constantine II and Constans in 337. Constantius ruled in the East, waging a war against the Persians. He crushed the rebellion by Magnentius and the Western army in 350–353. In 361, Constantius died of illness while en route to face his cousin Julian, who had been declared emperor by the Western army. An Arian Christian, Constantius sponsored Ulfilas, the so-called apostle to the Goths.

Cosmas Indicopleustas (fl. c. 525–550): Greek merchant of Alexandria who visited India in about 550 and composed *Christian Topography*, in which he reconciled Greek geography with Christian doctrine. He proposed a single landmass of three equal continents in the form of a box, with Jerusalem in the center—a worldview passed on to medieval Christendom.

Cyprian of Carthage (a.k.a. **Thasciius Caecilius Cyprianus**; d. 258): Saint and bishop (250–257) who composed in Latin numerous tracts on issues of baptism of *lapsi*, readmission of heretics into the church, and Episcopal authority. He was martyred during the persecution of Valerian.

Cyril (c. 376–444): Patriarch of Alexandria (412–444) who elevated Alexandria to the leading see of the Eastern Roman world. He condemned the doctrines of Nestorius in his *Twelve Anathemas* and defined the tenets of the Trinity and Mary Theotokos, so that his writings were accepted at the Third and Fourth Ecumenical Councils.

Demetrius of Alexandria (d. 231): Bishop of Alexandria (189–231) who appointed Origen to succeed Clement as the head of the Catechetical School. In 230, Demetrius protested the ordination of Origen by Theoctistus of Caesarea in 230 so that Origen retired to Caesarea Maritima.

Dio Chrysostom (a.k.a. **Dio the Golden Mouthed**; c. 40–120): Greek sophist and philosopher born at Prusa, Bithynia, in northwestern Asia Minor. Dio taught at Rome until he was banished by Emperor Domitian. A convert to Stoicisim, Dio left some 80 orations on a host of subjects.

Diocletian (245–316; r. 284–305): Roman emperor. A humble Dalmatian soldier declared emperor by the Eastern army, Diocletian ended the crisis of the 3rd century and retired from the throne 305. His administrative, monetary, and fiscal reforms established the Dominate, or late Roman state. He created collegial rule, the so-called tetrarchy, whereby imperial power was shared by two senior emperors called Augusti and two junior emperors called Caesars. In 305, Diocletian retired from public life to his fortress palace of Spalato (modern Split, Croatia).

Dionysius Exiguus (c. 470–544): A monk of the Scythian community at Tomi, on the shores of the Black Sea. He calculated the reckoning of Easter and devised the system of dating by A.D. (*Anno Domini*).

Domitian (a.k.a. **Titus Flavius Domitianus**; 51–96; r. 81–96): The younger son of Vespasian who succeeded his popular brother Titus as emperor. Domitian warred against the Chatti in 82–85, but he faced criticism for setbacks in Dacia and for his treaty with their king, Decebalus, in 92. Suspicious by nature, Domitian terrorized the Senate after 93, so that he was murdered by a palace plot.

Dioscorus (d. 454): Patriarch of Alexandria (444–451) and successor to Cyril. He failed to impose the Monophysite doctrine as the Orthodox faith. He was condemned and deposed at the Fourth Ecumenical Council (451).

Epictetus of Hierapolis (55–136): Stoic philosopher who arrived at Rome as the slave of Epaphrodites, freedman secretary of Emperor Nero, studied Stoic philosophy with Gaius Musonius Rufus, and acquired his freedom. In 93, Epictetus, along with several other philosophers, were banished from Rome on the orders of Domitian. His writings on moral conduct gained him admirers among the senatorial class and from Emperor Hadrian.

Epicurus (341–270 B.C.): Athenian philosopher who taught the goal of avoiding pain and finding pleasure by a balanced moral life. He established a school known as the Garden, and his doctrines, dubbed Epicureanism, were popular among the ruling classes of the Hellenistic world and Roman Empire. Epicurus based his cosmology on the early atomists, and so he concluded the gods took no note of human affairs.

Epiphanius of Salamis (c. 320–403): Native of Roman Palestine and monk who consecrated bishop of Salamis, Cyprus, in 367. He compiled a compendium *Against Heresies* (*Panarion*) in 374–377 that is a major source for early sectarian Christianity.

Eugenius (a.k.a. **Flavius Eugenius**; r. 392–394): Grammarian elevated as Western emperor by Arbogast, *magister militum* of the Western army, and backed by the Senate. He was defeated, captured, and executed after his defeat at the Battle of Frigidus on September 6, 394.

Eusebius (260–340): Bishop of Caesarea (314–340) and friend of Emperor Constantine. He composed important pastoral theological works, the most important of which was his *Ecclesiastical History*, the prime source for early Christianity. Eusebius set the standard for later Christian historians. He also composed a life of Constantine, the main source for the emperor's conversion in 312, and the *Tricennial Oration* (336), praising Constantine as the ideal Christian ruler.

Ezana (c. 325–360): King of Axum who received missionaries from Alexandria and converted to Christianity, thereby founding the Ethiopian church.

Fabian (r. 236–250): Pope respected by African and Italian bishops and credited with missions to cities in Gaul. He was martyred during the persecution of Trajan Decius on January 20, 250.

Galen of Pergamon (a.k.a. Aelius Galenus; 129–205): Physician and philosopher born of a prominent family with Roman citizenship. A product of the Second Sophistic movement, Galen wrote extensively on human physiology and biology. He studied at the Asclepieion and was physician to gladiatorial schools at Pergamon and Rome. He was also physician to the young Emperor Commodus. In his writings, Galen makes a number of references to Christians and martyrdoms.

Galerius (a.k.a. **Gaius Galerius Valerius Maximianus**; c. 250–311; r. 305–311): Balkan officer created Caesar of the East in 293. He married Diocletian's daughter Galeria Valeria. In 305, Galerius succeeded Diocletian as Augustus of the East, but his political arrangements denied the succession to both Constantine and Maxentius (each the son of an emperor), so that civil war erupted after 306. Galerius was credited with the initiative for the Great Persecution in 303–313.

Gallienus (a.k.a. **Publius Licinius Egantius Gallienus**; 218–268; r. 253–268): Son of Valerian I, Gallienus was proclaimed joint ruler with his father by the army of the Rhine. Gallienus failed to contain the Germanic invaders; thus the West seceded under the Gallo-Roman emperor Postumus (260–269), and the East fell under the control of Odenathus, the merchant prince of Palmyra. Christians fondly remembered Gallienus, however, because he halted the persecutions.

Gordian III (a.k.a. **Marcus Antonius Gordianus**; 225–244; r. 238–244): Grandson of Gordian I, the young Gordian III was proclaimed emperor by the Praetorian Guard and Senate at Rome in opposition to Maximinus I. His father-in-law and Praetorian prefect Gaius Furius Timisitheus directed policy after 240. In 242–244, Gordian took the field against the Persian Shah Shāpūr I. The young emperor was slain in a mutiny, staged by his prefect, Philip the Arab (who had succeeded Timistheus in 243).

Gratian (a.k.a. **Flavius Gratianus**; 359–383; r. 367–383): The elder son of Valentinian I, he made his court at Treveri. Gratian pursed anti-pagan measures and promoted Nicene Christianity. In 383, he was betrayed and murdered near Lugdunum (Lyon) by supporters of Magnus Maximus, who had been proclaimed emperor by the army of Britain.

Gregory Nazianzus (329–390): Born near Nazianzus in Cappadocia, he entered a religious life in 361 and was staunch opponent to the pagan emperor Julian II. He was ordained Bishop of Sasima in Cappadocia in 372 and then patriarch of Constantinople in 380. Classically educated, Gregory penned important refutations of Arianism and treatises on the nature of the Holy Spirit, views accepted at the Second Ecumenical Council in 381.

Gregory of Nyssa (335–394): Saint and bishop of Nyssa (372–394). Born at Caesarea in Cappadocia, he was the younger brother to Saint Basil of Caesarea. Gregory penned important tracts on the Trinity and the omnipotence of God, thereby rejecting the views of Origen and the pagan Neoplatonists.

Gregory Thaumaturgus (a.k.a. **Gregory the Wonderworker**; 213–270): Bishop of Neocaesarea in Asia Minor (240–270) who studied with Origen at Caesarea Maritima in 231–239. He was credited with aggressive proselytizing among pagans in eastern Asia Minor, but these exploits now appear to be anachronistic creations by his hagiographer, Gregory of Nyssa.

Gregory the Illuminator (c. 257–313): Apostle to the Armenians. Educated as a Christian and studied at Caesarea in Cappadocia, in about 301 Gregory baptized King Tiridates III, although there is reason to believe that Tirdiates embraced Christianity later, following the example of Constantine.

Hadrian (a.k.a. **Publius Aelius Hadrianus**; 76–138; r. 117–138): Fatherless child reared as the ward of his second cousin and future emperor Trajan and his wife, Plotina. In 100, Hadrian married the emperor's grand-niece Sabina. He later succeeded his adoptive father Trajan. Hadrian relinquished Trajan's eastern conquests. By inclination an architect and philhellene, Hadrian was unpopular with the Senate, but he proved a brilliant emperor. Hadrian was also a tireless traveler who patronized the cities of the Roman East.

Hegesippus (c. 110–180): Reportedly a convert from Judaism and the earliest known Christian chronicler. His work was a major source for Eusebius's *Ecclesiastical History*, but it does not survive.

Helena (a.k.a. **Flavia Julia Helena**; c. 246–330): Saint, first wife of Constantius I, and mother of Constantine I. In about 289, Constantius divorced Helena so that he could marry Theodora, daughter of Maximianus, Augustus of the West. In 326–328, Helena traveled to Jerusalem and Bethlehem, where she reportedly found the True Cross.

Herod Agrippa I (10 B.C.–A.D. 44; r. A.D. 41–44): Grandson of Herod the Great, Herod Agrippa was educated at Rome, where he became a boyhood friend of the future Roman emperor Claudius. In 41, Claudius appointed Herod Agrippa king of Jews. He initiated building programs and won the affection of his Jewish and Samaritan subjects. In 44, he died before he could raise a rebellion against Rome.

Herod Antipas (c. 20 B.C.–A.D. 39; r. 4 B.C. –A.D. 39): Son of Herod the Great and Malthace of Samaria who succeeded to the throne of Galilee and Peraea (east of the Jordan) after his father's death. He is remembered in the New Testament for ordering the execution of John the Baptist. In 39, he was deposed and exiled to Lugdunum on the orders of Caligula.

Herod the Great (74–4 B.C.; r. 37–4 B.C.): Second son of Antipater of Idumaea who rose in Hasmonaean service and was appointed governor of Galilee in 49 B.C. From 43 B.C., Herod adroitly exploited his friendship with leading Romans, first Marc Antony and then Octavian, so that he ousted the Hasmonaean dynasty and ruled the Jewish lands from 37 B.C. in the interests of Rome. Herod built on a grand scale, notably Caesarea Maritima and the fortress of Masada. He was despised by his Jewish subjects as a tyrant and a slack adherent to Judaism. In the Gospel of Matthew, he is charged with the Slaughter of the Innocents.

Herodotus (c. 490–425 B.C.): Called the father of history, Herodotus was born at Halicarnassus on the shores of Asia Minor and traveled widely in the Persian Empire and Greece. His *History*, about the wars between the Greeks and Persians, contains invaluable observations on religious practices and Greek attitudes, notably books 2 (Egypt), 3 (Persia and Babylon), and 4 (Scythia).

Hesiod (c. 750–700 B.C.): Boeotian poet inspired by the Muses under Mount Helicon who composed in epic verse *Works and Days* and *Theogony*. Hesiod was regarded as second only to Homer; his *Theogony* gives the first literary definition of the gods and myths of Greece.

Homer (fl. c. 750 B.C.): Reputedly a native of Smyrna, this blind poet was credited with the composition of the epic poems the *Iliad* and the *Odyssey*, which were regarded as the foundation of Hellenic religious beliefs.

Honorius (a.k.a. **Flavius Honorius**; 384–421; r. 395–421): Second son of Theodosius I and Aelia Flaccillia; created Augustus in 393 and succeeded as Western emperor in 395. Real power was in the hands of Stilicho down to 408. Honorius, at his capital at Ravenna from 402 on, witnessed the loss of northwestern and Spanish provinces.

Horace (a.k.a. **Quintus Horatius Flaccus**; 65–8 B.C.): Poet and soldier. Born at Venusia and son of a freedman, Horace fought for the Republican cause at Philippi (42 B.C.), but he was pardoned and promoted at the court of Augustusthrough the efforts of Maecenas. His works include *Carmen Saeculare* (chorus for the Saecular Games of 17 B.C.), *Odes*, Epodes, Epistles, Satires, and *Ars Poetica*. He is considered the master of the Roman lyric and poet laureate of the Golden Age.

Hosius of Cordoba (257–359): Bishop before 300, he suffered exile during the Great Persecution of 303–305. In 313, he was invited to Treveri, where he advised the emperor Constantine on doctrinal matters. After the death of Constantine, Hosius staunchly opposed the Arian policies of Constantius II.

Hypatia (c. 360–415): Daughter of the mathematician Theon (c. 335–405) who taught mathematics and astronomy at Alexandria. She succeeded to the head of the pagan philosophical school at Alexandria in 400 and so was perceived as a threat by Patriarch Cyril. In 415, she was assaulted and hacked to pieces by a crowd of monks. Her works do not survive, but she apparently wrote commentaries on philosophy and astronomy.

Iamblichus of Chalcis (c. 250–325 A.D.): Neoplatonist theurgist from Syria who studied with Porphyry at Rome. Iamblichus composed *De mysteriis* (*On the Mysteries*), an exposition of theurgy and the efficacy of sacrifice that influenced Julian and Proclus. He also composed three treatises on mathematics and a tract on the Pythagorean life.

Ignatius of Antioch (d. c 107): Saint and bishop. He wrote seven letters that offer the first insight into the authority and role of bishops in apostolic churches.

Irenaeus (d. c. 202): Native of Smyrna, saint, bishop of Lugdunum (Lyon), and Christian apologist and theologian. He wrote an eyewitness account of the persecution at Lugdunum in 177 and an important refutation of the Gnostics, *Against Heresies*.

James the Righteous (d. 62) Called the brother of Jesus by Saint Paul (Galatians 1:19). He succeeded to the authority of the Jerusalem church after the crucifixion.

Jerome (a.k.a. **Sophronius Eusebius Hieronymus**; c. 347–420): Saint and philosopher. A native Latin speaker of Dalmatia who mastered rhetoric and philosophy, he assumed an ascetic life and was ordained a priest in about 378 or 379. He translated the Bible from Greek into Latin, a version called the Vulgate. He enjoyed the patronage of leading aristocratic ladies of Rome. From 388, he settled as an ascetic near Bethlehem.

John Chrysostom (349–407): Patriarch of Constantinople (398–405). A brilliant orator, he asserted the primacy of Constantinople over the Eastern churches and clashed with the emperor Arcadius.

John of Amida (c. 507–585): A Monophysite ascetic trained in the Syrian tradition. As bishop of Ephesus (535–575), he carried out aggressive efforts to convert pagans in Western Asia Minor.

John the Baptist (c. 6 B.C.–A.D. 36): A prophet and hailed forerunner of Jesus (*prodromos*) in the Synoptic Gospels. He baptized Jesus at Bethany beyond the Jordan River. He was arrested and beheaded on orders of Herod Antipas to please the seductive Salome, daughter of Herodias (c. 14–71). His followers included the founders of Mandaeism, a faith that accepted John the Baptist as prophet, but not Jesus. There is no direct evidence that the Essenes influenced John the Baptist.

Josephus (a.k.a. **Flavius Josephus**, b. c. 37): A prominent Pharisee and historian of the first rank who composed an eyewitness account of the Jewish War of 66–73 A.D. His *Antiquities of the Jews* is invaluable for Jewish religious attitudes and custom. He also composed an apology for Judaism in two books, *Contra Apionem*.

Jovian (a.k.a. **Flavianus Jovianus**; 337–364; r. 363–364): a Nicene Christian commanding the imperial guard who was elected as emperor after the death Julian during the retreat from Ctesiphon in 363. Jovian surrendered provinces in Mesopotamia to Shah Shāpūr II in exchange for the safe return of the Roman army. In February 364, Jovian was found dead in his tent during the march to Constantinople.

Judas Maccabaeus (a.k.a. **Judah Maccabee**; d. 160 B.C.): Jewish priest and son of Mattathias of the Hasmonaean house who led the revolt against Seleucid king Antiochus IV Epiphanes (175–164 B.C.), who sought to Hellenize the cult of Yahweh at Jerusalem. In 167–163 B.C., Judas won spectacular victories, acquiring the nickname Maccabaeus ("hammer" in Aramaic), and he reoccupied and rededicated the Temple at Jerusalem.

Julia Domna (170–217): Daughter of Gaius Julius Bassianus, equestrian and high priest of the cult of Baal at Emesa (identified with Helios and Sol). The beautiful and intelligent wife of Septimius Severus (193–211), she presided over a court of savants and artists. She was mother to the emperors Caracalla and Geta.

Julia Mamaea (180–235): The second daughter of Julia Maesa, sister of Julia Domna, and the equestrian Julius Avitus. She was mother of the emperor Severus Alexander and guided imperial policy. She was murdered, along with her son, by mutinous soldiers of the Rhine army.

Julian II (a.k.a. **Julian the Apostate** or **Flavius Claudius Julianus**; 332–363; r. 360–363): Nephew of the first Christian emperor, Constantine I, he survived the purge of 337 and was raised and educated in the wastes of Cappadocia. Devoted to the classics, Julian secretly renounced his Christianity in 351. Promoted to Caesar in 355, Julian brilliantly cleared Gaul of Germanic invaders, and he was proclaimed emperor by the Western army. His brief reign saw the restoration of paganism to civic life; his reforms were cut short by his untimely death while on campaign in Persia. His works include orations, philosophical tracts, hymns to Helios and Magna Mater, and critiques on Christian dogma.

Julius Caesar (a.k.a. **Gaius Julius Caesar**; c. 100–44 B.C.): Statesman, general, and author who championed the popular cause in the late Roman Republic. As proconsul of Gaul, he forged an invincible army and overthrew the Republic in a civil war (49–45 B.C.). His dictatorship marked the birth of a Roman monarchy, but his disregard for Republican conventions led to his assassination.

Justin the Martyr (103–165): Christian apologist who wrote (in Greek) two Apologies and *Dialogue with Typhro*.

Justinian I (a.k.a. **Justinian the Great**; 483–565; r. 527–565): Byzantine (Eastern Roman) emperor. Justinian succeeded his uncle and adoptive father Justin I as a mature, experienced ruler of 46. The greatest emperor since Constantine, he restored imperial rule in the Italian Peninsula and Africa. His most enduring achievements are Hagia Sophia and the *Corpus Iuris Civilis*.

Juvenal (a.k.a. **Decimus Junius Juvenalis**; c. 60–140): Roman lawyer and satirist whose surviving 16 satires represent a fraction of his poems in five books.

Kartir Hangirpe, (c. 240–280): Religious advisor to Shahs Shāpūr I, Hormizd I, and Bahrām I. He reorganized Iranian religious practices and stressed the universal, aniconic worship of Ahura Mazdā, claiming to have restored the pure teachings of Zoroaster. He also opposed Mani and likely instigated the arrest and crucifixion of Mani in 276. *See* **Zoroaster**.

Lactantius (a.k.a. **Lucius Caecilius Firmianus Lactantius**; c. 240–320): Roman rhetor and tutor to Crispus, eldest son of Constantine I. Born in Roman Africa, he taught rhetoric at Nicomedia. In about 315, he composed *On the Deaths of the Persecutors* (*De mortibus persecutorum*), the prime source for and the earliest report of the conversion of Constantine in 312.

Leo I (a.k.a. **Leo the Great**; c. 400–461): Pope (440–461), politician, and theologian. Born in Tuscany, he laid the foundations of the medieval papacy. He composed the *Tome* in 449, the first major Latin work on the nature of Christ; it was accepted as canonical at the Council of Chalcedon (451). He persuaded Attila the Hun to withdraw from Italy in 452, thereby making the papacy the moral authority of the Roman West.

Libanius of Antioch (314–394): Pagan rhetorician and sophist of Antioch who trained talented young men, pagan and Christian, destined for imperial service. He was friend to the emperor Julian II, and yet he was allowed to present an oration protesting the desecration of temples in 383–388 to Theodosius I. Sixty-four orations of Libanius—along with commentaries, rhetorical exercises, and over 1,500 letters—have survived.

Licinius I (a.k.a. **Gaius Valerius Licianus Licinius**; c. 263–325; r. 308–324): A veteran officer, Licinius was elevated as Augustus of the West by Galerius after Severus II had been defeated and executed by Maxentius. In 311, Licinius succeeded to the Balkan provinces. In 313, he contracted an alliance with Constantine and married Constantine's half-sister Constantia. That same year, he defeated Maximinus II Daza and took over the eastern provinces. Twice—in 314 and 323–324—Licinius clashed with Constantine. Licinius was defeated and deposed by Constantine in 324; he was executed in 325. Licinius issued jointly with Constantine the Edict of Milan in 313. Initially tolerant of Christians, Licinius was criticized for persecution of Christians during his final war with Constantine.

Lucian of Samosata (c. 125–180): Greek satirist and brilliant prose stylist, he composed works on religious themes, including *Dialogues of the Gods*, *Banquet of Philosophers*, and a life of the false prophet Alexander of Abonouteichos.

Loukas of Cyrene (d. 116): Messianic leader of the Jewish rebellion in Cyrene in 115–116.

Macarius (c. 300–390) Saint and Egyptian ascetic who established *lavrae* ("cells") whereby holy men could live in support of each other—an innovation that led to the establishment of monastic houses.

Macrobius (a.k.a. **Ambrosius Theodosius Macrobius**; 395–423): Pagan grammarian and Neoplatonic philosopher. He wrote *Saturnalia*, a learned discussion on literary and religious topics set in the house of his patron Vettius Agorius Praetextatus. He also wrote a commentary on the "Dream of Scipio" in Cicero's *De re publica*.

Magnentius (a.k.a. **Flavius Magnus Magnentius**; c. 303–353; r. 350–353): Born of a German family settled in Gaul, Magnentius commanded the cavalry under Constans. In 350, the Western army revolted, declaring Magnentius emperor and slaying Constans. In the ensuing civil war, Constantius II defeated Magnentius, who committed suicide. The fighting weakened defenses on the Rhine so that in 355–357, Franks and Alemanni overran Gaul.

Magnus Maximus (a.k.a. **Flavius Magnus Maximus**; c. 335–388; r. 383-388): Soldier who rose in the service of Count Theodosius and then Emperor Gratian. In 380, he succeeded to the command of the army of Britain. In response to the antipagan laws, in 383, Magnus Maximus rebelled and invaded Gaul. Gratian was deserted and murdered. In 387, Magnus Maximus invaded the Italian Peninsula so that Valentinian II fled to Constantinople. In 388, Theodosius I defeated Magnus Maximus at the Battle on the Save. He fled to Aquileia, surrendered, and was executed.

Mani (216–276): Prophet and founder of the dualist monotheistic religion Manichaeism. Born into a community of Elcesaites, an ascetic sect of Judaizing Christians, near Ctesiphon in Babylonia, between 218 and 228 Mani experienced mystical visions, and in 240–242 he traveled to India, where he might have conversed with Buddhist monks. He returned to Persia and gained favor at the court of Shāpūr I. His teaching, however, offended Kartir and the strict Zoroastrians, who likely contrived his arrest and crucifixion by Shah Bahrām I in 276. Mani's writings, originally written in Syriac, have survived in translations.

Marc Antony (a.k.a. **Marcus Antonius**; c. 83–30 B.C.): Lieutenant of Julius Caesar and triumvir in 44–31 B.C., he ruled the Roman East after 44 B.C.; his defeat at Actium and subsequent suicide marked the end of the Roman civil wars.

Marcian (a.k.a. **Flavius Valerius Marcianus**; c. 390–457; r. 450–457): An officer of Illyrian origin, Marcian was elected to the Senate of Constantinople. In 450, the empress Aelia Pulcheria married Marcian, who was hailed Eastern Roman emperor. Marcian refused payment of tribute to Attila the Hun, reformed the Eastern army, and presided over the Fourth Ecumenical Council (451).

Marcion of Sinope (c. 85–160): Christian theologian and editor of the New Testament. In 143–144 he emigrated to Rome. He produced his own edited version of the New Testament based on the letters of Paul and the Gospel of Luke. His teachings were rejected and condemned at the first reported synod at Rome, presided over by Pope Anicetus. Marcion then founded his own church that flourished into the 5th century.

Marcus Aurelius (a.k.a. **Marcus Annius Verus** or **Marcus Aurelius Antoninus**; 121–180; r. 161–180): Son of Annius Verus and nephew of Emperor Antoninus Pius (r. 138–161). He was adopted by Antoninus Pius in 138 and was promoted to Caesar (heir apparent) in 139. A brilliant general, modest ruler, and conscientious administrator, Marcus Aurelius is regarded as the best of the Five Good Emperors. His *Meditations* are letters on the oral precepts of Stoic philosophy.

Maternus Cynegius (d. 388): Christian from Spain who rose in the service of Theodosius I. As prefect of the East (384–388), he initiated riots by monks against pagan temples and synagogues. In protest, the pagan rhetorician Libanius wrote his *Pro templis* (*On the Temples*), an oration delivered to Theodosius I.

Maxentius (a.k.a. **Marcus Valerius Maxentius**; c. 278–312; r. 306–312 A.D.): Son of Maximianus, Maxentius revolted at Rome and declared himself emperor after he had been denied the succession by Galerius. Maxentius controlled Italy and Africa. In 312, he was defeated and slain by Constantine at the Battle of Milvian Bridge.

Maximianus (a.k.a. **Marcus Aurelius Valerius Maximianus**; c. 250–310; r. 286–305): A Pannonian comrade of Diocletian, Maximianus was promoted as Augustus in the West. He abdicated in 305 but reentered politics, first as co-emperor with his son Maxentius and then with his son-in-law Constantine. He committed suicide at Massilia in 310 after he failed to raise a revolt against Constantine.

Maximinus II Daza (a.k.a. **Galerius Valerius Maximinus Daia**; c. 270–313; r. 309–313): Nephew of Galerius, he was named Caesar of the East in 305. Devoted to the old gods, Maximinus persecuted Christians. In 309, he proclaimed himself Augustus and warred against Galerius and later Licinius. In 313, defeated by Licinius, he died a refugee at Tarsus.

Maximinus I Thrax (a.k.a. **Gaius Julius Verus Maximinus**; 173–238; r. 235–238) A Thracian peasant who rose through the ranks to the equestrian order. In 235, he was proclaimed emperor after the murder of Severus Alexander. His reign marked the inception of 50 years of civil wars. The first soldier-emperor of low social origins, Maximinus was detested by the landed classes despite his success in waging frontier wars. In 238, a revolt that began in Africa and spread to Rome precipitated his downfall.

Maximus of Ephesus (d. 372): Neoplatonist philosopher and student of Porphyry. He instructed the future emperor Julian in philosophy and theurgy at Pergamon in 351–352.

Melito of Sardis (d. c. 180): Perhaps bishop of Sardis, he wrote an apology in Greek addressed to Emperor Marcus Aurelius. He also expressed his anxiety over Judaism and so reflected the fact that Jews occupied a favored position at Sardis.

Minucius Felix (c. 150–270): This otherwise anonymous figure wrote the earliest surviving Latin apology, *Octavius*, set as a debate between Christian Octavius and pagan Caecilius Natalis.

Montanus (c. 150–200): Credited with apocalyptic revelations from the Holy Spirit either in 157 or 172, Montanus and his associates, Maximilla and Priscilla, offered a so-called New Prophecy that promised redemption only to the elect. Montanus challenged the authority of bishops in apostolic churches, who condemned Montanus as a heretic and convert from paganism. Montanist churches, however, survived in Asia Minor into the 7th century.

Nero (a.k.a. **Lucius Domitius Ahenobarbus**; 37–68; r. 54–68): The last Julio-Claudian emperor. Nero was the son of Gnaeus Domitius Ahenobarbus and Agrippina the Younger (the great-granddaughter of Augustus). In 49, his mother married Claudius and secured Nero's adoption as Claudius's heir. Nero took the name Nero Claudius Caesar. In 54, Nero succeeded as emperor, but he craved popularity as an artist and therefore entrusted the affairs of state to his ministers down to 62, when he assumed direct control. By his amoral and outrageous conduct, he alienated the ruling classes and legions and thus precipitated his downfall and suicide in 68. In 64, Nero ordered the first persecution of Christians at Rome.

Nestorius (b. c. 386): Brilliant theologian at Antioch who, on the recommendation of Theodosisus II, was elevated to patriarch of Constantinople (429–431). He taught that Mary was Christokos, or mother of the human nature of Christ. His views were condemned at the Third Ecumenical Council (431); he was deposed and exiled. His followers established a Nestorian church in Persian Mesopotamia or rejoined the imperial church under the Formula of Reunion (433).

Nonnus of Panopolis (c. 375–425): Pagan poet of a prominent Greco-Egyptian family who composed the epic *Dionysiaca,* the myths and traditions of the god Dionysus.

Octavian: *See* **Augustus**.

Odenathus (a.k.a. **Septimius Odenathus**; r. 262–267): Merchant prince of the caravan city Palmyra, Roman senator, and Roman general (*dux*). He imposed his authority over the Roman eastern frontier after the capture of Valerian I in 260. In 262, he imposed a treaty on Shah Shāpūr I. He was murdered at Emesa.

Opamonas (fl. 2nd century A.D.): Leading citizen of Rhodiapolis who listed on his funerary monument gifts totaling nearly 500,000 denarii to the cities and sanctuaries of Lycia between 114 and 153. Opromoas epitomizes the values of *philopatris* and *philotimia* in the Roman age.

Origen (185–254): Brilliant Christian theologian. Born at Alexandria of a Christian family and studied under Saint Clement, whom he succeeded as head of the Catechetical School. He was sent a number of diplomatic missions by Bishop Demetrius of Alexandria. In 230, Origen removed himself to Caesarea Maritima because Demetrius protested Origen's ordination. Origen wrote numerous commentaries on books of the Bible and pastoral works, establishing the discipline of exegesis and typology. In 215–217, Origen composed *On First Principles*, the first serious theological work that reconciled Christian faith and Platonic philosophy. He also produced the *Hexapla*, a study of the Hebrew and Greek texts of the Old Testament. His views on cosmology and salvation were later condemned at the Fifth Ecumenical Council in 553.

Ovid (a.k.a. **Pubius Ovidius Naso**; 43 B.C.–17 A.D.): Poet and lawyer who initiated the silver age of Latin literature. Born at Sulmona, he was in A.D. 8 banished by Emperor Augustus to the city of Tomi (Constantia) on the Black Sea. A prolific writer, he composed *Metamorphoses*, an epic poem on Greek and Roman mythology, and *Fasi*, on the holidays of the Roman sacred calendar.

Pachomius (c. 290–346): Saint and pagan convert to Christianity who undertook an ascetic life, founding the first monastery at Tabennesi in Upper Egypt in 323.

Patrick (c. 387–460): Saint and son of a Roman decurion who was enslaved by Irish pirates at age 16; he escaped to Gaul and entered the monastery of Lerins. Commissioned apostle to the Irish, Patrick sailed to Ireland in around 432 or 433 and preached in Ulster, establishing a church at Armagh.

Paul (a.k.a. **Paul of Tarsus**; c. 5–67): Saint and early Christian writer and missionary. Born to wealthy Pharisee family with Roman citizenship, after his conversion on the road to Damascus in about 35, Paul defined the universal message of Jesus as the conversion of the wider pagan world. He conducted three missions establishing churches in the Greek cities of Asia Minor and Greece in 46–48, 49–52, and 53–57. At the council of Jerusalem (c. 48), Peter and James the Righteous accepted Pauline converts in a compromise. Paul was arrested and imprisoned at Caesarea Maritima in 58–59. He was conveyed to Rome and martyred in the wake of the Great Fire. His seven Epistles (Romans, 1 and 2 Corinthians, Galatians, 1 Thessalonians, Philippians, and Philemon) are fundamental to Christian theology.

Paulus Orosius (375–418): Christian apologist who studied under Saint Augustine of Hippo. Orosius wrote *History against the Pagans*, a work in seven books, to refute pagan critics who said that abandonment of the worship of the gods led to Rome's decline. Orosius's apology is a detailed narrative listing disasters suffered by pagans due to their ignorance of God and the true faith.

Pausanias (fl. late 2nd century A.D.): Greek author of the *Description of Greece*, a tour guide to the sites and shrines of Greece in the Roman age. It is filled with information about heroes, gods, and cult practices.

Peregrinus Proteus (c. 95–165): Cynic philosopher born at Parium, Mysia. According to Lucian, Peregrinus had contact with early Christians and adopted the ascetic life of an itinerant Cynic. His abusive and outrageous conduct earned him expulsion from Rome on the order of Emperor Antoninus Pius. At the Olympic Games in 165, he immolated himself just east of the sanctuary.

Peter (a.k.a. **Simon Cephas**; d. c. 67): Saint and one of the 12 original disciples of Jesus Christ. Born Bethsida in the Galilee, Peter figures as the leading apostle in the Synoptic Gospels, and he was the first to enter the empty tomb of Jesus. He actively proselytized in the Levant after the crucifixion and, according to the Acts of the Apostles, supported the admission of Pauline converts at the Council of Jerusalem in the year 48. He arrived at Rome in about 63 and was martyred, along with Saint Paul, in the persecutions after the Great Fire.

Philip I (a.k.a. **Philip the Arab** or **Marcus Julius Philippus**; r. 244–249): An equestrian of Arabian origin who succeeded Timisitheus as Praetorian prefect of Gordian III in 243. Philip instigated the murder of Gordian and so succeeded as emperor. He concluded a treaty with Shāpūr at the price of 500,000 aurei. Philip faced rebellions in Pannonia and the East in protest to his fiscal exactions. In 249, he was defeated and slain by Trajan Decius, who had been hailed emperor by the Danube legions.

Philip the Evangelist (fl. c. 35–80): Saint and one of the seven deacons of the Jerusalem church, who converted Simon Magus and the Ethiopian eunuch at Gaza. He preached in the cities of Samaria, and later traditions placed him and his four virgin daughters, who were prophetesses, at Hierapolis (Pamukkale) in Asia Minor.

Philo of Alexandria (c. 15 B.C.–45 A.D.): Jewish thinker and Platonist who headed the prosperous Jewish community of Alexandria and represented Jewish interests in the embassy to Emperor Caligula in protest of the laws requiring sacrifice in A.D. 39–40. A prolific writer, Philo used Platonic analysis and schemes in *On the Creation* to elucidate the Jewish faith and so set the model for Christian Platonic thinkers.

Philostratus (a.k.a. **Lucius Flavius Philostratus**; c. 170–247): Athenian sophist and stylist associated with the court of the empress Julia Domna, wife of Septimius Severus. His works include *Lives of the Sophists* and a biography of Apollonius of Tyana, the Neopythagorean magician and miracle worker of the 1st century. His *Life of Apollonius* is sometimes regarded as a response to the Gospels.

Plato (428–348 B.C.): Athenian philosopher and disciple of Socrates (470–399 B.C.) who founded the Academy and defined Western philosophy. He was from a noble family and despised the Athenian democracy. His dialogue *Timaeus*, composed around 360 B.C., defined all subsequent Greek and Roman speculation on cosmology and morality. His philosophical dialogues also set the standard of literary Attic Greek prose.

Pliny the Younger (a.k.a. **Caius Caeilius Plinus Secundus**; 61–112): Roman senator from northern Italy and adopted son of a famous naturalist, Pliny penned letters to Emperor Trajan that reveal the workings of civic life in Asia Minor during the Roman peace.

Plotinus (205–270): Born at Lycopolis, Egypt. Plotinus gained the favor of Emperor Gallienus. He defined Neoplatonism, and his disciple Porphyry compiled Plotinus's teachings into the *Enneads*. Plotinus's vision of the Great Chain of Being and synthesis of Platonic thought provided the intellectual basis for the revival of the pagan cults by Emperor Julian (360–363).

Plutarch of Chaeronea (c. 45–120): Platonic philosopher, biographer, and scholar born at Chaeronea, Boeotia, in central Greece. He studied at both Athens and Rome and was a friend of Emperor Trajan. His works include the *Moralia*, 60 essays on a wide range of topics, and *Parallel Lives of Greeks and Romans*.

Polycarp of Smyrna (fl. 2nd century A.D.): Saint and bishop martyred at an uncertain date during a persecution in c. 150–155. He established the role of bishops in apostolic churches and was in the forefront of fixing the Christian canon by editing the books of the New Testament.

Pompey (a.k.a. **Gnaeus Pompeius Magnus**; 106–48 B.C.): The most talented of Sulla's lieutenants, Pompey rose to be the most celebrated general of the late Roman Republic by series of extraordinary commands. He sided with the Senate against Julius Caesar in 49 B.C., and he was defeated at Pharsalus (48 B.C.) and fled to Egypt, where he was treacherously murdered.

Pontius Pilate (r. 26–36): Roman procurator of Judaea and fifth equestrian governor of Roman Palestine (Judaea and Samaria, notorious for his inept and venal rule. In the Synoptic Gospels, Pilate is presented as reluctant to order the crucifixion of Jesus.

Porphyry of Tyre (c. 232–304): Greek Neoplatonic philosopher who wrote a life of his mentor, the philosopher Plotinus, a work *Against the Christians* (15 books), and a historical chronicle from the fall of Troy to about A.D. 270.

Posidonius of Apamea (135–51 B.C.): Stoic philosopher, historian, and astronomer who studied under Panaetius at Athens. Favorable to Rome, he traveled the lands of the western Mediterranean, writing on geography and ethnography. In his philosophical writings, he refined Plato's doctrine on the soul (*pysche*) and Stoic cosmology.

Praetextatus (a.k.a. **Vettius Agorius Praetextatus**; (315–384): An illustrious pagan senator who was urban prefect in 367 and Praetorian prefect in 384. He and his equally illustrious wife Aconia Fabia Paulina patronized the cults of Rome, protested the anti-pagan legislation of Gratian and Valentinian II, and sponsored traditional letters.

Priscilla and **Maximilla** (fl. mid-2nd century A.D.): Prophetesses and associates of Montanus, through whom the Paraclete (Holy Spirit) was believed to have spoken.

Proclus (c. 410–485): Brilliant Neoplatonic thinker and theurgist who was born of wealthy family in Lycia but studied in Athens under Syrianus and succeeded the latter as head of the Academy in Athens. His *Elements of Theology, Platonic Theology*, and *Elements of Physics* are the climax of Greek philosophical thinking. He composed commentaries on Plato's *Timaeus* and *Alcibiades I*, as well as religious hymns.

Quintus of Smyrna (fl. 4th century A.D.): Pagan poet who composed the epic *Posthomerica*, a work of more than 20,000 lines (twice the length of the *Iliad* and the *Odyssey* combined), which told of events at Troy after Homer's epic leaves off.

Rufinus of Aquileia (c. 350–410): Roman monk who translated Greek theological and historical writings into Latin. In 372, he traveled to Alexandria and then resettled at Jerusalem, where he disputed with Saint Jerome the doctrines of Origen. In 397, Rufinus returned to Rome and translated and adapted into Latin Origen's *On First Principles*.

Salutius (c. 340–370): Author of the Latin treatise *On the Gods and the Cosmos*, a pagan defense of theurgy. A friend to Emperor Julian II, Salutius is sometimes identified with Flavius Salutius, prefect of Gaul (361–363) and consul (363), or with Saturninius Secundus Salutius, Praetorian prefect of the East (361–367), who declined the emperorship after the death of Julian.

Seneca (a.k.a. **Lucius Annaeus Seneca**; 1 B.C.–A.D. 65): Stoic philosopher and tutor of Emperor Nero who was born of a noble Hispano-Roman family of Cordoba. He was exiled from Rome by Emperor Claudius in 41. Agrippina the Younger, fourth wife of Claudius, had Seneca recalled in 49 as a tutor to the future emperor Nero. In 54–62, Seneca and Lucius Afranius Burrus, the Praetorian prefect, acted as regent ministers for Nero. Seneca retired in 62 and was implicated in the Pisonian Conspiracy of 65. He was forced to commit suicide. Seneca wrote philosophical essays, moral letters, and tragedies. He epitomized the Stoic philosopher in public service during the Principate.

Septimius Severus (a.k.a. **Lucius Sepimius Severus**; 146–211; r. 193–211): A native of Lepcis Magna, Africa, who became legate of Upper Pannonia in 193. In 193–195, he defeated his rivals in the second civil war of imperial Rome and founded the Severan dynasty. Septimius Severus made harsh reprisals against his opponents in the Senate, but he secured the frontiers and forged links with the provincial elites, especially those in the East and Africa. He was succeeded by his sons Caracalla and Geta.

Severus Alexander (a.k.a. **Marcus Aurelius Severus Alexander**; 208–235; r. 222–235): Son of Julia Mamaea and the senator Gessius Marcianus, he was the last Severan emperor. In 221, he was promoted to Caesar by his cousin Emperor Elagabalus (r. 218–222), whose devotion to the orgiastic rites of the Syrian sun god of Emesa compromised the dynasty. In contrast, Severus Alexander ruled judiciously under the guidance of his mother, Julia Mamaea. His inconclusive wars against the Persians and Germans led to his assassination by mutinous soldiers of the Rhine army.

Severus II (a.k.a. **Flavius Valerius Severus**; c. 260–307; r. 306–307): An Illyrian officer who was created by Caesar of the West by Galerius in 305. In 306, after the death of Constantius I, Galerius elevated Severus II to Augustus of the West. In 307, Severus invaded the Italian Peninsula, but his soldiers defected, and he fell into the hands of Maxentius, who executed him.

Shāpūr I (r. 241–272): The second Sāsānid shah of Persia, who waged three successful campaigns against the Roman Empire (242–244, 253–255, and 258–260). In 260, he captured Emperor Valerian. He sacked Antioch, the third city of the Roman Empire, in either 253 or 260. Odenathus, prince of Palmyra, compelled Shāpūr to negotiate a peace.

Shāpūr II (r. 309–379): Sāsānid shah of Persia who pursued aggressive policies against Armenia and Rome. In 255–261, he waged a desultory frontier war over the Roman fortresses of Mesopotamia. In 363, he checked the invasion of Julian and compelled Jovian to surrender the strategic fortresses of Mesopotamia, thereby giving Persia the initiative in future wars against Rome.

Shimon bar Kokhba (a.k.a. **Simon ben Kosiba**; r. 132–135): Ruler of Judaea during the Second Jewish Revolt. He was accepted as Messiah by the rabbi Akbia, but in later rabbinical writings he was denounced as Simon bar Kozeba ("son of lies").

Simon Magus (fl. 1ˢᵗ century A.D.): Samaritan magician and convert to Christianity. Simon was accused by Saint Peter of sales of offices (that is, the sin of simony) in Acts 8:9–24). Christian authors condemned Simon as the founder of heresy. Gnostic apocryphal works were attributed to Simon and his reputed followers, the Simonians.

Symeon Stylites (c. 390–459): Christian ascetic who followed the example of Saint Antony. During his last 37 years, he spent his life atop a pillar east of Antioch as a symbol of his withdrawal from the world. He was hailed as the most pious saint of the Roman East, respected by the emperors Theodosius II and Marcian.

Symeon Stylites the Younger (521–597): Born at Antioch, he survived the great plague and so dedicated himself to an ascetic life in imitation of his namesake, living atop a pillar for 68 years.

Symmachus (a.k.a. **Quintus Aurelius Symmachus**; c. 340–402): The most distinguished Roman pagan senator of the 4ᵗʰ century and an accomplished man of letters. He served as proconsul of Africa (373), urban prefect (384–385), and consul (391). He presided over the pagan cultural and literary revival of Rome. In a series of orations (*relationes*), he pleaded for the restoration of the Altar of Victory to the Senate house (*Curia*) in 382–390. He supported Magnus Maximus in 387–388, but Theodosius pardoned him, and he retired from public life after 391.

Synesius of Cyrene (373–414): Philosopher and bishop of Ptolemais, Synesius studied philosophy at Alexandria under Hypatia and then at Athens in 395–399. He was drawn to embrace Christianity through philosophy, and in 410 he was ordained bishop. Besides his philosophical writings, Synesius urged the emperors Arcadius and Theodosius II to discontinue the use of Germanic tribal regiments in favor of native Roman soldiers.

Tacitus (a.k.a. **Publius Cornelius Tacitus**; 56–after 120): From a northern Italian or southern Gallic provincial family, Tacitus entered a senatorial career under Vespasian. In 77, he married Julia, daughter of Gnaeus Julius Agricola. In 97, he was consul, and in 112–113, he was proconsul of Asia. He is the greatest historian of imperial Rome. He wrote *Annals* and *Histories*, covering the periods 14–68 and 68–96, respectively. He also wrote *Germania*, *Agricola*, and *Dialogus de oratoribus*. In *Annals*, Tacitus reports the persecution of Christians by Nero in 64.

Tatian (c. 120–180) translated the Gospels from Greek into Syriac. His *Diatessaron* was a single narrative reconciling the four Gospels.

Tertullian (a.k.a **Quintus Septimius Florens Tertullianus**; c. 160–c. 220): Lawyer and Christian apologist at Carthage who wrote the first major Christian works in Latin. Of foremost importance was his *Apology*, defending Christianity.

Thecla (fl. mid 1st century A.D.): A legendary female apostle mentioned in the *Apocryphal Acts of Saints Paul and Thecla*, written in 2nd century A.D., perhaps by a Montanist. She was an early convert of Paul at Iconium, rejecting marriage and living an ascetic life. She miraculously escaped the arena at Pisidian Antioch and established ascetic communities at Iconium (modern Konya), Seleucia ad Calycadnum (Silifke), and Nicomedia (Izmit). Her tomb near Seleucia became a celebrated pilgrimage site in the 4th century.

Themistius of Constantinople (317–391): Pagan rhetorician and philosopher born of a noble family in Asia Minor, he was a loyal servant at Constantinople to successive emperors between Constantius II (r. 337–361) and Theodosius I (r. 379–395). Constantius II elected Themistius, although a pagan, into the Christian senate of Constantinople (355). Themistius served as proconsul (358) and urban prefect (359–360). He favored Julian II, but he was respected as the senior pagan senator by Julian's Christian successors. Thirty-six orations of Themistius have survived, but his philosophical works and commentaries survive only in fragments.

Theodore of Sykeon (d. 613): A healing saint of Galatia and bishop of Anastasiopolis, he was famous for his miracles and exorcisms that inspired pagan villagers to convert.

Theodosius I (a.k.a. **Theodosius the Great**; c. 346–395; r. 379–395): The son of Count Theodosius, a leading general of Valentinian I, Theodosius rose to high command under Gratian. In 379, as Augustus of the East, Theodosius restored order in the Roman East. In 387, he married Galla, sister of Valentinian II (r. 375–392). In return, Theodosius defeated the usurper Magnus Maximus (r. 383–388), who had overthrown the Western emperor Gratian. A devout Nicene Christian, Theodosius summoned the Second Ecumenical Council in 381 and outlawed pagan sacrifices in 391–392. He faced a revolt of the Western army in 392–394. By the victory at Frigidus (394), Theodoius crushed the rebels and reunited the Roman Empire.

Theodosius II (a.k.a. **Flavius Theodosius**; 401–450; r. 408–450): The son of Aracdius and Eudocia, Theodosius succeeded as a minor. He proved a weak emperor directed by his older sister, Aelia Pulcheria, and his ministers, who were responsible for the Theodosian Walls, the *Theodosian Code* (438), and the Third Ecumenical Council (431).

Theophilus of Antioch (d. c. 183): Bishop who wrote the apology *Ad autolycum*, in which he advanced the doctrine of creation *ex nihilo* and a doctrine of the Trinity.

Thrasea Paetus (a.k.a. **Publius Clodius Thrasea Paetus**; c. 20–66): Roman senator and leading Stoic critic of Nero. Born at Patavium, he was *consul suffectus* in 56 and in 59 retired from the Senate in criticism of Nero's murder of his mother Agrippina and other outrageous conduct. In 66, Thrasea Paetus, perceived as the inspiration behind the Pisonian Conspiracy of 65, was forced to commit suicide on the orders of Nero.

Tiberius (a.k.a. **Tiberius Claudius Nero**; 42 B.C.–A.D. 37; r. A.D. 14–37): The son of Livia Drusilla and her first husband Tiberius Claudius Nero (praetor in 42 B.C.), he was reared in the household of his stepfather Augustus. Tiberius was ill suited for the role of emperor; he withdrew to Capri and fell into depravity. During his reign, the crucifixion of Jesus occurred.

Tiberius Julius Alexander (fl. 1st century A.D.): Born in the reign of Tiberius, he renounced his Judaism and entered imperial service, serving as procurator of Judaea (46–48) and prefect of Egypt (68–69). He first declared for Vespasian as emperor in the civil war of 69 and served on the staff of Titus at the siege of Jerusalem.

Timothy (d. c. 80): The associate of Saint Paul during his second (49–52) and third (56–57) missions to the churches of Asia Minor and Greece. He is the recipient of Paul's Epistles 1 and 2 Timothy and possible author of many of the Deutero-Pauline letters in the New Testament. He was later reported to have been bishop of Ephesus (65–80), a tradition likely based on the chronicle of Hegesippus.

Tiridates III (250–339; r. 285–339): Arsacid king of Armenia who was a loyal ally of Rome in the wars against the Persians. In 301, he reportedly converted to Christianity and was baptized by Gregory the Illuminator. There is reason to believe that Tiridates might have converted after the conversion of Emperor Constantine I.

Thomas Didymus (fl. 1st century A.D.): Saint and one of Jesus Christ's 12 apostles, he was known as Doubting Thomas upon seeing Jesus after the resurrection (John 20:28). In the *Acts of Saint Thomas*, written in the early 2nd century A.D., Thomas was credited with missions to the cities of India and to the Parthian Empire. The reports are plausible, and Thomas would have traveled on ships crossing the Erythraean Sea (Indian Ocean). Thomas is thus the first apostle to have preached outside the Roman Empire.

Trajan (a.k.a. **Marcus Ulpius Traianus**; 52–117; r. 98–117): The son of the senator and namesake of a Hispano-Roman family of Italica. Trajan was adopted by Nerva (r. 96–98) and so succeeded as the first Roman emperor of provincial origin. Trajan conquered Dacia (101–102; 105–106), smashed Parthian power (113–117), and brought the Roman Empire to its territorial zenith. He initiated a spectacular building program at Rome. Hailed *optimus princeps*, Trajan founded the third dynasty of imperial Rome and was succeeded by his adopted son, Hadrian.

Trajan Decius (a.k.a. **Gaius Messius Quintus Traianus Decius**; 201–251; r. 249–251): A Pannonian provincial who attained senatorial rank under Severus Alexander and legate of Upper Pannonia, he was declared emperor by the Danube legions. He defeated and slew the emperor Philip at Verona in 249. Trajan Decius was defeated and slain by the Goths at Abrittus in Lower Moesia. He initiated the first empire-wide persecution of Christians in 250–251.

Trebonianus Gallus (a.k.a. **Gaius Vibius Trebonianus Gallus**; r. 251–253): A legate of Trajan Decius, he was declared emperor by the Roman army after Decius's death. Gallus faced attacks by northern barbarians and Persians. In 253, he was defeated and slain by Aemilian, governor of Moesia, whom the Danube legions had declared emperor.

Ulfilas (a.k.a. **Wulfila**; 311–381): Arian bishop of the Goths consecrated at the synod of Antioch in 341. As missionary to the Goths, Ulfilas adapted the Greek alphabet to Gothic and translated the Bible into Gothic in 341–343.

Valens (a.k.a. **Flavius Valens**; c. 328–378; r. 364-378): Born of a military family in Pannonia, he served under Julian and Jovian. In 364, his brother Valentinian I created Valens emperor of the East. A devoted Arian Christian, Valens faced opposition from the Nicene bishops. His Persian war was inconclusive. In 378, he was decisively defeated and slain by the Goths at Adrianople.

Valentinian I (a.k.a. **Flavius Valentinianus**; 321–375; r. 364–375): Born to a Pannonian military family, he was a senior officer acclaimed emperor by the Eastern army after the death of Jovian. Valentinian appointed his brother Valens emperor of the East and campaigned against the Germans on the Rhine and Upper Danube, where he strengthened fortifications. He was succeeded by his two sons, Gratian (r. 367–383) and Valentinian II (r. 375–392).

Valentinian II (a.k.a. **Flavius Valentinianus**; 371–392; r. 375–392): The son of Valentinian and Justina and half-brother of Gratian. In 375, he was declared joint emperor and resided at Mediolaunum (Milan) under the influence of his mother and Bishop Ambrose of Milan. Reared as a staunch Nicene, Valentinian supported anti-pagan measures that precipitated the revolt of Magnus Maximus. In 387, he fled to Constantinople and allied with Theodosius I against Magnus Maximus. In 388–392, Valentinian was restored as emperor of the West, and he was murdered on the orders of Arbogast.

Valentinus (c. 100–160): A noted Gnostic teacher and thinker born at Alexandria who founded school at Rome. His dualist cosmology, based on allegorical myths and middle Platonic principles, were rejected by Christians as heretical. The *Gospel of Truth*, among the texts found at Nag Hammadi, was penned by Valentinus.

Valerian I (a.k.a. **Publius Licinius Valerianus**; c. 195–260; r. 253–260): A senator of noble origins who became legate of Raetia in the civil war of 253. He was proclaimed emperor by the Rhine legions and defeated his rival Aemilian. Valerian issued the second empire-wide persecution of Christians in 258–260. Valerian faced barbarian assaults along the northern and eastern frontiers. He waged two Persian wars (253–256 and 258–260). He was treacherously captured by Shah Shāpūr in 260 and died in captivity.

Vetranio (d. c. 360; r. 350): Officer of the Illyrian army who was proclaimed emperor by his army in opposition to Magnentius. Vetranio checked Magnentius's advance, declared his loyalty to Constantius II, and abdicated and retired when Constantius II arrived. Vetranio minted the first coins carrying the labarum with the Latin inscription *In hoc signo victor eris*, the words Constantine was reported to have seen before the Battle of Milvian Bridge in 312.

Vergil (a.k.a. **Publius Vergilius Maro**; 70–19 B.C.): One of the most important poets of ancient Rome. Born at Mantua in Cisalpine Gaul (northern Italy), he was a friend of Horace. His patrons included Maecenas, Asinius Pollio, and Augustus. A poetic genius, Vergil composed the national Roman epic, the *Aeneid* and the pastoral poems *Eclogues* (or *Bucolics*) and *Georgics*. He shares with Horace the rank of poet laureate of the Augustan court.

Vigilius (r. 537–555): Pope elected with the support Empress Theodora so that he could work for religious unity with the Monophysites. An exile at Constantinople after the Gothic recapture of Rome in 546, he refused to compromise the papal position and so opposed Justinian at the Fifth Ecumenical Council (553). His arrest, exile, and premature death undermined Justinian's popularity in the Western church.

Xenophon of Ephesus (fl. early 2nd century A.D.): Novelist of the Second Sophistic movement who wrote the *Ephesian Tale*, a fanciful romance between Anthia and Habrocomes. The story provides details of cult practices and social mores in the Roman East.

Zeno (c. 425–491; r, 474-491): An Isaurian officer, he married Ariadne, daughter of Emperor Leo I, and so succeeded as Eastern Roman emperor. He sought reconciliation with the Monophysites by issuing the *Henotikon* (482), and he crushed serious rebellions of the provincial armies.

Zeno of Citium (335–263 B.C.): A merchant turned philosopher and founder of Stoicism. From 301 B.C., he taught in the Stoa Poikile at Athens because he could not afford a proper school. His ethnical and philosophical writings survive in fragments.

Zenobia (a.k.a. **Septimia Zenobia**; r. 267–272): The wife of Odenathus of Palmyra and mother of Vaballathus. In 267, she succeeded her husband's extraordinary position in the Roman East. Styling herself as Empress Augusta, she advanced her son Vaballathus as emperor in 270. In 270–271, Palmyrene forces occupied Asia Minor, Palestine, and Egypt. In 272, she was defeated by Aurelian and allowed to retire to a Campania villa.

Zoroaster (c. 625–550 B.C.): Prophet and reputed author of the oldest *gathas* in the Avesta, therefore claimed as the founder of Zoroastrian monotheism. He was believed to have originated from Eastern Iran. *See* **Kartir Hangirpe**.

Zosimus (c. 480–515): Greek historian who wrote *New History*, in which he attributes the decline of Roman power to the rejection of the gods in favor of Christianity.

Bibliography

Primary Sources

Ammainus Marcellinus. *The Later Roman Empire, A.D. 354–378.* Translated by Walter Hamilton. New York: Penguin/Viking, 1986. An abridged modern translation.

———. *Roman History.* 3 vols. Loeb Classical Library. Translated by C. Rolfe. Cambridge, MA: Harvard University Press, 1939—1950. The complete history of Ammianus with later chronicle *Excerpta Valensiana* included in volume 3.

The Ante-Nicene Fathers: Translations of the Writings of the Fathers down to A.D. 325. Vols. 1–10. Buffalo, NY, 1885–1896. Reprint, Peabody, MA: Henrickson Publishers, 1994. Indispensable translations of all Christian authors prior to the Council of Nicaea.

Apuleius. *The Golden Ass.* Translated by E. J. Kennedy. Baltimore: Penguin Classics, 1999.

Aristides, Aelius. *Aelius Aristides and the Sacred Tales.* Translated by C. A. Behr. Amsterdam, The Netherlands: Adolf M. Hakkert, 1968.

Athanasius. *The Life of Saint Antony and the Letter to Marcellinus.* Translated by R. C. Gregg. Mahwah, NJ: The Paulist Press, 1979.

Augustine. *The City of God against the Pagans.* Translated by R. W. Dyson. Cambridge: Cambridge University Press, 1998. Recommended translation.

———. *Confessions.* Translated by Henry Chadwick. Oxford: Oxford University Press, 2009. Excellent recommended translation and introduction.

Celsus. *On True Doctrine: A Discourse against the Christians.* Translated by R. J. Hoffman. Oxford: Oxford University Press, 1987. Text reconstructed from the quotations by Origen.

Cicero, M. Tullius. *De re publica, de legibus*. Vol. 16 of the Loeb Classical Library. Translated by C. W. Keyes. London: William Heinemann, 1928. "Dream of Scipio" in book 6 of *De re publica* is the most elegant Latin exposition of the Stoic cosmology.

Clement of Alexandria. *Works*. Loeb Classical Library. Translated by G. W. Butterworth. Cambridge, MA: Harvard University Press, 1919.

Copenhaven, Brian P. *Hermetica. The Greek Corpus Hermeticum and the Latin Asclepius in a New English Translation with Notes and Introduction.* Cambridge: Cambridge University Press, 1992. Late antique pagan mystical texts.

Dawes, Elizabeth A. S., and Norman H. Baynes, trans. *Three Byzantine Saints: Contemporary Biographies of Saint Daniel the Stylite, Saint Theodore of Sykeon, and Saint John the Almsgiver.* Yonkers, NY: Saint Vladimir's Seminary Press, 1977. The lives of these three saints of the 6th and 7th centuries are vital sources on the conversion of the countryside.

Doran, Robert, trans. *Stewards of the Poor: The Man of God, Babbula, and Hiba in Fifth-Century Edessa.* Kalamazoo, MI: Cistercian Publications, 2006. Important translation of the role of bishops at Edessa (modern Urfa) as patrons of the power.

Eusebius. *The History of the Church*. Rev. ed. Translated by G. W. Williamson. Baltimore: Penguin Classics, 1990. Recommended translation of this indispensable source.

———. *The Life of Constantine*. Translated by Averil Cameron and Stuart G. Hall. Oxford: Oxford University Press, 1999. Superb edition with excellent notes and introduction.

Gardmer, Iain, and Samuel N. Lieu. *Manichaean Texts from the Roman Empire.* Cambridge: Cambridge University Press, 2004. Definitive modern translations.

Hadot, Pierre. *Plotinus or the Simplicity of Vision*. Translated by Michael Chase. Chicago: University of Chicago Press, 1991. Best modern translation and discussion of Plotinus's mystical vision.

Hardy, Edward R., trans. and ed. *The Christology of the Later Fathers*. Philadelphia: The Westminster Press, 1964. Translations of the crucial texts for the First Four Ecumenical Councils.

Iamblichus of Chalcis. *De mysteriis*. Translated by Emma C. Clarke, John M. Dillon, and J. P. Hershbell. Leiden, The Netherlands: Brill, 2004.

Irenaeus. *Irenaeus of Lyons*. Translated by Robert M. Grant. New York: Routledge, 1996. Recommended modern translation.

———. *Saint Irenaeus of Lyons: Against Heresies*. Reprint ed. N.p.: CreateSpace (www.amazon.com), 2010. Reprint from Alexander Roberts, James Donaldson, and A. Cleveland Coxe, eds. Ante-Nicene Fathers volume.

Josephus. *Antiquities of the Jews*. Vols. 5–11. Loeb Classical Library. Translated by Henry St. John Thackeray and Ralph Marcus. Cambridge, MA: Harvard University Press, 1930–1965. Fundamental source for Jewish history.

Josephus, Flavius. *The Jewish Wars*. Translated by B. Radice. Rev. ed. Baltimore: Penguin Classics, 1984.

Justin Martyr. *Saint Justin Martyr: The First and Second Apologies*. Translated by L. W. Barnard. Mahwah, NJ: Paulist Press, 1996.

Julian. *Works*. 3 vols. Loeb Classical Library. Translated by W. C. Wright. Cambridge, MA: Harvard University Press, 1913–1923.

Lactantius. *On the Manner in Which the Persecutors Died*. Whitefish, MT: Kessinger Publishing, 2004; reprint of the translation from Ante-Nicene Christian Library, vol. 21, edited by Alexander Roberts and James Donaldson. Edinburgh: T and T. Clark, 1871.

Layton, Bentley, trans. and ed. *The Gnostic Scriptures: A New Translation with Annotations and Introductions*. Garden City, NY: Anchor Books. 1995. The indispensable modern translation of Gnostic texts with superb commentary.

Louth, Andrew, and M. Saniforth, ed. and trans. *Early Christian Writings: The Apostolic Fathers*. Baltimore: Penguin Classics, 1987.

Lucian. *On the Syrian Goddess*. Translated by J. J. Lightfoot. Oxford: Oxford University Press, 2005.

―――. *Selected Dialogues*. Translated by Desmond Costa. Oxford: Oxford University Press, 2005. Excellent modern translations especially for the dialogues on Pergerinus and Alexander of Abonouteichos.

―――. *Works*. 8 vols. Loeb Classical Library. Translated by A. M. Harmon. Cambridge, MA: Harvard University Press, 1968–1979. Volume 4 includes the life of Alexander of Abonouteichos.

MacMullen, Ramsay, and Eugene N. Lane, eds. *Paganism and Christianity.* Minneapolis: University of Minnesota Press, 1992. Important translations of many inscriptions, legal texts, and other documents not otherwise available.

Marcus Aurelius. *Meditations*. Translated by M. Hammond. Baltimore: Penguin Classics, 2006. The reflection of the emperor who was the quintessential Stoic.

Musurillo, Herbert, ed. and trans. *Acts of the Christian Martyrs*. Oxford: Clarendon Press, 1972. Recommended translations for the early acts of the Christian martyrs.

Nixon, C. E. V., and Barbara S. Rodgers. *In Praise of Later Roman Emperors: The Panegyrici Latini*. Berkeley: University of California Press, 1994. Translation and discussion of the late Roman panegyrics essential for imperial ideology.

Origen. *On First Principles*. Translated by G. W. Butterworth. New York: Peter Smith Publishers, 1973. Recommended translation.

Philo of Alexandria. *On Creation: Interpretation of Genesis*. Vol. 1. Loeb Classical Library. Translated by F. H. Colson and G. H. Whitaker. Cambridge, MA: Harvard University Press, 1929. Crucial Platonized cosmology of the most learned Jewish scholar of the Roman era.

Philostratus. *The Life of Apollonius of Tyana*. 2 vols. Loeb Classical Library. Translated by C. P. Jones. Cambridge, MA: Harvard University Press, 2005–2006.

Plato. *Timaeus and Critias*. Translated by D. Lee. Baltimore: Penguin Classics, 1972. The indispensable Platonic dialogues on cosmology.

Pliny the Younger. *The Letters of Pliny the Younger*. Translated by B. Radice. Baltimore: Penguin Classics, 1963. Letters, book X, 96–97 contain the exchange between Pliny and Trajan on Christians.

Plotinus. *The Enneads*. Translated by Stephen MacKenna. London: Faber, 1969. Older, literate translation.

Plutarch. *Moralia*. Vol. 5. Loeb Classical Library. Translated by Frank Cole Babbit. Cambridge, MA: Harvard University Press, 1968. Contains Plutarch's essay on the moral and philosophical meaning of the myth of Serapis and Isis.

Porphyry. *Against the Christians: The Literary Remains*. Translated by R. J. Hoffman. Amherst, NY: Prometheus Books, 1994. Reconstructed text of Porphyry's critique.

Procopius. *The Secret History*. Translated by Peter Sarris and G. A. Williamson. Baltimore: Penguin Classics, 2007.

———. *Works*. 7 vols. Loeb Classical Library. Translated by H. B. Dewing. Cambridge, MA: Harvard University Press, 1914–1940. Primary source on the reign of Justinian.

Rees, Roger, ed. and trans. *Diocletian and the Tetrarchy*. Edinburgh: University of Edinburgh Press, 2004. Modern translation of legal texts, inscriptions, and other sources vital for the Great Persecution.

Richardson, Cyril C., ed. *Early Christian Fathers*. New York: Collier Books, 1995. Recommended modern translation of the works of key church fathers before the Council of Nicaea. Excellent introduction and notes.

Tacitus, Cornelius P. *The Annals of Imperial Rome*. Translated by Michael Grant. Baltimore: Penguin Classics, 1956. Includes an eyewitness account of the persecution of 64.

Theophilus of Antioch. *Ad autocylum*. Translated by Robert M. Grant. Oxford: Clarendon Press, 1970.

Tertulllian. *Apologia and De spectaculis*. Minucius Felix. *Octavius*. Loeb Classical Library. Translated by T. R. Glover and Gerald H. Rendall. Cambridge, MA: Harvard University Press, 1931.

Vermes, Geza, trans. *The Complete Dead Sea Scrolls in English*. Rev. ed. Baltimore: Penguin Books, 2004. Excellent translation and introduction by leading scholar.

Wilkinson, John, trans. *Egeria's Travels*. 3rd ed. Warminster: Aris and Phillips, 1999. Translation of the first account of a pilgrimage to the tomb of Saint Thecla and the Holy Land.

Zosimus. *New History*. Translated by Ronald T. Ridley. Sydney: Australian Association for Byzantine Studies, 1982. Modern translation of this polemical pagan historian.

Secondary Literature

Alföldi, Andrew. *A Conflict of Ideas in the Late Roman Empire: The Clash between the Senate and Valentinian*. Translated by Harold Mattingly. Oxford: Clarendon Press, 1979.

————. *The Conversion of Constantine and Pagan Rome*. Translated by Harold Mattingly. Oxford: Oxford University Press, 1948.

Anderson, James C. Jr. *Roman Architecture and Society*. Baltimore: Johns Hopkins University Press, 1997.

Arnold, Edward Vernon. *Roman Stoicism, being Lectures on the History of Stoic Philosophy with Special Reference to its Development within the Roman Empire*. Cambridge: Cambridge University Press, 1911.

Athanassiadi-Fowden, Polymnia. *Julian and Hellenism: An Intellectual Biography*. Oxford: Oxford University Press, 1981. Arguing that Julian was a devotee of Mithras.

Atkins, Margaret, and Robin Osborne, eds. *Poverty in the Roman World*. Cambridge: Cambridge University Press, 2009.

Ayres, Lewis. *Nicaea and Its Legacy: An Approach to Fourth-Century Trinitarian Theology*. Oxford: Oxford University Press, 2004.

Barker, John. *Justinian and the Later Roman Empire*. Madison: University of Wisconsin Press, 1966. Mediocre narrative of the reign.

Barnes, Timothy D. *Athanasius and Constantius: Theology and Politics in the Constantinian Empire*. Cambridge, MA: Harvard University Press, 1993.

————. *Constantine and Eusebius*. Cambridge, MA: Harvard University Press, 1986. Arguing for an implausible rapid conversion of the Roman world.

————. *The New Empire of Diocletian and Constantine*. Cambridge, MA.: Harvard University Press, 1982. Controversial reconstruction of late Roman chronology.

————. *Tertullian: A Historical and Literary Study*. Oxford: Oxford University Press, 1985.

Barrow, Reginald H. *Prefect and Emperor: Relationes*. Oxford: Oxford University Press, 1973. Study with text and discussion on the dispute over the Altar of Victory in 382–390.

Beckwith, John. *Early Christian and Byzantine Art*. New Haven, CT: Yale University Press, 1986.

Bigg, Charles. *The Christian Platonists of Alexandria*. Oxford: Clarendon Press, 1888. Thoughtful essays on Saint Clement and Origen.

Bowersock, G. W. *Augustus and the Greek World*. Oxford: Oxford University Press, 1982.

———. *Greek Sophists in the Roman Empire*. Oxford: Oxford University Press, 2003. Concise introduction to the leading figures of the Second Sophistic movement.

———. *Hellenism in Late Antiquity*. Ann Arbor: University of Michigan Press, 1990.

———. *Julian the Apostate*. Cambridge, MA: Harvard University Press, 1978.

Brandon, S. G. F. *Jesus and the Zealots: A Study of the Political Factor in Primitive Christianity*. New York: Charles Scribner's Sons, 1967. Controversial study on the political aspects of Jesus's teachings; excellent on the turbulent politics of Roman Palestine in the 1st century A.D.

Bregman, Jay. *Synesius of Cyrene, Philosopher-Bishop*. Berkeley: University of California Press, 1982. Model study of the conversion of the pagan intellectual classes in late antiquity.

Brown, Peter. *Augustine of Hippo*. Berkeley: University of California Press, 1967. Brilliant biography evoking the world of the late antiquity; a masterpiece.

————. *The Body and Society: Men, Women, and Sexual Renunciation in Early Christianity*. Rev. ed. New York: Columbia University Press, 2008. Brilliant and recommended discussion of asceticism and spirituality.

————. *The Cult of Saints: Its Rise and Function in Latin Christianity*. Chicago, IL: Chicago University Press, 1981.

————. *The Making of Late Antiquity*. Cambridge, MA: Harvard University Press, 1977. Thoughtful essays on the social and spiritual changes; superb read.

————. *Poverty and Leadership in the Later Roman Empire*. Waltham, MA: Brandeis University Press, 2001. Excellent on the role of bishops in late antiquity.

————. *Power and Persuasion in Late Antiquity: Towards a Christian Empire*. Madison: University of Wisconsin Press, 1992. Concise and masterful analysis of the power of rhetoric.

————. "The Rise and Function of the Holy Man in Late Antiquity." *Journal of Roman Studies* 61 (1971): 80–101; reprinted in *Society and the Holy in Late Antiquity*. Berkeley: University of California Press, 1982. Seminal article.

————. *Society and the Holy in Late Antiquity*. Berkeley: University of California Press, 1982. Reprint of seminal articles.

————. *The World of Late Antiquity: A.D. 150–750*. New York: W. W. Norton and Company, 1989. Concise introduction.

Brown, Raymond E. *The Churches the Apostles Left Behind*. New York: Paulist Press, 1984

————. *An Introduction to New Testament Christology*. New York: Paulist Press, 1994.

Brown, Raymond E., and John P. Meier. *Antioch and Rome: New Testament Cradles of Catholic Christianity*. New York: Paulist Press, 1983. Important scholarly study on the early traditions about Saints Paul and Peter.

Browning, Robert. *Justinian and Theodora*. Piscataway, NJ: Gorgias Press, 2009.

Burckhadt, Jakob. *The Age of Constantine the Great*. Translated by Moses Hadas. Berkeley: University of California Press, 1983. Classic rationalist study by brilliant humanist and scholar of the 19th century.

Burkert, Walter. *Ancient Mystery Cults*. Cambridge, MA: Harvard University Press, 1987.

———. *Greek Religion*. Translated by John Raffan. Cambridge, MA: Harvard University Press, 1985.

———. *Homo Necans: The Anthropology of Ancient Greek Sacrificial Ritual and Myth*. Translated by Peter Bing. Berkeley: University of California Press, 1983. Recommended modern study.

Burrell, Barbara. *Neokoroi: Greek Cities and Roman Emperors*. Leiden, The Netherlands: Brill, 2004. Learned study on the role of the imperial cult in Greek cities.

Cameron, Alan. *The Last Pagans of Rome*. Oxford: Oxford University Press, 2011. Newest and indispensable study of the decline of paganism after the 391–392 laws.

Cameron, Averil. *The Mediterranean World in Late Antiquity: A.D. 395–600*. 2nd ed. New York: Routledge, 2011. Excellent introduction.

Chitty, D. J. *The Desert, A City: A Introduction to the Study of Egyptian and Palestinian Monasticism under the Christian Empire*. Yonkers, NY: St. Vladimir's Seminary Press, 1977.

Chuvin, Pierre. *A Chronicle of the Last Pagans*. Translated by B. A. Archer. Cambridge, MA: Harvard University Press, 1990.

Corcoran, Simon. *The Empire of Tetrarchs: Imperial Pronouncements and Government, A.D. 284–324*. Rev. ed. Oxford: Oxford University Press, 2000.

Cornford, Francis M. *Plato's Cosmology: The Timaeus of Plato*. London: Kegan Paul, Trench, Trubner and Co., 1937; Reprint, Indianopolis: Hackett Publishing, 1997. Outstanding analysis by a leading scholar of Plato.

Cumont, Franz. *The Mysteries of Mithra*. Translated by Thomas J. McCormack. Chicago: Open Press, 1903; Reprint, F.Q. Legacy Books, 2010. Seminal work on the cult of Mithras.

———. *Oriental Religions in Roman Paganism*. Translated by Grant Showerman. New York: Dover Books, 1956; Reprint, Charleston, SC: Biblo Bazaar, 2007. Seminal work on mystery cults.

Dietz Maribel. *Wandering Monks, Virgins and Pilgrims: Ascetic Travel in the Mediterranean World, A.D. 300–800*. State College: Pennsylvania State University Press, 2005.

Digeser, Elizabeth DePalma. *The Making of a Christian Empire: Lactantius and Rome*. Ithaca, NY: Cornell University Press, 2000.

Dill, Samuel. *Roman Society in the Last Century of the Western Empire*. 2nd ed. London: Macmillan, 1899. Still a superb evoking of the literary and cultural life of late pagan Rome and the Senate.

Dillon, John. *The Great Tradition: Further Studies on the Development of Platonism and Early Christianity*. Aldershot, UK: Ashgate Publishing, 1997.

———. *The Golden Chain: Studies in the Development of Platonism and Christianity*. Brookfield, VT: Variorum, 1990.

———. *The Middle Platonists: A Study of Platonism, 80 B.C. to A.D. 200*. Ithaca, NY: Cornell University Press, 1977. Indispensable study.

Dodds, Eric R. *The Greeks and the Irrational*. Berkeley: University of California Press, 1951. Provocative work on Greek religious values.

———. *Pagan and Christian in the Age of Anxiety: Some Aspects of the Religious Experience from Marcus Aurelius to Constantine*. Cambridge: Cambridge University Press, 1991. Classic study on the pagan spiritual crisis.

Drake, H. A. *Constantine and the Bishops: The Politics of Intolerance*. Baltimore: Johns Hopkins University Press, 2002. A controversial view of the politics of conversion based on modern analogies from political science.

Drijvers, Hendrik Jan Willem. *Helena Augusta: The Mother of Constantine the Great and the Legend of Her Finding of the True Cross*. Leiden. The Netherlands: Brill, 1992. Excellent scholarly work.

Eadie, John, ed. *The Conversion of Constantine*. Pittsburgh, PA: Krieger Publishing, 1977. Excellent introduction of sources and excerpts of the modern controversy.

Elsner, John. *Imperial Rome and Christian Triumph: The Art of the Roman Empire, A.D. 100–450*. Oxford: Oxford University Press, 1999. Recommended introduction to aesthetics and arts.

Finn, Richard. *Almsgiving in the Later Roman Empire: Christian Promotion and Practice (313–450)*. Oxford: Oxford University Press, 2006.

Fishwick, Duncan. *The Imperial Cult in the Latin West: Studies in the Ruler Cult in the Western Provinces of the Roman Empire*. Leiden, The Netherlands: Brill, 2005.

Fowden, Garth. *The Egyptian Hermes: A Historical Approach to the Late Pagan Mind*. Princeton, NJ: Princeton University Press, 1986. Study of late pagan mysticism.

———. *Empire to Commonwealth: Consequences of Monotheism in Late Antiquity*. Princeton, NJ: Princeton University Press, 1994. Insightful work on the role of monotheism across Eurasia between A.D. 300 and 700.

Fox, Robin Lane. *Pagans and Christians*. New York: HarperCollins, 1988. Popular and literate work on the conversion.

Frend, William Hugh Clifford. *The Donatist Church: A Movement of Protest in Roman North Africa*. 2nd ed. Oxford: Clarendon Press, 1985. Classic study.

———. *Martyrdom and Persecution in the Early Church: A Study of Conflict from Maccabees to Donatus*. Oxford: Blackwell, 1965; Reprint, Grand Rapids, MI, 1981. Seminal and magisterial work; indispensable.

———. *The Rise of Christianity*. Philadelphia: Fortress Press, 1984. Excellent reference work on Christianity; dated on scholarship about paganism.

———. *Rise of the Monophysite Movement: Chapters in the History of the Church in the Fifth and Sixth Centuries*. Cambridge: Cambridge University Press, 1972.

Garnsey, Peter. *Social Status and Legal Privilege in the Roman Empire*. Oxford: Oxford University Press, 1970.

Garnsey, Peter, and Richard Saller. *The Roman Empire: Economy, Society and Culture*. Berkeley: University of California Press, 1987. Recommended introduction.

Gibson, Elsa. *The "Christians for Christians" Inscriptions of Phrygia*. Missoula: The Scholars Press, 1978. Collection and translations of the pre-Nicene Christian funerary monuments of the Upper Tembris valley in Asia Minor.

Goodman, Martin. *The Ruling Classes of Judaea: The Origins of the Jewish Revolt against Rome, A.D. 66–70*. Cambridge: Cambridge University Press, 1966. Excellent on the social and political conditions for Jews under Roman rule.

———. *State and Society in Roman Galilee, A.D. 132–212*. Totowa, NJ: Rowman and Allanheld, 1983.

Grant, Robert M. *Augustus to Constantine: Thrust of the Christian Movement in to the Roman World*. New York: Collins Press, 1971. Recommended introduction.

———. *Formation of the New Testament*. London: Hutchinson Press, 1965. Superb discussion of the issue.

———. *Gnosticism and Early Christianity*. New York: Columbia University Press, 1954.

Green, Tamara. *The City of the Moon: The Religious Traditions of Harran*. Leiden, The Netherlands: Brill, 1992. Learned study for the survival of paganism at Carrhae (Harran) into the 10th century.

Gregory, Kent. *Vox Populi: Popular Opinion and Violence in the Religious Controversies of the Fifth Century A.D.* Columbus: Ohio State University Press, 1979. Fine on the urban riots and ecclesiastical politics of the Great Councils.

Guthrie, W.K.C. *The Greeks and Their Gods*. Boston: Beacon Press, 1955. Dated classic study on Greek religion.

Harl, Kenneth W. *Civic Coins and Civic Politics in the Roman East, 180–275 A.D.* Berkeley: University of California Press, 1987. Arguing against the spiritual decline of paganism.

———. *Coinage in the Roman Economy, 300 B.C.–A.D. 700*. Baltimore: Johns Hopkins University Press, 1996. Reassessment of the impact of debasement of the coinage.

———. "From Pagan to Christian in the Cities of Asia Minor." *Urban Centers and Rural Contexts in Late Antiquity*. Vol. 3 in Shifting Frontiers in Classical Antiquity. Edited by John Eadie and Thomas Burns. East Lansing: Michigan State University Press, 2001.

———. "Sacrifice and Pagan Belief in Fifth- and Sixth-Century Byzantium." *Past and Present* 128 (August 1990): 7–27.

Hatlie, Peter. *The Monks and Monasteries of Constantinople, c. 350–850.* Cambridge: Cambridge University Press, 2007.

Herrin, Judith. *The Formation of Christendom.* Princeton, NJ: Princeton University Press, 1987. Thoughtful synthesis of cultural and religious change between A.D. 300 and 800.

Harris, William V. *Ancient Literacy.* Cambridge, MA: Harvard University Press, 1989.

Hirschfeld, Yizhar. *The Judean Desert Monasteries in the Byzantine Period.* New Haven, CT: Yale University Press, 1992.

Holman, Susan R. *The Hungry Are Dying: Beggars and Bishops in Roman Cappadocia.* Oxford: Oxford University Press, 2001.

Holum, Kenneth G. *Theodosian Empresses: Women and Imperial Dominion in Late Antiquity.* Berkeley: University of California Press, 1989. Excellent on the role of Christian empresses as patrons of holy men and conversion.

Hopkins, Keith. "Murderous Games." *Death and Renewal.* Cambridge: Cambridge University Press, 1983. Seminal study on the role of gladiatorial combats and cult of blood in the Roman arena.

Hunt, Edward D. *Holy Land Pilgrimage in the Later Roman Empire, A.D. 312–460.* Oxford: Oxford University Press, 1982. Excellent.

Jones, Arnold H. M. *Constantine and the Conversion of Europe.* London: Macmillan, 1948. Available from the University of Toronto Press MART (Medieval Academy Reprints for Teaching), 1970.

———. *The Decline of the Ancient World.* London: The Longman Group, 1975. Strong on institutional and legal history.

————. *The Greek City from Alexander to Justinian*. Oxford: Clarendon Press, 1940. Fundamental study with excellent citation of sources.

Jones, C. P. *Culture and Society in Lucian*. Cambridge, MA: Harvard University Press, 1986.

————. *Kinship Diplomacy in the Ancient World*. Cambridge, MA: Harvard University Press, 1999.

————. *The New Heroes in Antiquity: Achilles to Antinoos*. Cambridge, MA: Harvard University Press, 2010.

————. *Plutarch and Rome*. Oxford: Clarendon Press, 1971.

————. *The Roman World of Dio Chyrsostom*. Cambridge, MA: Harvard University Press, 1979. Excellent view of the social and cultural world of the Second Sophistic movement.

Kaegi, Walter E., Jr. *Byzantium and the Decline of Rome*. Princeton, NJ: Princeton University Press, 1968. Important study on how the Christian elite of Constantinople theologically and ideologically redefined themselves in light of the decline of the Roman West.

Kaster, Robert A. *Guardians of Language: Grammarian and Society in Late Antiquity*. Berkeley: University of California Press, 1988.

King, Noel Q. *The Emperor Theodosius and the Establishment of Christianity*. London: Westminster Press, 1960.

Kitzinger, Ernst. *Byzantine Art in the Making: Main Lines of Stylistic Development in Mediterranean Art, 3rd–7th Century*. Cambridge, MA: Harvard University Press, 1980. Provocative and wide-ranging essays.

Koester, Helmut, ed. *Ephesos: Metropolis of Asia. An Interdisciplinary Approach to its Archaeology, Religion, and Culture*. Vol. 41 in Harvard Theological Studies. Valley Forge, PA: Trinity Press International, 1995.

―――――, ed. *Pergamon, Citadel of the Gods: Archaeological Record, Literary Description, and Archaeological Development*. Vol. 46 in Harvard Theological Studies. Valley Forge, PA: Trinity Press International, 1995.

Krautheimer, Richard. *Early Christian Architecture*. 4th ed. New Haven, CT: Yale University Press, 1984. Recommended.

―――――. *Three Christian Capitals: Topography and Politics*. Berkeley: University of California Press, 1987. Excellent study on role of Christian capitals (Milan, Rome, and Constantinople) in Christianization.

Lenski, Noel. *The Crisis of the Roman Empire: Valens and the Roman State in the Fourth Century A.D.* Berkeley: University of California Press, 2002. With excellent chapter on Arianism and paganism.

Liebeschuetz, J. H. W. G. *Continuity and Change in Roman Religion*. Oxford: Oxford University Press, 1975. Recommended for ritual and practice.

Lieu, Samuel. *Manichaeism in the Later Roman Empire and Medieval China: A Historical Study*. Manchester: Manchester University Press, 1985. The standard study based on source.

L'Orange, Hans Peter. *Art Forms and Civic Life in the Late Roman Empire*. Princeton, NJ: Princeton University Press, 1965. Provocative study on changes in society and religion reflected in art and architecture.

Luck, Georg, trans. *Arcana Mundi*. Baltimore: Johns Hopkins University Press, 1985. Translations and discussion of magical texts from the Roman world.

MacCormack, Sabine. *Art and Ceremony in Late Antiquity*. Berkeley: University of California Press, 1982. Learned study with an important discussion on the influence of Christainity in shaping late Roman ideology.

MacMullen, Ramsay. *Changes in the Roman Empire: Essays in the Ordinary*. Princeton, NJ: Princeton University Press, 1990. Seminal articles on social history republished.

————, *Christianizing the Roman Empire, A.D. 100–400*. New Haven, CT: Yale University Press, 1986. Social forces at work in conversion.

————. *Constantine*. New York: Routledge, 1987. Excellent on the social world of Constantine.

————. *Enemies of the Roman Order: Treason, Unrest, and Alienation in the Empire*. Cambridge, MA: Harvard University Press, 1966. Recommended.

————. *Roman Government's Response to Crisis, 235–337 A.D.* New Haven, CT: Yale University Press, 1972. Essays on transformation wrought by crisis.

————. *Paganism in the Roman Empire*. New Haven, CT: Yale University Press, 1982. Indispensable.

————. *The Second Church: Popular Christianity A.D. 200–400*. Atlanta: Society of Biblical Literature, 2010. Provocative study of popular Christianity.

Mainestone, Rowland J. *Hagia Sophia: Architecture, Structure, and Liturgy of Justinian's Great Church*. London: Thames and Hudson, 1997.

Matthews, John. *Western Aristocracies and the Imperial Court, A.D. 364–425*. Oxford: Oxford University Press, 1975.

Markus, Robert A. *Christianity in the Roman World*. London: Thames and Hudson, 1978.

Maxwell, Jaclyn L. *Christianization and Communication in Late Antiquity: John Chrysostom and His Congregation in Antioch*. Cambridge: Cambridge University Press, 2009. Sensitive study of the impact of sermons on ordinary Christians.

Meeks, Wayne R. *First Urban Christians. The Social World of Saint Paul*. New Haven, CT: Yale University Press, 2003. Seminal and recommended study.

Meyendorff, John. *Imperial Unity, Christian Divisions: The Church from 450 to 680 A.D.* Yonkers, NY: St. Vladimir's Seminary Press, 1989. Superb discussion.

Miller, Patricia Cox. *Biography in Late Antiquity: A Quest for the Holy Man.* Berkeley: University of California Press, 1983.

———. *Dreams in Late Antiquity: Studies in the Imagination of a Culture.* Princeton, NJ: Princeton University Press, 1984.

Momigliano, Arnaldo. *Conflict of Paganism and Christianity in the Fourth Century.* Cambridge: Cambridge University Press, 1970. Provocative study.

Moorhead, John. *Justinian.* London: Longman Group, 1994. Fine introduction.

Mylonas, George E. *Eleusis and the Eleusinian Mysteries.* Princeton, NJ: Princeton University Press, 1961.

Naiden, F. S. *Ancient Supplication.* Oxford: Oxford University Press, 2006. Indispensable study reinterpreting the nature of Greek and Roman cults and rituals.

Nickelsburg, George W. E. *Jewish Literature between the Bible and the Mishnah.* 2nd ed. Minneapolis: Fortress Press, 2005.

Nilsson, Martin P. *The Dionysiac Mysteries in the Hellenistic and Roman Age.* New York: Arno Press, 1975.

Nock, Arthur D. *Conversion: The Old and the New Religion from Alexander the Great to Augustus.* Oxford: Oxford University Press, 1933. Classic study.

Norris, Richard A. *God and World in Early Christian Theology: A Study in Justin Martyr, Irenaeus, Tertullian, and Origen.* London: Black, 1967. Useful introduction.

Odahl, Charles M. *Constantine and the Christian Empire.* New York: Routledge, 2004. Recommended biography.

Osborn, Eric. *Irenaeus of Lyons*. Cambridge: Cambridge University Press, 2005.

Parke, Herbert William, and Donald Ernest W. Wormell. *The Delphic Oracle*. Vols. 1–2. Oxford: Oxford University Press, 1956.

———. *The Oracles of Apollo in Asia Minor*. London: Croom Helm, 1985.

Parvis, Sara. Justin Martyr and His World. Minneapolis: Fortress Press, 2007.

Patterson, Lloyd G. *God and History in Early Christian Thought*. New York: Seabury Press, 1967.

Pelikan, Jaroslav. *The Emergence of the Catholic Tradition (100–600)*. Chicago: University of Chicago Press, 1975. Classic study by leading scholar on theology.

Perkins, Anne L. *Art of Dura-Europos*. Oxford: Oxford University Press, 1973. Important study on the Jewish and Christian arts.

Potter, David. *The Roman Empire at Bay, A.D. 180–395*. New York: Routledge, 2004. The best one-volume study on the late Roman world.

Price, Simon. *Rituals and Power: The Imperial Cult in Roman Asia Minor*. Cambridge: Cambridge University Press, 1986. Seminal study on ruler cults and nature of pagan worship.

Rapp, Claudia. *Holy Bishops in Late Antiquity: The Nature of Christian Leadership in the Age of Transition*. Berkeley: University of California Press, 2005.

Richardson, Cyril C. *The Christianity of Ignatius of Antioch*. New York: AMS Press, 1967.

Rist, John M. *Plotinus: The Road to Reality*. Cambridge: Cambridge University Press, 1977.

————. *Stoic Philosophy*. Cambridge: Cambridge University Press, 1969. Excellent study by a leading scholar.

————. *The Stoics*. Berkeley: University of California Press, 1978. Essays on the leading Roman senatorial Stoics and critics of the emperor.

Robinson, Thomas A. *Ignatius of Antioch and the Parting of the Ways: Early Jewish-Christian Relations*. Grand Rapids, MI: Baker Academic Press, 2009.

Rogers, Guy M. *The Sacred Identity of Ephesos: Foundation Myths of a Roman City*. New York: Routledge, 1991.

Rogers, Rick. *Theophilus of Antioch: The Life and Thought of a Second-Century Bishop*. Lexington, MA: Lexington Books, 2000.

Roller, Lynn E. *In Search of God the Mother: The Cult of Anatolian Cybele*. Berkeley: University of California Press, 1999. The indispensable study.

Rosen, William. *Justinian's Flea: The First Great Plague and the End of the Roman Empire*. Baltimore: Penguin Books, 2007. Excellent essays on the impact of the plague on religious and social life.

Rousseau, Philip. *Basil of Caesarea*. Berkeley: University of California Press, 1998. Model study of the role of bishops in cities.

————. *Pachomius: The Making of a Community in Fourth Century Egypt*. Berkeley, 1985. The major study.

Sainte Croix, G. E. M. de. "Why Were the Early Christians Persecuted?" *Past and Present* 26 (1963): 6–38. Seminal article on the legal proceedings at trials of Christians.

Saltzman, M. R. *The Making of a Christian Aristocracy: Social and Religious Change in the Western Roman Empire*. Cambridge, MA: Harvard University Press, 2002.

Sambursky, S. *The Physical World of Late Antiquity*. Princeton, NJ: Princeton University Press, 1987. Concise recommended work on pagan cosmology.

Sandwell, Isabella. *Religious Identity in Late Antiquity: Greeks, Jews, and Christians in Antioch*. Cambridge: Cambridge University Press, 2007. Model study of legal and social change wrought by Christianization.

Schott, Jeremy M. *Christianity, Empire, and the Making of Religion in Late Antiquity*. Philadelphia: University of Pennsylvania Press, 2008.

Schweitzer, Albert. *The Mysticism of Saint Paul*. Baltimore: Johns Hopkins University Press, 1998 Reprint.

––––––. *The Quest of the Historical Jesus*. New York: Dover Publications, 2005. Reprint of the 1906 edition.

Segal, Alan F. *Paul the Convert: The Apostolate and Apostasy of Saul the Pharisee*. New Haven, CT: Yale University Press, 1992. Excellent study.

––––––. *Rebecca's Children: Judaism and Christianity in the Roman World*. Cambridge, MA: Harvard University Press, 1986. Provocative, recommended study.

Segal, J. B. *Edessa, the Blessed City*. Piscataway, NJ: Gorgias Press, 2001. Model study of the Christianizing of a Roman city.

Shaw, Gregory. *Theurgy and the Soul: The Neoplatonism of Iamblichus of Chalcis*. Philadelphia: University of Pennsylvania Press, 1967.

Sherwin-White, Adrian N. *Racial Prejudice in Imperial Rome*. Cambridge: Cambridge University Press, 2010. Recommended.

Smallwood, E. Mary. *The Jews under the Roman Rule from Pompey to Diocletian*. Boston: Brill, 2001. The classic and recommended study.

Smith, Morton. *Jesus the Magician*. New York: Barnes and Noble, 1993. Controversial study, but excellent on popular Judaism of the 1st century A.D.

Swain, Simon. *Hellenism and Empire: Language, Classicism, and Power in the Greek World, A.D. 50–250*. Oxford: Oxford University Press, 1998. The scholarly study on the Second Sophistic movement.

Talbert, Richard J. A. *Rome's World: The Peutinger Map Reconsidered.* Cambridge: Cambridge University Press, 2010. Crucial for Roman worldviews.

Taylor, Lily R. *The Divinity of the Roman Emperor*. Middleton, CT: American Philological Association, monograph no. 1, 1931.

Tougher, Shau, trans. and ed. *Julian the Apostate*. Edinburgh: Edinburgh University Press, 2007.

Toynbee, Jocelyn M. C. *Death and Burial in the Roman World*. Baltimore: Johns Hopkins University Press, 1971.

Trebilco, Paul. *Jewish Communities in Asia Minor*. Cambridge: Cambridge University Press, 1981. Survey of the archaeological, literary, and epigraphic evidence.

Trevett, Christine. *Montanism: Gender, Authority, and New Prophecy*. Cambridge: Cambridge University Press, 2002. Controversial study on the social aspects of Montanism.

Trigg, Joseph W. *Origen*. New York: Routledge, 1998.

———. *Origen: The Bible and Philosophy in the Third-Century Church*. Atlanta: John Knox Press, 1983.

Trombley, Frank R. *Hellenic Religion and Christianization: c. 370–529*. 2 vols. Leiden, The Netherlands: Brill, 2001. Learned study with collection of the sources.

Tyson, Joseph B. *Marcion and Luke-Acts: A Defining Struggle*. Charleston: University of South Carolina Press, 2006.

Van Dam, Raymond. *Families and Friends in Late Roman Cappadocia.* Philadelphia: University of Pennsylvania Press, 2003. Excellent on the roles of bishops.

————. *The Roman Revolution of Constantine.* Cambridge: Cambridge University Press, 2009. Important study.

Veyne, Paul. *Bread and Circuses: Historical Sociology and Political Pluralism.* Translated by Brian Pearee. Introduction by Oswyn Murray. London: Penguin Press, 1976. Brilliant study of the ethos of pagan gift giving in the Hellenistic and Roman ages.

Vermes, Geza. *Jesus the Jew.* Minneapolis: Fortress Press, 1981. Recommended work by a leading scholar of Judaism.

Vermeule, Emily. *Aspects of Death in Early Greek Art and Poetry.* Berkeley: University of California Press, 1981. Still the best study on Greek notions of the afterlife.

von Harnack, Adolf. *Marcion: The Gospel of an Alien God.* Translated by J. E. Steely and L. D. Bierma. Eugene, OR: Wipf and Stock, 2007. The classic study on Marcion and a modern English translation.

————. *The Mission and Expansion of Christianity in the First Three Centuries.* Translated by James Moffat. 2nd ed. New York: G. P. Putman's Sons, 1924. The classic and indispensable.

von Simson, Otto Georg. *Sacred Fortress: Byzantine Art and Statecraft in Ravenna.* Princeton, NJ: Princeton University Press, 1987.

Waddell, Helen. *The Desert Fathers.* New York: Vintage, 1998.

Wallis, Richard T. *Neoplatonism.* London: Duckworth Publishers, 2008.

Watson, A. *Aurelian and the Third Century.* New York: Routledge, 1999. Model study on the changes wrought by the so-called crisis of the 3rd century.

Watts, Edward J. *Riot in Alexandria: Tradition and Group Dynamics in Late Antique Pagan and Christian Communities.* Berkeley: University of California Press, 2010.

Weinstock, Stefan. *Divus Julius.* Oxford: Oxford University Press, 1972. Scholarly study on the creation of the ruler cult at Rome.

Weitzmann, Kurt, ed. *The Age of Spirituality: A Symposium.* New York: The Metropolitan Museum of Art, 1980.

Weitzmann, Kurt, and Herbert Kessler. *The Frescoes of the Dura Synagogue and Christian Art.* Washington, DC: Dumbarton Oaks, 1990.

Wilken, Robert L. *The Christians as the Romans Saw Them.* 2nd ed. New Haven, CT: Yale University Press, 2003. Excellent study and recommended.

———. *John Chrysostom and the Jews: Rhetoric and Reality in the Late Fourth Century.* New Haven, CT: Yale University Press, 1983. Seminal study on the origins of medieval anti-Semitism.

Witt, Reginald E. *Isis in the Ancient World.* Baltimore: Johns Hopkins University Press, 1997.

Yadin, Yigael. *Bar-Kokhba: The Rediscovery of the Legendary Hero of the Second Jewish Revolt against Rome.* New York: Random House, 1971. Popular account strong on archaeology by a leading Israeli scholar.